THE MENTOR'S GUIDE TO BIBLICAL ELDERSHIP

TWELVE LESSONS FOR MENTORING ELDERS

Alexander Strauch
& Richard Swartley

Lewis & Roth Publishers

P. O. Box 469 Littleton, Colorado 80160 U. S. A.

Biblical Eldership Mentor's Guide

ISBN: 0-93608-312-3

Copyright © 1996 by Lewis & Roth Publishers. All rights reserved.

Cover Design: Stephen T. Eames (EamesCreative.com)
Editors: Stephen and Amanda Sorenson
Typography: Tim Howard

Printed in the United States of America
Eighth Printing / 2008

To receive a free catalog of books published by Lewis & Roth Publishers, call toll free: 800-477-3239. If you are calling from outside the United States, please call 719-494-1800.

Lewis & Roth Publishers
P.O. Box 469
Littleton CO 80160
www.lewisandroth.com

CONTENTS

OLD TESTAMENT ELDERS - JOB

Lesson 1 explores Job's life as a model of the Old Testament elder. We will examine the duties and deficiencies of Israel's elders and will note the failure of Job's colleagues to compassionately and tactfully minister to him during his intense suffering. This lesson will help you think and act like a biblical, Christlike elder. The lesson covers pages 121-124, 186-202, 227-238.

MEN OF SOUND DOCTRINE AND WISDOM - ACTS 15:1-35; 21:18-25

Lesson 2 sets forth the biblical imperative that elders know Bible doctrine so that they will be adequately equipped to judge doctrinal disputes and provide wise, godly counsel and leadership for the congregation. As you will discover throughout the *Guide*, biblical elders must be men of the Word. The biblical standard for pastor elders is that they be able to teach and defend sound Christian doctrine. Elders who are biblically inadequate are actually a curse to the church, not the blessing God would have them be. This lesson is intended to help you evaluate your preparedness as a teacher and defender of Christ's doctrine. It will also touch briefly on the elder-congregation relationship and the need for elders to be men of wisdom who know how to lead the congregation in godly decision making. The pages to be read are 17-22, 125-133, 291-295.

THE FIRST ELDER APPOINTMENTS - ACTS 14:23
"GUARD YOURSELVES" - ACTS 20:28*a*

In this lesson we will be confronted by the significance of Acts 14:23 to the New Testament doctrine of eldership and learn to think accurately about the Greek word for "appointed," which is frequently misinterpreted to mean church election or ordination.

Most of the lesson covers Acts 20:28*a*: "Be on guard for yourselves." Shepherds cannot guard others from Satan's many deceptions if they do not first guard their own souls. This lesson reinforces the Lord's call for elders to be men of the Word and of prayer. The pages to be read are 133-147.

PROTECTING THE FLOCK FROM FALSE TEACHERS - ACTS 20:18-35
THE SOURCE OF THE ELDERS' STRENGTH - ACTS 20:32, 36-38
THE PAULINE MODEL FOR ELDERS - ACTS 20:33-35

Lesson 4 deals with the elders' solemn duty to protect their flock from "savage wolves," that is, false teachers. It covers Paul's farewell message to the Ephesian elders in Acts 20:18-35. An elder who desires to be a faithful guardian of Christ's Word and flock must become thoroughly familiar with this Scripture passage. It answers the question of who places elders in the local church as overseers and pastor shepherds, and establishes the inestimable worth of the body of Christ, which elders are called to guard from Satanic workers.

The second half of the lesson addresses the elders' need to trust in God and His Word for strength and guidance. It also explores Paul's example of self-employment and generosity to others. The reading covers pages 17-22, 27-29, 31-34, 109-115, 140-159.

HUMBLE SERVANTS AND THE CHIEF SHEPHERD - 1 PETER 5:3*b*-5
HARD-WORKING MEN - 1 THESSALONIANS 5:12, 13

Lesson 5 covers 1 Peter 5:1*a*, 3*b*-5 and 1 Thessalonians 5:12, 13. Peter exhorts elders to shepherd the flock through the power of personal example and encourages them with the promises of the glorious return of the "Chief Shepherd" and the "crown of glory." Finally, he calls elders, as well as the flock, to clothe themselves with humility so that all may live together in peace.

Paul's exhortation to the congregation at Thessalonica reinforces the elders' task of leading and admonishing the congregation. In order to bear this great responsibility, pastor elders must be self-disciplined, highly committed disciples of the Master. Clearly, board elders cannot pastor a local church: only hard-working, self-disciplined, shepherd elders can.

Like Peter, Paul also calls the congregation and its leaders to work for peace and to love one another. Without humility, love, and peace there is little hope of experiencing the joys of Christlike community and effective pastoral leadership. The pages to be read are 161-174, 249-252.

TEAM LEADERSHIP - PHILIPPIANS 1:1, 1 TIMOTHY 5:17, 18

Lesson 6 examines the plurality of overseers mentioned in Philippians 1:1, the equating of overseers with elders, the significance of church leadership terminology, the importance and practice of team leadership, and the principle of "first among equals."

The major focus of the lesson is on learning how to work with fellow elders in Christian harmony, which is not an easy task. Becoming a good team player takes years of effort and commitment. The key to team leadership is *agapē* love. The lesson covers pages 31-50, 101-117, 174-180.

QUALIFIED LEADERS - 1 TIMOTHY 3:1-15

The major emphasis of lesson 7 is the necessity of church elders being "above reproach." The lesson also reviews Paul's purpose in writing 1 Timothy, the Ephesian elders' failure to protect the church from false teaching, the faithful saying of 1 Timothy 3:1, and the qualifications for overseers. The pages to be read are 67-83, 181-202.

HONORING AND DISCIPLINING ELDERS - 1 TIMOTHY 5:17-25

Lesson 8 surveys 1 Timothy 5:17-25, one of the most significant New Testament passages on the doctrine of Christian eldership. It focuses on elders who deserve double honor because of their capable leadership and diligent labor in the Word and explains the necessity of evaluating each elder's gifts.

The passage also addresses the difficult issue of disciplining elders who have been proved guilty of sin. The lesson emphasizes the need for leaders to be courageous in exposing sin, to judge justly, and to follow the New Testament precautions in appointing elders. The pages to be read are 206-224.

APPOINT ONLY QUALIFIED MEN - TITUS 1:5-11

Lesson 9 reviews Paul's instructions to Titus and the underdeveloped churches on the Island of Crete that were facing attack from false teachers. Paul sets forth the qualifications for elders: church elders must control personal anger, be hospitable, be faithful to Christian doctrine, and be able to exhort in sound doctrine and refute false teachers. The lesson also examines the terms "ordination" and "appointment," and the unbiblical division between clergy and laity. The lesson covers pages 104-106, 111-114, 202-205, 225-238, 284-288.

SHEPHERD GOD'S FLOCK IN GOD'S WAY - 1 PETER 5:1-3

In lesson 10, Peter's farewell exhortations to the elders of northwestern Asia Minor in 1 Peter 5:1-3 are considered. We examine the urgent apostolic imperative for elders to shepherd God's flock, that is, to be all that shepherds should be to the flock. This lesson will help you think practically about your time commitment to the shepherding task and your personal contribution to the shepherding team.

Furthermore, this passage is an urgent call for pastor elders to shepherd the flock in a distinctly Christlike way-willingly, eagerly, and as godly models of Christ-not as authoritarian tyrants or hirelings. Christian elders are to be loving, servant leaders. The lesson requires that you read chapter 5, "Servant Leadership," in *Biblical Eldership*. It covers pages 9-31, 85-98, 114, 149, 239-248.

CARING FOR THE POOR - ACTS 11:29, 30; 20:35
PRAYING FOR THE SICK - JAMES 5:13-16

Lesson 11 addresses the elders' attitude toward the poor and needy, and the character qualities necessary in the men who administer the church's charitable funds. The second half of the lesson deals with the elders' responsibility to the sick, as described in James 5:14, 15. To be a Christlike shepherd, the elder must be compassionate toward those who suffer. In ministering to the sick, the pastor elder must be a man of faith, prayer, and wise counsel. The pages to be read are 29-31, 156-159, 253-263; also referenced are pages 188-202, 228-238.

SPIRITUAL WATCHMEN - HEBREWS 13:17
SUBMISSION TO AUTHORITY - HEBREWS 13:17
MALE LEADERSHIP - 1 TIMOTHY 2:9-3:2*a*

The final lesson explores Hebrews 13:17. We discuss the institutional church model versus the community church model, and the joys and heartaches of leading God's people. In addition, the subject of submission to church elders, a matter of great disdain to modern man, is studied.

The lesson also reviews chapter 3 of *Biblical Eldership*, "Male Leadership." This is not only an issue related to God's plan for male-female relationships in the home and church, but is an issue of biblical integrity and authority that is of utmost importance to the Lord's people. The lesson covers pages 51-66, 265-273.

ACKNOWLEDGMENTS

Enthusiastic words of thanks are given to Anne Swartley who has spent untold hours refining *The Mentor's Guide to Biblical Eldership*. Without her, *The Mentor's Guide* would not be the valuable tool it is today. Her work has been a labor of love on behalf of God's people.

Thanks are also due to Todd Leapold for his critique of each lesson as a mentoree; to John Ellis for his analysis of each lesson as an experienced shepherd elder; to the elders of the First Evangelical Free Church in Lakeland, Florida who worked through the *Study Guide to Biblical Eldership* together, resulting in many helpful suggestions; and to Barbara Peek for proofreading the final copy.

AUTHORS

ALEXANDER STRAUCH and his wife, Marilyn, reside in Littleton, Colorado, near their four married daughters. Mr. Strauch is a gifted Bible teacher and an elder at a church in Littleton where he has served for over 30 years. Other works by Mr. Strauch include: *Biblical Eldership*, *A Study Guide to Biblical Eldership*, *The Biblical Eldership Booklet*, *Meetings That Work*, *The New Testament Deacon*, *The New Testament Deacon Study Guide*, *Agape Leadership*, *The Hospitality Commands*, and *Men and Women: Equal Yet Different*.

RICHARD SWARTLEY lives with his wife Anne in Wayne, Pennsylvania. He is a retired senior systems engineer from Lockheed Martin and a seminary graduate. The Swartleys have four children and are the authors of *Right Start*, a premarital mentoring program. Mr. Swartley, a founding elder of Church of the Saviour in Wayne, is also the author of *Eldership in Action: Through Biblical Governance of the Church*.

Introduction
How to use *The Mentor's Guide to Biblical Eldership*

Friends of ours who are elders in another church were discussing the need to train more men for eldership. As they sought suitable material for training potential elders, one reminded the others that, "No one ever trained us!" Unfortunately, this assessment could be echoed by 95 percent of all elders and deacons.

WHY TRAIN MEN FOR ELDERSHIP?

The lack of elder and deacon training is an extremely critical problem. We are not training the very men who lead and have oversight of our churches. We erroneously believe that our serving elders and deacons understand spiritual oversight and care, but in fact our churches are filled with elders and deacons who confess that they are unprepared and untrained for their work. Even Bible schools and seminaries, for the most part, do not prepare men to provide spiritual care or leadership for a congregation.

This lack of training is not uncommon among organizations that operate in a familial manner. A leading news magazine reported on the amazing strength of America's family-owned businesses, estimating that "nearly 50 percent of the nation's gross national product" was produced by family-owned firms.[1] After enumerating many positive aspects of the family-owned business, however, the article reported that its chief weakness is its failure to train the next generation of family leaders: "On the whole, only a third of family-owned companies survive into the second generation because founders often are too busy to plan ahead or because they lack confidence in their young."[2]

The local church is an extended family that does God's business. Like many family-owned businesses, local churches fail to train the next generation of leaders. Church leaders are frequently too preoccupied with the work of the church or lack vision for training future leaders. They have seriously underestimated both the need and their responsibility. Like flowers in spring, leaders who are ready to bless the flock will not appear without planting or preparation.

Kenneth O. Gangel, a biblically sound expert in church management and training, is right on target when he points out, "The key to reproducing leadership is to clearly plan for it."[3] "Church leaders," exhorts Gangel, "need to produce leaders who will reproduce leaders precisely as it is done in the family-through experience, instruction, and modeling."[4]

9

Training men for future leadership and ministry should not be a novel concept to the Christian who is familiar with what the Bible teaches. Our Lord and Savior Jesus Christ spent a significant part of His public ministry preparing for the future. He patiently poured His life into twelve men, training them to be the future leaders of the church. He was a master teacher and mentor. Scottish biblical professor and writer, A. B. Bruce (1831-1899), in his standard-setting work, *The Training of the Twelve*, writes:

> "Follow Me," said Jesus to the fishermen of Bethsaida, "and I will make you fishers of men." These words ... show that the great Founder of the faith desired not only to have disciples, but to have about Him men whom he might train to make disciples of others. . . . Both from His words and from His actions we can see that He attached supreme importance to that part of His work which consisted in training the twelve. In the intercessory prayer [John 17:6], e.g., He speaks of the training He had given these men as if it had been the principal part of His own earthly ministry. And such, in one sense, it really was. The careful, painstaking education of the disciples secured that the Teacher's influence on the world should be permanent; that His kingdom should be founded on the rock of deep and indestructible convictions in the minds of the few, not on the shifting sands of superficial evanescent impressions on the minds of the many.[5]

Like his Lord, Paul was also a discipler of men. He had his Timothys, and he expected his Timothys to train others: "The things which you have heard from me in the presence of many witnesses, entrust these to faithful men who will be able to teach others also" (2 Tim. 2:2). Paul expected that when Timothy departed from Ephesus he would leave in place trained, faithful men who would continue the development of future teachers and leaders.

Local church elders are to be faithful men who are determined to train other faithful men. Elders must understand that the shepherding-leading task includes planning for ongoing leadership for the flock. As spiritual overseers of the congregation, elders have a special obligation to recognize, develop, and establish those to whom the Spirit has given the desire to shepherd God's people.

The fact that the Spirit plants in some men the desire to shepherd does not eliminate the elders' responsibility to prayerfully search for potential shepherd elders and to challenge, recognize, mentor, and appoint such men. The Holy Spirit uses people to help others discover and develop their gifts. The Holy Spirit also requires that elders protect the church from pushy, deceived people who think they are gifted and motivated by the Spirit when in reality they are not. Such people are in fact a detriment to the church. So, the elders must actively participate in the process of selecting, examining, and training prospective elders. Whether they intend to or not, elders encourage or stifle the development of new elders.

It should not be assumed that men trained in a seminary are exempt from the need for specialized preparation for the responsibilities of being a pastor elder. Unfortunately, seminaries train a man to be the leader of "his own" congregation rather than an equal participant on an elder council. Seminary graduates who receive significant preparation in the application of scriptural principles to the governance and care of the church are a blessed exception to the rule.

Furthermore, and significantly more important, if current elder councils intend to have doctrinally sound and competent shepherd elders to serve and preserve their churches' distinctives in the future, then they must actively train, guide, and pray for quality men *now*.

Elder training is essential to the church's response to the great commission. Our Lord's command to go, to teach, and to make disciples of all the nations–in other words, the discipleship process–cannot be sustained without elders. In any mission field, whether it be local or at a great distance culturally, the planting of new churches is paced by the availability of elders. The stability of those new churches and their ability to grow will be determined by the maturity of their founding elders.

THE TERM "PASTOR ELDER"

Throughout both the *Study Guide* and *The Mentor's Guide*, as in *Biblical Eldership*, elders are referred to as "shepherd elders" or "pastor elders." This is to counter the considerable amount of unscriptural thinking about elders that exists today. When most Christians hear of church elders, they think of lay church officials, committeemen, executives, policymakers, or advisors to the pastor. They do not expect church elders to teach the Word or be involved pastorally in the lives of people. We refer to such elders as "board elders." They are not true biblical elders.

The contemporary, church-board concept of eldership is irreconcilably at odds with the New Testament's definition of eldership. According to the New Testament concept, elders lead the church, teach and preach the Word, protect the church from false teachers, exhort and admonish the saints in sound doctrine, visit the sick and pray, and judge doctrinal issues. To use biblical terminology, elders shepherd, oversee, lead, and care for the local church. Therefore, to communicate accurately the New Testament concept of eldership, it is necessary to explain that the New Testament term *elder* means "pastor elder," "shepherd elder," or "pastor." Throughout both *Guides*, we use these terms interchangeably to distinguish between "board elder," the unscriptural concept, and "shepherd elder," the biblical concept. For further explanation of the differences, read pp. 15-17, 31-34 in *Biblical Eldership*.

ELDER QUALIFICATIONS

Since the New Testament so emphatically emphasizes the moral and spiritual qualifications of elders, we underscore them throughout this *Guide*. Most elder leadership problems can be traced directly to the failure on the part of an elder or the body of elders to act according to a specific New Testament character qualification. As there is such a profound depth of wisdom contained in each Spirit-given qualification, elders need to be thoroughly familiar with each. If you need help defining the New Testament elder qualifications, read pp. 188-202 and 228-238, in *Biblical Eldership*. See p. 17 of this introduction for a complete list.

USING THE STUDY GUIDE AND THE MENTOR'S GUIDE

The *Study Guide to Biblical Eldership: Twelve Lessons for Mentoring Men for Eldership* is designed primarily as a mentoring tool for training prospective new elders. It consists of twelve lessons based on the revised and expanded edition of Alexander Strauch's *Biblical Eldership: An Urgent Call to Restore Biblical Church Leadership* (1995). The *Study Guide to Biblical Eldership* is to be used by the prospective new elder (the mentoree or trainee) under the direction of a mentoring elder. The prospective elder reads *Biblical Eldership* (the revised edition of 1995) and works through the lessons in the *Study Guide to Biblical Eldership*. After completing each lesson, he meets with his mentoring elder to discuss the questions and assignments.

The Mentor's Guide to Biblical Eldership is for the mentoring elder only, not the trainee. It is the leader's guide to the *Study Guide to Biblical Eldership*. Elders are busy men, and many may not have the time or adequate resources to prepare for mentoring their mentorees. Therefore, *The Mentor's Guide* provides the mentoring elder with extensive answers to all the questions in the *Study Guide* (in the appropriate space below each question), as well as extended commentary (at the bottom of each page). *The Mentor's Guide* supplies helpful exposition on select Scripture passages used in the questions, suggestions on how to best utilize the questions and assignments and which points need emphasis or clarification, helpful quotations from other authors, and insights for the mentoring elder.

It is essential that the mentoring elder interact directly with the material in *Biblical Eldership* and the *Study Guide* and form his own responses before he helps a mentoree evaluate his answers. Therefore, we highly recommend that the mentoring elder personally work through the lessons in the *Study Guide to Biblical Eldership*. After completing each lesson from the *Study Guide*, the mentoring elder should evaluate his own work in light of the answers and comments in *The Mentor's Guide*.

PREPARATION FOR A MENTORING PROGRAM

Before mentoring men for eldership, acting church elders must be perfectly clear about what the New Testament teaches about elders. Elders cannot train others biblically if they are not biblically and accurately taught themselves. *Biblical Eldership* was written to satisfy this need for clarification of the scriptural doctrine and practice of biblical eldership.

If church elders are not well versed in the subject of biblical eldership, they should study *Biblical Eldership* and complete the *Study Guide* prior to training others. The best outcome for a church will result if the entire current elder council works through the *Study Guide* individually, then meets to discuss their insights and to compare them with the answers and commentary in *The Mentor's Guide*. Furthermore, if the present elders have not yet mentored others, they should begin praying that God's Spirit will give them the vision for the joy of mentoring, a keen eye for spotting potential elders, and a burning desire to invest time in future church leaders. Few things in life are more meaningful than training others for God's service.

Realistically, it will take time for elders to prepare themselves for mentoring others. Discipling is not easy. In *Jesus Christ, Disciplemaker*, Bill Hull pinpoints the reasons: "True disciplemaking is difficult because it entails change, it takes a long time, and it is hard to visualize. It is teeming with both possibilities and problems."[6]

Here is a simple, broad overview of the steps involved in selecting, training, examining, and appointing elders. For a more in-depth treatment, read pp. 277-295 of *Biblical Eldership*. The detailed steps required to select, mentor, and examine prospective elders will vary according to the size of your congregation, what is appropriate for your culture, and the available mentoring personnel. Nevertheless, careful planning and prayerful, conscientious execution are in order.

1	2	3
Personal desire based on Spirit-motivation moves a brother to: ■ diligently study the Scriptures ■ instruct others in the Word ■ sacrificially care for and serve the congregation	Elders observe a brother's: ■ spiritual maturity ■ godly character ■ years of faithful, fruitful, and loving service ■ doctrinal soundness ■ spiritual giftedness	Elders consult (either formally or informally) with the brother as to his desire for eldership and future life plans. Or, a brother speaks to the elders about his desire to become a shepherd elder. ■ If there is a positive response by both parties . . .
⮕	⮕	⮕
4	**5**	**6**
Elders agree to formally invite the brother into a mentoring-training relationship, looking to God for future direction, timing, and detailed plans. ■ After a positive mentoring experience . . .	Elders, with the congregation, formally examine (1 Tim. 3:10) the prospective elder's ■ doctrine ■ character ■ capabilities If the approval to be an elder is given . . .	Elders publicly appoint and install the candidate to the church eldership.
⮕	⮕	

PREPARING THE MENTOREE OR TRAINEE

Scripture states most emphatically that a new convert cannot be an elder (1 Tim. 3:7) and that a man is not to be appointed an elder in a hasty manner (1 Tim. 5:22). Thus the *Study Guide* is designed for mature Christian men who are *already actively involved* in local church service, teaching, and leadership. It is for those who know the Scriptures, are knowledgeable in basic Bible doctrines, and agree with the doctrinal positions of the local church. It is for those who desire pastoral eldership (1 Tim. 3:1), and those whom the elders have selected for training for possible eldership. It is assumed that those who use the *Study Guide* are experienced in serving in the church and are well-known by the elders.

Before any brother is formally invited to start the *Study Guide to Biblical Eldership*, he should be approved as a trainee by the eldership and assigned to a primary mentoring elder. *He should also be told at the start that entering the mentoring process does not guarantee that he will be appointed an elder at its conclusion.* In fact, the program may reveal that the candidate does not truly desire, is not gifted for, is unable to make the commitment to, or does not yet have the maturity required for biblical eldership.

Depending on the mentoree's experience, knowledge, skills, personal desire, and needs, the lessons can be accomplished in six months or spread out over a year or two. The lessons should be used in a flexible manner, depending on the mentoree's progress and interest in moving forward. The *Study Guide* is demanding by virtue of the seriousness of the task, and each lesson requires between three to five hours of preparation. In addition, most lessons require about an hour and a half for the mentoring elder and mentoree to review and discuss the mentoree's work. Although this *Guide* was prepared to be used in a mentoring relationship, an aspiring elder can use the *Study Guide* in a self-directed study if no elder in the church is available to mentor him.

The *Study Guide* is not designed to be a general leadership training manual. It is a specialized leadership training course intended only for those who aspire to be pastor elders and for the congregation's emerging elders, as surfaced by its current elders. Churches should provide other specific leadership training for all leaders and ministry directors.

THE ROLE OF THE STUDY GUIDE IN PREPARING ELDERS

The *Study Guide to Biblical Eldership* is designed to provide mentoring elders with three crucial elements for training prospective elders:

1. **A thorough study of what the Bible teaches about elders and eldering**

   An often neglected but critically essential requirement for training new elders is the study of the biblical texts on eldership and Christian leadership. The *Study Guide* directs the trainee through all the New Testament passages on eldership, using *Biblical Eldership* as an in-depth commentary. Lesson 1 begins with Old Testament elders (chapter 7 of *Biblical Eldership*). The *Guide* then moves through Acts (also chapter 7), followed by all the epistles (chapters 8-13). The *Study Guide* also refers to the first six chapters of *Biblical Eldership* as they relate to the eldership texts of Scripture. **Therefore, before starting lesson 1 of the *Study Guide*, the mentoree should read the introduction and the first six chapters of *Biblical Eldership*.**

   Only the Spirit of God, using the Word of God, can instill in the hearts and minds of men God's will for what they should be and do as shepherds of God's precious flock. Therefore, an elder trainee needs to saturate his mind with God-breathed words on biblical eldership. Only when he is "constantly nourished on the words of the faith and of the sound doctrine" will he be "a good servant of Christ Jesus" (1 Tim. 4:6).

2. **Practical ideas for developing prospective elders' pastoral skills and personal spiritual growth**

Elder trainees need much practical instruction in preparing for eldership. Since *Biblical Eldership* is largely a doctrinal, expository book, it offers little practical counsel for prospective elders. The *Study Guide* supplements *Biblical Eldership* by providing probing questions, self-evaluations, warnings, assignments, useful suggestions, and recommended reading material.

Throughout the *Study Guide*, many books are recommended for study or purchase as resource material. Mentorees may not be able to afford such an investment, so we suggest that the church purchase these books for an elders' resource library. It is important that basic books are at hand for training leaders and elders.

To maximize the trainee's practical experience, it is essential that he attend elders' meetings while working on these lessons. *Elders' meetings are an extraordinarily effective and essential training ground for emerging elders.* They are a virtual school of advanced pastoral training. Observing experienced leaders is fundamental to the mentoring process. While training the Twelve, Jesus was the model. He provided maximum exposure for His disciples to observe His methods of evangelism, the priority of prayer in His life, His compassion for suffering people, His leadership style, and His absolute faithfulness to the will and Word of God. The more exposure the mentoree has to the elders at work, the more effective the mentoring process will be. In addition, trainees should seek opportunities to accompany the elders in their pastoral duties. In-service training is always effective.

3. **A guide to facilitate a mentoring relationship between an experienced elder and an elder trainee**

If a church is blessed with a well-trained council of elders, the *Study Guide* provides an organized format to be used by elders in mentoring men preparing to share that responsibility in the future. This *Guide* provides the structure for a mentoring elder and mentoree to study all the biblical texts on elders and the book *Biblical Eldership*. It also allows the mentoring elder to share his personal insights into Scripture; his personal spiritual journey and growth; and his experiences, failures, and successes as a shepherd of God's people.

Please be aware that a number of assignments and questions may require much more effort than the lesson schedule allows. Your mentoree should list these items on the inside back cover of the *Guide*. When he has completed the *Study Guide*, help him prioritize the postponed items and schedule time to work on each.

SUGGESTIONS FOR EFFECTIVE MENTORING

So that you may derive the greatest benefit from your mentoring relationship, we recommend that both the mentoring elder and the trainee read the book, *Connecting: The Mentoring Relationships You Need To Succeed in Life*, by Paul D. Stanley and J. Robert Clinton. It is available from your local bookstore or from Lewis & Roth (800-477-3239). It is without question the finest book available on spiritual mentoring. Stanley and Clinton briefly define mentoring as "a relational experience through which one person empowers another by sharing God-given resources."[7] Their expanded definition reads:

> Mentoring is a relational process between [a] mentor, who knows or has experienced something and transfers that something (resources of wisdom, information, experience, confidence, insight, relationships, status, etc.) to a mentoree, at an appropriate time and manner, so that it facilitates development or empowerment.[8]

Stanley and Clinton dispel false ideas about mentoring and challenge us to seek different kinds of mentoring relationships throughout life for our continued growth.

In a church with several capable elders, one elder does not have to mentor a trainee through all twelve lessons of the *Guide*. As Stanley and Clinton explain, there is no one "ideal," or "all-encompassing mentor" for each of us for life,[9] so different elders should be involved with the trainee in specific areas of mentoring.

> When seeking a mentor, don't look for an ideal person who can do the whole range of mentoring functions. Few of these exist, if any. But if the mentoring needs are specified, someone is usually available who can mentor to that need. We believe that mentors are part of God's development plan for each of His followers. He will provide them as you "ask and seek."[10]

An elder who is more doctrinally astute should mentor prospective elders in the importance of knowing Bible doctrine (lessons 2, 4, and 8), for example, while an elder who is gifted in counseling and ministering to families should cover lesson 7. An elder who is devoted to prayer should guide the mentoree through lesson 3. This gives trainees the opportunity to learn from several mentoring elders and to draw from their particular strengths, experience, and gifts. However, one elder should be the primary mentoring elder for the trainee in order to provide close accountability for the overall training.

Mentoring should not end when a man becomes a pastor elder. The best learning actually occurs when one is in the process of serving. Furthermore, new elders need the closest mentoring. They need on-the-job training, guidance, counsel, rebuke, correction, love, and encouragement. Since the first few years as a pastor elder are the most strategic for growth in his shepherding ministry, it is imperative that experienced elders seize this opportunity to deliberately pass on their wisdom, knowledge, and skills to their new colleagues. In this way, the eldership is successfully perpetuated, guaranteeing future pastoral care for the local church.

ELDER QUALIFICATIONS

1 Timothy 3:2-7

1. Above reproach
2. The husband of one wife
3. Temperate [self-controlled, balanced]
4. Prudent [sensible, good judgment]
5. Respectable [well-behaved, virtuous]
6. Hospitable
7. Able to teach
8. Not addicted to wine
9. Not pugnacious [not belligerent]
10. Gentle [forbearing]
11. Peaceable [uncontentious]
12. Free from the love of money
13. Manages his household well
14. Not a new convert
15. A good reputation with those outside the church

Titus 1:6-9

1. Above reproach
2. The husband of one wife
3. Having children who believe
4. Not self-willed
5. Not quick-tempered
6. Not addicted to wine
7. Not pugnacious
8. Not fond of sordid gain
9. Hospitable
10. Lover of what is good [kind, virtuous]
11. Sensible [see prudent]
12. Just [righteous conduct, law-abiding]
13. Devout [holy, pleasing to God, loyal to His Word]
14. Self-controlled
15. Holds fast the faithful [trustworthy NIV] Word, both to exhort and to refute

1 Peter 5:1-3

1. Not shepherding under compulsion, but voluntarily
2. Not shepherding for sordid gain, but with eagerness
3. Not lording it over the flock, but proving to be an example

---

[1] Steve Huntley, with Jeannye Thornton, "The Silent Strength of Family Businesses," *U. S. News & World Report* (April 25, 1983), p. 47.

[2] Ibid., p. 50.

[3] Kenneth O. Gangel, *Feeding and Leading* (Wheaton: Victor, 1989), p. 313.

[4] Ibid., p. 309.

[5] A. B. Bruce, *The Training of the Twelve* (1871; reprinted Grand Rapids: Kregel, 1988), pp. 12, 13. Descriptions and dates are provided in this *Guide* only for those authors not previously identified in *Biblical Eldership*.

[6] Bill Hull, *Jesus Christ, Disciplemaker* (Grand Rapids: Revell, 1984), p. 94.

[7] Paul D. Stanley and J. Robert Clinton, *Connecting: The Mentoring Relationships You Need To Succeed in Life* (Colorado Springs: NavPress, 1992), p. 33.

[8] Ibid., p. 40.

[9] Ibid., pp. 45, 46.

[10] Ibid., p. 45.

Lesson 1
Old Testament Elders

LESSON OVERVIEW

Every prospective shepherd elder needs good role models to learn from and to follow. God's book, the Bible, provides us with many inspiring examples of godly men and women. In their excellent book on mentoring, Paul Stanley and Robert Clinton call such an example an "Historical Model," meaning "a person now dead whose life or ministry is written in a(n) (auto)biographical form and is used as an example to indirectly impart values, principles, and skills that empower another person."[1]

Lesson 1 explores Job's life as a model of the Old Testament elder. We will examine the duties and deficiencies of Israel's elders and will note the failure of Job's colleagues to compassionately and tactfully minister to him during his intense suffering. This lesson will help you think and act like a biblical, Christlike elder.

JOB, A MODEL ELDER

"There was a man in the land of Uz whose name was Job, and that man was blameless, upright, fearing God and turning away from evil" (Job 1:1).

> Read pages 186-202, 227-238. It is assumed that you have previously read pages 9-117.

1. Using a Bible dictionary, encyclopedia, or other reference tool,[2] briefly describe who Job is and what the book of Job is about.

   The book of Job is about a godly man who lived prior to Abraham. Job was a respected and prosperous leader (elder) of his community. The book addresses God's justice in light of the suffering of the righteous.

---

1. Job was a respected and prosperous leader, an elder of his community. Through a series of sudden, catastrophic events, Job lost his wealth, family, and health. His friends blamed Job's heartbreaking sufferings on his personal unconfessed sins. They tried to convince Job that he was receiving only what he rightfully deserved from God. Although Job himself could not understand God's harsh and mysterious treatment, he stubbornly disagreed with his friends' counsel. At the conclusion of the book, Job meets God and learns that He is the absolute, infinite sovereign over all creation. Job repents of his pride and foolishness in questioning God and trusts anew in God's justice, goodness, and inscrutable wisdom. Since pastor elders help people deal with life-and-death problems and address the puzzles and mysteries of life, they need to master the awe-inspiring theology of this remarkable OT book.

2. The verses below describe Job's personal character traits and his actions as a community leader.

    a. As you read each passage, mark with an "E" each reference that substantiates that Job was an elder.

    b. Where appropriate, summarize what Job did that a shepherd elder should do.

    c. Consider the New Testament qualifications of an elder on the list below and, using the numbers 1 through 11 that correspond to those qualifications, identify each passage that contains similar qualifications.

        1 **Above reproach** (1 Tim. 3:2; pp. 188, 228)
        2 **Hospitable** (1 Tim. 3:2; p. 194)
        3 **Respectable** [well-behaved, virtuous] (1 Tim. 3:3; p. 193)
        4 **Gentle** [forbearing] (1 Tim 3:3; p. 197)
        5 **Free from the love of money** (1 Tim. 3:3; p. 198)
        6 **Manages his household well** (1 Tim. 3:4; p. 199)
        7 **Lover of what is good** [kind, virtuous] (Titus 1:8; p. 233)
        8 **Just** [righteous conduct, law-abiding] (Titus 1:8; p. 234)
        9 **Devout** [holy, pleasing to God, loyal to His Word] (Titus 1:8; p. 235)
        10 **Faithful to God's Word** (Titus 1:9; pp. 235, 236)
        11 **Able to teach and exhort, and to refute false teachers** (Titus 1:9; pp. 236, 237)

Job 1:1 There was a man in the land of Uz whose name was Job, and that man was blameless, upright, fearing God and turning away from evil.

   Example: b. Job was blameless, God-fearing; c. 1, 8, 9

Job 1:4, 5 And his sons used to go and hold a feast in the house of each one on his day, and they would send and invite their three sisters to eat and drink with them. It came about, when the days of feasting had completed their cycle, that Job would send and consecrate them, rising up early in the morning and offering burnt offerings according to the number of them all; for Job said, "Perhaps my sons have sinned and cursed God in their hearts." Thus Job did continually.

   b. Job was the spiritual leader of his family; c. 6, 9

Job 1:1 Take special note of the Spirit's instructive description of Job. Oh, that God may say these things of us! As a mentoring elder, it is your responsibility to help the emerging elder see the vital importance of Job's example. Christian men need models of godly conduct and leadership. Your mentoree's encounter with Job could implant a permanent image in his mind. God the Holy Spirit chose to give us the example of Job for a purpose.

Job 1:4, 5 Job was the spiritual leader of his family. He prayed regularly for the spiritual condition of his children. He was an example of a godly father. Ask your mentoree about his prayers for his wife and children. Does he pray regularly for his children's spiritual welfare?

Job 4:1-4 Then Eliphaz the Temanite answered, "If one ventures a word with you [Job], will you become impatient? But who can refrain from speaking? Behold you [Job] have admonished [instructed] many, and you have strengthened weak hands. Your words have helped the tottering to stand, and you have strengthened feeble knees."

b. Job taught and admonished in order to strengthen others; c. 7, 11

Job 23:11, 12 My foot [Job's] has held fast to His path; I have kept His way and not turned aside. I have not departed from the command of His lips; I have treasured the words of His mouth more than my necessary food.

b. Job set an example; c. 1, 8, 9, 10

Job 29:7, 8 When I [Job] went out to the gate of the city, when I took my seat in the square, the young men saw me and hid themselves, and the old men arose and stood.

a. E; b. Job was a respected elder; c. 1, 3

Job 29:12-17 Because I delivered the poor who cried for help, and the orphan who had no helper. The blessing of the one ready to perish came upon me, and I made the widow's heart sing for joy. I put on righteousness, and it clothed me; my justice was like a robe and a turban. I was eyes to the blind and feet to the lame. I was a father to the needy, and I investigated the case which I did not know. I broke the jaws of the wicked and snatched the prey from his teeth.

Job 4:1-4 Job's beloved friend, Eliphaz, generously acknowledged Job's excellent character and abundant service in the past. Noble Job had helped many needy people. He had instructed and counseled those who faced life-crippling afflictions. He helped sufferers bear the heavy burdens of life. Job was a source of strength, comfort, knowledge, and encouragement to many weak, struggling people. Job was a man to be counted on for practical help, loving sympathy, and wise counsel.

Job 23:11, 12 Job provided to his community an inspiring example of unwavering loyalty to God's Word and a life of obedience to God's commands. God was the supreme master and guide of his life. Job loved and followed God's ways and instructions, which had been handed down from godly predecessors like Noah and Shem. Indeed, Job prized God's ordinances more than his necessary food. It was God's will, not his own, that mattered in his life. In the face of many alternative lifestyles and tempting, idolatrous religions, Job clung tenaciously to God's moral and spiritual path. He was a living example of godliness in an ungodly world.

Note: Jesus said that the greatest commandment is to love the Lord God "with all your heart, and with all your soul, and with all your mind. This is the great and foremost commandment. The second is like it, you shall love your neighbor as yourself" (Matt. 22:37-39). Job is a marvelous example of an elder who loved God with all his might and loved his neighbor as himself. Job had his priorities straight, and illustrates true, biblical religion.

Job 29:7, 8 In ancient times, *gate* meant the open space at the gate of the city, the official meeting place where business and justice were openly conducted. The elders of the city sat at the gate to hear disputes and administer justice for the community. This passage tells us that Job was a highly respected elder of his community.

Job 29:12-17 Job was a champion of the poor, the widow and orphan, and the feeble in body and mind. He befriended the helpless. He was a protector and guardian. He provided comfort for the dying, legal defense from unscrupulous oppressors and creditors for orphans and widows, and assured that justice was administered to all. Although he was an active and important man in the community, Job was not too busy to help those who were suffering or who could not repay his kindness. He was always generous, watching out for the needs of others. He was like a father to those who had no one to help them. He was a minister of mercy.

Job's moral integrity was well-known. He hated injustice and oppression. A living model of service, loving-kindness, courage, and justice, he had a great social impact on his community. What an inspiring model of Christlike compassion and love for people Job provides for us. See James 1:27.

b. Job cared for the needs of the downtrodden and administered justice for the oppressed; c. 4, 7, 8

Job 29:21 "To me they listened and waited, and kept silent for my counsel."

a. E; b. Job was a teacher and wise counselor; c. 11

Job 30:25 "Have I not wept for the one whose life is hard? Was not my soul grieved for the needy?"

b. Job showed compassion to the needy; c. 4, 7

Job 31:1 "I have made a covenant with my eyes; how then could I gaze [look lustfully NIV] at a virgin?"

b. Job set a moral example; c. 1

Job 31:24-34 "If I have put my confidence in gold, and called fine gold my trust, if I have gloated because my wealth was great, and because my hand had secured so much; if I have looked at the sun when it shone or the moon going in splendor, and my heart became secretly enticed, and my hand threw a kiss from my mouth, that too would have been an iniquity calling for judgment, for I would have denied God above. Have I rejoiced at the extinction of my enemy, or exulted when evil befell him? No, I have not allowed my mouth to sin by asking for his life in a curse. Have the men of my tent not said, 'Who can find one who has not been satisfied with his meat'? The alien has not lodged outside, for I have opened my doors to the traveler. Have I covered my transgressions like Adam, by hiding my iniquity in my bosom, because I feared the great multitude, and the contempt of families terrified me, and kept silent and did not go out of doors?"

b. Job was free from the love of money and demonstrated that lifestyle. He rejected pride. Job provided for his household and guests. He had the right attitude toward his own sin; c. 1, 2, 4, 5, 6, 7, 8, 9

Job 29:21 Sought after for his wisdom and guidance, Job helped many people. He had enormous influence for good on their minds and spirits. In today's world, which is full of lies and manipulation, men need wise, biblical counselors. To be such a counselor, however, one needs to know God and His Word.

Job 30:25 Job sympathized with those who were suffering or in need. He was never unfeeling or uncaring. Like our Lord, he hurt with those who hurt and mourned with those who mourned.

Job 31:1 Job was above reproach in male-female relationships. This is an extremely important verse to direct men in their battle against sexual lust. The first step for a man is to follow Job's example and commit himself to controlling his wandering, lustful eyes.

Job 31:24-34 Job was a hospitable man. He opened his home to needy travelers and strangers. He was big-hearted and sacrificially generous with his time, money, and effort. Job was free from the love of money and demonstrated that lifestyle. He rejected the pride of wealth and self-accomplishment. He did not worship wealth or created, heavenly objects like the sun and moon, as most people did in his day. He trusted only in God, creator of heaven and earth. Job did not gloat over the misfortunes of his enemies. He was not small, petty, or cruel.

3. In summary, what was Job's attitude toward people?

Job was a humble and compassionate leader who was both loving and just in all his dealings with people. He was Christlike in his relationships.

The following observation is from a letter by Hudson Taylor, founder of the China Inland Mission and one of the greatest missionaries of all time. He wrote about the lack of tact and sensitivity some missionaries displayed toward the Chinese. May his words remind us of the importance of grace and tact in dealing with people:

"Some persons seem really clever in doing the right thing in the worst possible way, or at the most unfortunate time. Really dull, or rude persons will seldom be out of hot water in China; and though earnest and clever and pious will not effect much. *In nothing do we fail more, as a Mission, than in lack of tact and politeness.*"
—Hudson Taylor[3]

---

4. Job complained that his three friends, who may also have been elders, were miserable comforters. **"You are all worthless physicians"** (Job 13:4). **"Sorry comforters are you all"** (Job 16:2). Many elders today think and act like Job's friends. So that you will not become a worthless physician of the soul, observe the negative characteristics in Job's friends that shepherds of God's people should avoid. List those that appear in these passages.

Job 6:14, 15 "For the despairing man [Job speaking] there should be kindness from his friend; so that he does not forsake the fear of the Almighty. My brothers [Job's friends] have acted deceitfully like a wadi [a seasonal stream], like the torrents of wadis which vanish."

Example: lack of compassion, inconsistent, useless

Job 12:5a "He who is at ease holds calamity in contempt."

Job 6:14, 15 Job expected basic human comfort and sympathy from his three friends. Instead they let him down and left him bitterly frustrated. A *wadi* is a seasonal stream in the desert. In the rainy season it is a fast-moving torrent, but to the thirsty traveler in the heat of the drought, the dry wadi is a crushing disappointment. Job asserts that his friends are like a wadi in that they have failed to provide brotherly kindness and relief for their dying companion. How disillusioning! When Job needed them, his friends proved to be useless and impotent.

Job 12:5a It is common for those who are at ease financially and physically vigorous to look with contempt on the poor and ill. Not having suffered personally, they lack sympathy and compassion for those who do. Feeling superior and successful, blind and oblivious, they even assume the right to judge others. Job's friends are the same. They believed Job to be responsible for his misfortune and deserving of the consequences. In their minds, his situation did not require compassion or understanding, but confrontation and verdicts.

This is an important passage for elders to take to heart. Elders are often blessed and successful. They may find it difficult to respond to or sympathize with those who continually fail or are chronically ill. Nevertheless, this is the wrong attitude, born of ignorance and pride. Any good we enjoy is a result of God's grace and mercy. Rather than making us proud, the good we enjoy should cause us to turn the glory back to God. JAMES 1 v 17

Insensitivity, lack of compassion, arrogance, judgmental verdicts

Job 13:4 "But you smear with lies; you are all worthless physicians."

Lying, lack of integrity, critical spirit, ineffective leadership

Job 16:1-4 Then Job answered, "I have heard many such things; sorry comforters are you all. Is there no limit to windy words? Or what plagues you that you answer? I too could speak like you, if I were in your place. I could compose words against you and shake my head at you."

Arrogance, pride, lack of compassion or godly wisdom, judgmental, refusal to own the afflicted's problem

Job 19:1-5 Then Job responded, "How long will you torment me, and crush me with words? These ten times you have insulted me; you are not ashamed to wrong me. . . . If indeed you vaunt yourselves against me, and prove my disgrace to me."

Harmful, unjust, unloving, and proud

5. Restate Job 12:5*a* in your own words. Why is it important for those who provide spiritual care to understand and remember this text?

The man who has not experienced difficulties is often unsympathetic, perhaps even contemptuous of those who are. Unable or unwilling to visualize himself in similar circumstances, his judgments are simplistic, uninformed, and arrogant.

We elders and leaders must be careful not to let our lack of misfortune or trying experiences prevent us from being responsive and compassionate. We must empathize with those in our care. The truth is, we are not told nor do we know why some people suffer more than others.

Job 13:4 Job's counselors were charlatans. They totally misunderstood both Job's plight and God's inscrutable dealings with men. Their counsel was unbiblical and not to be trusted. In their finite reason, they played God, pronouncing charges without foundation in order to prove that Job was sinful and deserving of misfortune. With insinuations and lies, they smeared his reputation. Job's friends were like the counselor who further injures the sufferer with the judgment: "It's all in your head."

Job 16:1-4 Job's counselors proved to be of no consolation. Their irritating advice was simplistic, pious, and trite. Demanding and secure in their duty to correct Job, they quoted misconstrued Bible verses and clichés about life and suffering. At his angry response to their brilliant insights, they shook their heads in contempt. Job spoke sarcastically in this section, calling his friends miserable, inferior comforters.

Job 19:1-5 Unyielding, Job's friends mocked him repeatedly. They wounded him deeply with their pompous moralizing. Like many sincere people who want to help others, they degenerated into malicious critics, especially when Job disagreed with their advice and solutions.

ISRAEL'S ELDERS

"And they [the elders] shall bear the burden of the people with you"   (Numbers 11:17).

Read pages 121-124.

6. Practice pronouncing the following Greek words, and give their meanings:

presbyteros [prez BOO tuh rohs] (p. 124) ....*An elder (individual)*

presbyteroi [prez BOO tuh roy] (p. 124) ....*Elders (plural)*

presbyterion [prez boo TEH ree ohn] (pp. 123, 205) ....*A council of elders (collective)*

gerousia [geh roo SEE uh] (p. 123) ....*A council of elders (collective)*

7. Briefly define the eldership structure of government of the Old Testament (p. 39).

   A collective form of leadership in which the most qualified and respected men shared equally the leadership of the community: that is, in position, authority, and responsibility.

8. The divinely inspired New Testament is built on the divinely inspired Old Testament. A major reason why most Christians do not see or understand church eldership as practiced in the New Testament is that they do not know anything about the Old Testament elders. Robert B. Girdlestone (1836-1923), author of the classic *Synonyms of the Old Testament*, echoes this sentiment: "The importance of a right judgment of the position and functions of these [Old Testament] elders cannot well be overrated when we come to discuss the nature of the analogous office of presbyter in the NT."[4]

   Elders appear throughout the entire Bible, beginning with Genesis 50:7 and ending with Revelation 4:4, which describes the twenty-four elders who surround the throne of God. Since government by a council of elders has been a fundamental institution among the people of God all through biblical history, a study of New Testament church eldership must begin with an examination of what the Old Testament says about elders.

   List the responsibilities of the elders of Israel indicated in these Old Testament passages. Be sure to interpret these verses in their context.

Ex. 19:7, 8....................................*Official representatives of the people*

Lev. 4:13-15 ....*Led the congregation in repentance for sin*

Num. 11:16, 17............................*Took responsibility for leading the congregation*

Deut. 19:11, 12............................*Administered justice in accordance with Scripture*

Deut. 21:18-21 ....*Intervened in and judged families' problems*

Deut. 27:1 ....*Taught the congregation God's Word and exhorted them to obey it*

Deut. 31:9-12...............................*Instructed the congregation as to God's commands and exhorted them to obedience*

2 Sam. 5:3....................................*Represented the congregation in appointing leaders and accepting obligations*

Job 12:20 ....*Served and led with discernment*

Ezek. 7:26.....................................*Counseled the congregation wisely*

9. Although today's elders do not offer sacrifices, protect manslayers, or sit at the city gate, there are important similarities between the responsibilities of the Old and New Testament elders. List some of these similarities.

    As humble, God-fearing men, both the Old and New Testament elders were to be spiritual guides who were responsible to wisely and effectively lead and exhort the community. They were to know, teach, and uphold God's Word; to care for the community's well-being with sensitivity and compassion; and to protect the people by administering justice and dealing with sin and false doctrine.

Ex. 19:7, 8 When God spoke to the elders through Moses, it was the same as if He spoke to the people. That is why the OT elders were called "the elders of the people," or "the elders of the congregation." The elders were the chief men among the people.

Lev. 4:13-15 The elders were clearly the people's foremost representatives. They represented the entire nation in the sin offering and directed the congregation in spiritual matters, here in confession and repentance for sin.

Num. 11:16, 17 A select group of seventy, highly capable elders were chosen from among all Israel's elders to help Moses lead the congregation during the wilderness wanderings. These elders were given a measure of the Spirit to empower them to serve as co-shepherds with Moses in bearing the burden of the people.

Deut. 19:11, 12 The elders were to see that a murderer was brought to justice in accordance with the law.

Deut. 21:18-21 The elders were to judge the case of a rebellious son. Especially noteworthy is the elders' involvement in the family's protection, even hearing and judging the most intimate family matters.

Deut. 27:1 The elders were involved in the congregation's spiritual life. With Moses, the elders exhorted the people to obey the law of God.

Deut. 31:9-12 The elders and the priests were jointly responsible to read the law to the people every seven years. How could the elders administer the law if they and the people did not know it? Highlight this significant passage for your mentoree. In every age, elders must be men of the Book.

10. What highly significant lesson for elders do you find in Joshua 24:31?

Israel continued to follow the Lord as long as there were faithful elders who had experienced God's hand on Israel. Therefore, elders are responsible to uphold and teach God's message and to encourage the congregation to obey the Lord and His Word. Elders have an extraordinary impact on the spiritual life of the church, for its future spiritual health and success depend on them.

11. By and large, Israel's elders failed to meet their responsibility to uphold the law of God and protect the people. We also cannot assume that collective leadership will protect us from the consequences of corporate sin.

What were some of the root sins and failures of Israel's elders? Again, be sure to observe the context.

1 Sam. 4:1-11 ....*Believed they could manipulate God and deal with their enemies by controlling the symbol of His presence (ark)*

1 Sam. 8:4-9, 19, 20.....................*Rejected God's leadership and turned toward secular customs (earthly kings) for power and security, were enticed by worldly success and secular leadership fads, and were idolatrous in serving other gods*

1 Sam. 11:1-3 ....*When in trouble, acquiesced to fear and were subservient to men and secular patterns instead of depending upon God and His provision (Saul)*

2 Sam. 5:3; 17:1-4 ....*Disobeyed God by breaking covenant with God's anointed and supporting the popular opposition*

---

1 Sam. 4:1-11 The elders' unbiblical counsel in this situation demonstrates their utter ignorance of spiritual matters. Failing to recognize the chastening hand of God, of which they had ample warning (Deut. 28:25), the elders showed no more wisdom than their heathen Philistine neighbors. Superstitiously and unlawfully, they moved the ark of the covenant-that most sacred object of God's presence-exposing it to God's enemies, who captured it (1 Sam 4:22). These elders did not know God's Word or ways with His people. If they had known God, they would have first led the people in confession of sin and repentance. Then God would have delivered them from their enemies.

1 Sam. 8:4-9, 19, 20 The elders wanted to have a king so they could be like other nations around them. Accommodation to the spirit of the age is the age-old problem with which God's people struggle in every generation. The elders did not appreciate or understand their glorious privileges and distinctives as God's people, with God as their king and Lord. Moreover, the elders did not want to carry out their God-given responsibility to lead the people; they wanted an earthly king to bear the responsibility. Today many elders want a senior pastor, or the clergy in general, to lead.

1 Sam. 11:1-3 The fact that the elders of Jabesh-Gilead did not rely upon the Lord for help against the fearsome Ammonite army illustrates the unbelief at the root of their failures. Unbelief was their worst sin, the cause of most of their troubles. Sadly, the same failures–ignorance of His precious Word, earthly mindedness, little understanding of the exalted privilege of being in Christ, and unbelief–exist today among many of God's elders. As a result, the same multitude of spiritual problems abound among God's people at this present time.

2 Sam. 5:3; 17:1-4 After Absalom skillfully won the elders' loyalty, they broke their covenant with David (2 Sam. 17:4,15). How easily people–even elders–are fooled and misled by powerful, charismatic leaders.

1 Kings 21:5-11 ....*Did what was wrong out of fear of the powerful*

Ezek. 8:7-13 ....*Led the people in idolatry and were loyal to personal idols rather than to the Lord*

12. In light of your desire to become a godly leader or elder, write brief phrases that summarize the biblical standards for character and conduct for elders that you have gleaned from this study.

I must:

a. *Love God with all my heart and love my neighbor as myself*

b. *Fear God and turn away from evil*

c. *Know God's Word and see that it is obeyed*

d. *Demonstrate unswerving integrity*

e. *Be above reproach in male-female relationships*

f. *Be the spiritual leader of my home*

g. *Pray for my children*

h. *Be loving, compassionate, and available to God's people*

i. *Be tactful and sensitive when helping people*

j. *Be an effective servant leader by teaching, exhorting, encouraging, counseling, delegating, dealing with personal and corporate sin, and administering justice*

---

1 Kings 21:5-11 The account discloses how godless and fearful Israel's elders had become. At the urging of Queen Jezebel, the elders of Jezreel staged a mock trial and condemned an innocent Israelite, Naboth, to death. This enabled wicked King Ahab to seize the property Naboth had rightfully refused to sell him. The elders' action was a vile outrage against God's law and His people, an abomination of everything they were instructed to do in Deuteronomy. The very men who were commanded to protect the family and uphold God's law became its most heinous offenders.

Ezek. 8:7-13 In Babylon, the exiled elders of Judah visited Ezekiel for a report about the homeland (Jerusalem). To their dismay, Ezekiel received a vision of Jerusalem's abominable idolatry and further judgment, showing that the elders of Israel were the most heavily involved (Ezek. 8:11, 12). In his vision, Ezekiel saw Israel's seventy elders secretly worshipping the most detestable idols. Lacking the basic knowledge of God's omniscience, omnipresence, and lovingkindness, the elders even blamed God, saying, "The Lord does not see us; the Lord has forsaken the land" (Ezek. 8:12). What a contrast they are to the seventy elders who helped Moses ratify the covenant on Mount Sinai! So far had they strayed from God that judgment soon came upon them (Ezek. 9:6).

    k. *Guard against departures from God's Word or exchanging its directives for popular trends or secular concepts*

    l. *Take active ownership of, and give attention to, the local church's needs and condition*

    m. *Be a consistent and wise biblical counselor*

    n. *Continuously examine myself for closely-held opinions or loyalties that may become personal idols; be teachable*

    o. *Be aware of my personal pride, failings, and sin*

SCRIPTURE MEMORY ASSIGNMENT:

"There was a man in the land of Uz whose name was Job; and that man was blameless, upright, fearing God and turning away from evil" (Job 1:1).

---

[1] Paul D. Stanley and J. Robert Clinton, *Connecting: The Mentoring Relationship You Need to Succeed in Life* (Colorado Springs: NavPress, 1992), p. 147.

[2] We highly recommend that every elder own and use regularly *Talk Thru the Bible,* by Bruce Wilkinson and Kenneth Boa (Nashville: Thomas Nelson Publishers). For a good Bible dictionary, we recommend the *New Bible Dictionary,* by Tyndale House Publishers.

[3] A. J. Broomhall, *Refiner's Fire* (Robesonia: The Overseas Missionary Fellowship, 1985), p. 231.

[4] Robert Baker Girdlestone, *Synonyms of the Old Testament*, 3d ed. (Grand Rapids: Baker, 1983), p. 269.

Lesson 2
Men of Sound Doctrine and Wisdom

LESSON OVERVIEW

Although there are important similarities between Old and New Testament elders, it would be a mistake to consider the apostolic elder to be simply the Old Testament elder in a new era. To try to define the New Testament elder (Pauline elder) in terms of the Old Testament elder or the Jewish synagogue elder (of whom we know very little) is to distort the New Testament's teachings on eldership. The work and qualifications of the Christian elder are more clearly defined than those of the Old Testament elder. In the following eleven lessons, we will study the New Testament elder and work through the implications of these teachings for your own ministry.

Lesson 2 sets forth the biblical imperative that elders know Bible doctrine so that they will be adequately equipped to judge doctrinal disputes and provide wise, godly counsel and leadership for the congregation. As you will discover throughout the *Guide*, biblical elders must be men of the Word. The biblical standard for pastor elders is that they be able to teach and defend sound Christian doctrine. Elders who are biblically inadequate are actually a curse to the church, not the blessing God would have them be. This lesson is intended to help you evaluate your preparedness as a teacher and defender of Christ's doctrine. It will also touch briefly on the elder-congregation relationship and the need for elders to be men of wisdom who know how to lead the congregation in godly decision making.

JUDGING DOCTRINAL ISSUES

"Some men came down from Judea and began teaching the brethren, 'Unless you are circumcised according to the custom of Moses, you cannot be saved.' And when Paul and Barnabas had great dissension and debate with them, the brethren determined that Paul and Barnabas and some others of them should go up to Jerusalem to the apostles and elders concerning this issue."   Acts 15:1, 2

Review pages 17-22. Read pages 125-133, 291-295.

1. Do not be surprised by doctrinal controversy. The first Christians struggled over doctrinal issues. Even the apostles' presence did not prevent theological conflict. As we see in Acts 15, it is the elders' responsibility to deal with doctrinal controversy. Elders must be able to judge

opposing theological views, weigh arguments, discern error, deal with potentially explosive situations, arbitrate, and make sound, expeditious decisions.

a.   Should maintaining peace within the church always be the elder's goal? Support your answer from Paul's actions in Acts 15:1, 2.

No. Challenging an erroneous belief may be necessary to protect a core Christian doctrine. Paul could have kept the peace at Antioch by giving in to the Judaizers. By arguing against their distorted doctrines, he initially provoked dissension. Peace in the church is always the elder's long-term goal, but elders may have to raise the level of contention in the short term in order to deal with doctrinal error.

b.   According to Acts 15, what was the chief doctrinal issue debated by these first Christians?

The issue was whether a Gentile could become a Christian without first becoming a Jew and observing the ceremonial law, with compliance to be marked by circumcision.

c.   Outline the process used by the church in Jerusalem to resolve the controversy.

The involved parties debated the issue before the apostles and elders (15:6).
The leaders applied the teachings of Scripture to the issue (15:15-18).
Consensus among the apostles and elders was achieved, and the church was taught (15:25).
The congregation concurred.
Action was taken consistent with the consensus decision.

d.   What do we learn from the fact that the apostles did not settle this doctrinal issue with a simple, authoritative, apostolic decree, without debate and congregational involvement?

1a. To get a true sense of how passionately Paul felt about the importance of peace in the local church, read pp. 173, 174 of *Biblical Eldership,* especially the quotation by Fenton J. A. Hort. We cannot escape the tension that always exists between the peace and unity of the church and its doctrinal purity. This is why elders must be balanced, sensible, and wise.

1d. Consider Hort's judicious, and now classic, evaluation of the apostles' exercise of their Christ-given authority at the Jerusalem counsel:

> The letter itself at once implies an authority, and betrays an unwillingness to make a display of it. . . . The New Testament is not poor of words expressive of command . . . yet none of them is used [in Acts 15] . . . . But along with the cordial concurrence in the release of Gentile converts from legal requirements there [is communicated] a strong expression of opinion, more than advice and less than a command, respecting certain salutary restraints. A certain authority is thus implicitly claimed. There is no evidence that it was more than a moral authority; but that did not make it less real.[1]

Present-day elders have oversight authority in the church, but, as illustrated in Acts 15, it must be exercised in grace, restraint, and for the good of the gospel and the congregation.

The apostles' actions indicate they were convinced that consensus decision making by the elders (and apostles) was the surest means of knowing the mind of Christ. Authoritarian rule has no place in the church. The church must be taught and convinced of the Scriptural position on issues. Imposing decisions without leading the congregation to understand them is unbiblical.

e. Contrast Paul's attitude toward those who opposed him as recorded in Acts 15:1, 2; Gal. 1:6-9, 2:4-5; and 2:11-16, with his opinions recorded in Phil. 1:15-18. Compare with Mark 9:38-41. What determined the differences? What principles can you learn from this?

Paul was confrontive and willing to dispute issues having to do with access to salvation, but he did not react to personal opposition or the jealousy of other men when doctrinal principles were not at stake. Disagreement must be handled in such a way that our egos and pride do not determine our responses.

2. Select those elder qualifications that qualify elders to judge and resolve doctrinal conflict in a Christian manner and explain your reason for each selection. You may include several qualifications in a single explanation where appropriate.

1 Timothy 3:2-7	Titus 1:6-9	1 Peter 5:1-3
1. Above reproach	1. Above reproach	1. Not shepherding under compulsion, but voluntarily
2. The husband of one wife	2. The husband of one wife	2. Not shepherding for sordid gain, but with eagerness
3. Temperate [self-controlled, balanced]	3. Having children who believe	3. Not lording it over the flock, but proving to be an example
4. Prudent [sensible, good judgment]	4. Not self-willed	
5. Respectable [well-behaved, virtuous]	5. Not quick-tempered	
6. Hospitable	6. Not addicted to wine	
7. Able to teach	7. Not pugnacious	
8. Not addicted to wine	8. Not fond of sordid gain	
9. Not pugnacious [not belligerent]	9. Hospitable	
10. Gentle [forbearing]	10. Lover of what is good [kind, virtuous]	
11. Peaceable [uncontentious]	11. Sensible [see prudent]	
12. Free from the love of money	12. Just [righteous conduct, law-abiding]	
13. Manages his household well	13. Devout [holy, pleasing to God, loyal to His Word]	
14. Not a new convert	14. Self-controlled	
15. A good reputation with those outside the church	15. Holds fast the faithful [trustworthy NIV] Word, both to exhort and to refute	

2. Remind your mentoree that the *Study Guide* continually returns to these qualifications because the NT emphasizes them. Also, it is the best way to make sure that the characteristics are fixed in the emerging elder's thinking. For many, the NT elder qualifications are a standard that is never understood or remembered.

a.   *Example: **Above reproach, respectable:** The elder who is not above reproach will be discredited because of peripheral matters and be ineffective in pursuing the critical issues.*

b.   ***Holds fast the faithful Word, both to exhort and refute:** The elder must know the Word, interpret it correctly, and properly apply it to life situations. He must be capable of refuting error and willing to do so.*

c.   ***Sensible, prudent:** The elder must be able to make sound, wise arguments that clarify issues for the congregation.*

d.   ***Peaceable [uncontentious], not pugnacious:** If the elder has the reputation of being contentious, the substance of his argument will be discounted when he opposes individuals on important issues.*

e.   ***Not self-willed:** The elder must not insist on his own way, a quality that is necessary to achieve dialogue and to resolve doctrinal issues.*

f.   ***Self-controlled, not quick-tempered:** The elder must remain calm in contentious situations, controlling his temper lest it interfere with his judgment or credibility.*

g.   ***Gentle, not lording it over the flock but proving to be an example:** Elders must be forbearing when resolving conflict, thereby demonstrating the value of the people involved.*

h.   ***Just [righteous]:** The elder must be upright and truthful when judging doctrinal conflict in order to retain the congregation's trust.*

3.   Discuss whether each elder must possess all of these qualifications, or should the elder council as a whole fulfill these requirements?

Scripture is clear that each elder must possess all the qualifications. However, each elder will be more gifted in some qualifications than in others. Since the elders complement each others' strengths, an elder council's ministry effectiveness is greater than the sum of the individual elders' contributions.

4.   In order for you to qualify as a pastor elder, God requires that you be able to teach and exhort "in sound doctrine" and refute false doctrine (Titus 1:9). An elder who does not know the doctrines of Scripture is as useful as a lifeguard who does not know how to swim. P. T. Forsyth was right on target when he wrote, "The real strength of the Church is not the amount of its work but the quality of its faith. One man who truly knows his Bible is worth more to the Church's real strength than a crowd of workers who do not."[2]

When elders who have not attended seminary defer to seminary-trained pastors when settling doctrinal issues, what are the consequences?

    a.   *The church is not necessarily protected from doctrinal error. Historically, most theological error has emanated from seminaries.*

    b.   *The elders on the elder council are not serving as equal partners. As a result, they create a de facto, unbiblical hierarchy among the elders.*

    c.   *The deferring elders fail in their responsibilities to each other and to the flock.*

5.   Below are the major Bible doctrines you must know in order to teach and defend "sound doctrine." Indicate after each of the eight doctrines whether or not you are currently prepared to teach and defend it.

    a.   **BIBLIOLOGY,** the doctrine of the Bible: general and special revelation; the inspiration, infallibility, canonicity, illumination, and interpretation of the Bible.

    b.   **THEOLOGY PROPER,** the doctrine of God: the existence, attributes, and decrees of God; the Trinity.

    c.   **CHRISTOLOGY,** the doctrine of Christ: the divine-human natures of Christ and the hypostatic union; the offices and present ministry of Christ; the theophanies and prophecies of Christ.

    d.   **PNEUMATOLOGY,** the doctrine of the Holy Spirit: the personality and deity of the Holy Spirit; the Spirit's work in relation to Christ and in regenerating, baptizing, indwelling, gifting, and helping believers.

    e.   **SOTERIOLOGY,** the doctrine of salvation: the death of Christ, substitution, propitiation, reconciliation, justification by faith alone, regeneration, election, free will, grace, faith, perseverance.

    f.   **ANTHROPOLOGY AND HARMARTIOLOGY,** the doctrines of man and sin: the origin, fall, and nature of man; the definition of sin and imputation of sin.

    g.   **ECCLESIOLOGY,** the doctrine of the church: the relationship between Israel and the Church; the local church and the universal Church; the imagery used to describe the church (body, bride, priesthood, temple, flock); the government of the church; the ordinances of the church; evangelism, spiritual gifts, and ministry.

    h.   **ESCHATOLOGY,** the doctrine of last things: heaven, hell, return and rule of Christ, resurrection, judgment, and man's eternal state.

---

5. The best method here is to read through all eight doctrines with your mentoree, marking any term or concept with which he is unfamiliar and identifying areas of doctrinal deficiency. If your mentoree cannot precisely define *inspiration, propitiation,* etc., he is doctrinally unprepared to protect the flock from false teachers. Also, some men know their Bible well and are doctrinally sound, but are not familiar with theological terms such as *canonicity* or *hypostatic union.* They need help in defining and learning these terms.

6.   As an elder, you will work with people who hold differing theological views. When is tolerance appropriate, and when is it necessary to challenge a teaching as false and harmful to the church? Keep in mind that scriptural data for some doctrines is inconclusive, and faithful scholars who are committed to the authority of Scripture have disagreed on such doctrines throughout church history. However, on essential matters Scripture is clear, and adherence to these teachings is crucial to the spiritual health of the church.

a.   There are essential doctrines that are not negotiable and on which we will not compromise. List several examples.

b.   There are other doctrinal issues on which we must agree to disagree. List several examples of such issues that are treated this way in your church.

7.   The suggested resources and practical methods below can help you enhance your knowledge of Bible doctrine. Record your decisions as to which of these you need to invest in or implement in order to become doctrinally equipped to shepherd God's flock.

a.   For a basic introductory book on the foundational doctrines of Christianity, read *Know What You Believe: A Practical Discussion of the Fundamentals of the Christian Faith*, by Paul E. Little.[3] Also highly recommended is Little's companion volume, *Know Why You Believe*.[4]

For more advanced study, read *The Moody Handbook of Theology*, by Paul Enns.[5] Enns's book is an excellent reference tool even if you do not entirely agree with his theology. Elders should own basic reference tools for equipping themselves and for answering the biblical and doctrinal questions directed to them.

b.   For a systematic study of doctrine, start with *Decide for Yourself: A Theological Workbook*, by Gordon R. Lewis.[6] Lewis presents all the Scripture passages on each of the major doctrines, but requires that you work out your own conclusions. You will find that this book is an invaluable tool for studying Bible doctrine.

---

7. Several other doctrinal books on key subjects that should be available, by personal purchase, or in the church's elder library are:
    • John Walvoord, *Jesus Christ Our Lord* (Chicago: Moody, 1969).
    • Norman L. Geisler and William E. Nix, *A General Introduction to the Bible*, rev. ed. (Chicago: Moody, 1986). This is a large, expensive reference work, but it is an essential help in answering your questions concerning the Bible.
    • Charles Caldwell Ryrie, *The Holy Spirit* (Chicago: Moody, 1965).
    • John R. W. Stott, *The Cross of Christ* (Downers Grove: InterVarsity, 1986).
    • H. Wayne House, *Charts of Christian Theology and Doctrine* (Grand Rapids: Zondervan, 1992).

c.   Develop your own topical, Bible doctrine workbook. Add to this as you regularly read the Bible (see the next lesson). For example, when you find a passage that teaches Christ's divine nature, note the verse that refers to His deity on the workbook page designated "Christology - Divine Nature." Your notebook will be an excellent resource for quickly locating passages needed for teaching and answering questions.

d.   Teaching tapes are one of the most efficient tools for using time wisely and maintaining consistent growth in your knowledge of the Word and doctrine. Many men use the time they spend exercising or driving to listen to great Bible expositors teach the Scriptures. This will amount to many hours of Bible teaching over the years.

A number of churches that are well-known for their Bible teachers loan or give away teaching tapes. We always encourage churches and men to regularly order such series and urge them to start with a set on the book of Romans. It is absolutely essential that church leaders master the book of Romans because it represents the most systematic statement of Christian doctrine found in Scripture.

e.   Study theology or Bible through a reputable correspondence school. If you are able, take a theology course at a local Bible school or seminary.

Document your plans for further study and discuss them with your mentor.

8.   What arguments presented in *Biblical Eldership* refute James Bannerman's claim that Acts 15 supports the *necessity* for an ecclesiastical court that rules over the local church (pp. 125-130)? Bannerman asserts:

Now, in this narrative we have all the elements necessary to make up the idea of a supreme ecclesiastical court, with authority over not only the members and office-bearers within the local bounds of the congregations represented, but also the Presbyteries or inferior Church courts included in the same limits (p. 128).

a.   *The issue in question was referred to the Jerusalem church because the Judaizing teachers had come from Jerusalem, **not** because the church in Jerusalem was the superior body. The decision to go to the Jerusalem church for resolution was **voluntary** on the part of the Antioch church.*

b.   *The churches in other areas were not represented at the meeting in Jerusalem.*

c.   *In the epistles, no mention at all is made of a court higher than the local church's elder council. As a case in point, if a higher court had been established, it would have been called upon to deal with the problems at Ephesus.*

ELDERS AND THE CONGREGATION

"And the following day Paul went in with us to James, and all the elders were present. . . . And they said to him, 'You see, brother, how many thousands there are among the Jews of those who have believed, and they are all zealous for the Law; and they have been told about you, that you are teaching all the Jews who are among the Gentiles to forsake Moses, telling them not to circumcise their children nor to walk according to the customs. What, then, is to be done? They will certainly hear that you have come. Therefore do this that we tell you.'"
                                                                                                    Acts 21:18, 20*b*-23*a*

Review pages 291-295.

9.   The several meetings recorded in Acts 15 are important examples of how church leaders and congregations should meet together to resolve doctrinal problems. List the biblical obligations the elders have to the congregation and those the congregation has to its elders.

    a.   The elders' obligations to the congregation:

        Titus 1:7   *As stewards, elders are entrusted with the overall management of the church family.*

        1 Peter 5:3   *Elders are to be examples to the flock as they humbly resolve problems in the congregation without emphasizing their own authority.*

        Acts 20:28   *Elders, as shepherds, must stand guard over the congregation on behalf of Christ who purchased His people with His blood.*

Titus 1:7 Point out the significance of the Greek word for "steward," *oikonomos* (p. 231). This term is important for the emerging elder's view of his own identity and service as an elder.

1 Peter 5:3 Acts 6 and 15 provide concrete examples of Christian leaders who were examples to the flock. The apostles and elders did not flaunt their authority over the congregation, but were open and fair in their deliberations.

Acts 20:28 Acts 15 is a perfect example of elders who guard the flock from false teachers who come from within. As true guardians of the flock, the apostles and elders dealt fairly and decisively with false teaching.

b.   The congregation's obligations to its elders:

1 Thess. 5:12, 13	*Respect your elders. Appreciate, esteem them very highly in love for their oversight, hard work for you and the Lord, and admonishment.*
1 Tim. 5:17	*Honor especially those elders who excel in leadership, teaching, and preaching. Support financially those elders who devote themselves full time to the Lord's work.*
Heb. 13:7	*Follow your elders, imitating their way of life and faith.*
Heb. 13:17	*Obey and submit to the elders, making their work a joy rather than a burden.*
1 Tim. 5:19, 20	*Guard the reputation of the leadership. Protect elders from false accusations by refusing to listen to unsupported charges, but publicly rebuke those who are involved in sin.*
1 Tim. 3:10; cf.	*Support the testing (proving) of elders and deacons by giving*
1 Tim. 5:22	*Provide feedback on their fulfillment of their duties.*
1 Thess. 5:25	*Pray for your elders.*

10.   In leading their congregation so that it will make wise corporate decisions, church leaders must recognize and avoid certain dangers. What are these dangers? See pp. 293-295.

Manipulating and failing to lead the congregation in decision making by being preoccupied, irresponsible, indecisive, aloof, secretive, arrogant, independent, and proud. The greatest danger is in failing to pray and to lead the congregation in prayer.

11.   What are the key steps church leaders must take in order to lead the congregation in good decision making?

a.   *Understand the problem and prioritize components.*

---

1 Thess. 5:12, 13 Church people most often think of their elders' responsibilities to them, but the NT also emphasizes the congregation's serious obligations to its spiritual leaders. We hear much today about leadership failure, but there is even more congregational failure, which is seen in a neglect of learning from and following God's appointed leaders. Very little is written about this problem, but it is real and widespread. Remember Moses and the complaining, rebellious congregation he led through the wilderness. They resisted his leadership to the point of wanting to kill him. The congregation, not Moses, was derelict. Not all church problems are leader-produced.
10. Emphasize the chief dangers of prayerlessness and manipulating the congregation in decision making. Whenever elders manipulate their brothers and sisters, it is sin. God speaks through the body of believers *and* the elders.

b.   *Pray about solutions and encourage corporate prayer.*

c.   *Teach the congregation the applicable scriptural principles.*

d.   *Encourage and consider congregational input.*

e.   *Propose the wisest solution.*

f.   *Encourage the congregation's agreement and acceptance.*

g.   *Oversee church members as they implement the plan.*

PROVIDING COUNSEL AND RESOLVING CONFLICT

"Appoint elders in every city as I directed you, namely, if any man is . . . . able both to exhort in sound doctrine and to refute those who contradict. For there are many rebellious men, empty talkers and deceivers, especially those of the circumcision, who must be silenced because they are upsetting whole families, teaching things they should not teach for the sake of sordid gain."

Titus 1:5*b*, 6*a*, 9*b*-11

"Be diligent to present yourself approved to God as a workman who does not need to be ashamed, accurately handling the word of truth."   2 Timothy 2:15

Review pages 130-133.

12.   What problems, created by Paul's presence in Jerusalem, were the Jerusalem elders trying to resolve? See Acts 21:18-25.

The accusations against Paul, which were distortions of his actual conduct, were likely to adversely affect the witness to the Jews and to cause dissension within the church between the Christians who were still zealous for the law and those who were not.

"It is impossible to lead anyone without facing opposition. The leader must learn to take the heat. He will face opposition-it's an occupational hazard of every leader."   Charles Swindoll [7]

13.   Do you agree with the recommendations of the Jerusalem elders, or do you believe they acted improperly, out of fear? Why?

Agree. There was legitimate concern for the church's witness to the non-Christian Jews.

14. What does the apostle Paul's submission to the decision of the elders tell us about the governance of the church?

Paul did not exercise his apostolic authority, nor did the leaders act as autocrats. Both sought to submit to the consensus decisions of the elder council and believed God would work through the council to properly govern the church.

15. In Acts 15, the Jerusalem elders had to counsel Paul on how to quell false rumors and resolve potential division over his presence in Jerusalem. Draw from the following verses those characteristics that are necessary in the man who would be a wise, godly counselor.

Ps. 119:97-100   *Deep reflection on, study of, and obedience to God's Word*

Prov. 1:7   *Reverent submission to God's lordship*

Prov. 3:5-7   *Full trust in the Lord rather than in one's own understanding*

Prov. 4:6-9   *Lover of and seeker after wisdom and understanding*

Prov. 11:2   *Humility*

Ps. 119:97-100 "Meditation all the day" means a life of deep reflection and application of God's law to practical attitudes and choices. Such a person is always thinking of how God's Word applies to his daily life. Know God's Word first, then use it moment by moment. Remind your mentoree of Job's love for and obedience to God's Word (Job 23:11,12).

Prov. 1:7 The first prerequisite to true wisdom and knowledge is the "fear of the Lord," that is, reverential submission to and acknowledgment of the Lord God. As Martin Luther said, "There is God, and all else is dust." See Job 28:28. Charles Bridges explains this great OT concept:

> But what is the fear of the Lord? It is that affectionate reverence, by which the child of God submits himself humbly and carefully to his Father's law. God's wrath is so bitter, and his love so sweet, that there naturally arises an earnest desire to please Him. And also-in view of the danger of falling short because of his own weakness and temptations-a holy watchfulness and fear, so "that I may not sin against Thee." This enters into every thought and every activity of life.[8]

Pass on a love for the book of Proverbs to your mentoree. Wise men love wisdom literature and should own several good commentaries on Proverbs. One that is worthwhile is Derek Kidner's *The Proverbs, The Tyndale Old Testament Commentaries* (Downers Grove: InterVarsity, 1964).

Prov. 3:5-7 Note that a wise man trusts in God with "*all*" his heart and in "*all*" his ways. That means total commitment in every area of life. Equally important, he has a deep-seated distrust in his own natural, fleshly understanding. A wise man places his trust in the only infallible source of all knowledge-God Himself-not in any fallen, finite creature.

Prov. 4:6-9 In v. 6, wisdom is personified as a virtuous woman. Those who seek her find protection, safety, and security. Derek Kidner summarizes v. 7 well: "What it takes is not brains or opportunity, but decision. Do you want [wisdom]? Come and get it .... And with (or, at the cost of) all that you possess, ... at any cost."[9] The wise man seeks wisdom at all cost because he knows wisdom is of supreme value. Ask your mentoree what personal sacrifices he has made in order to acquire wisdom from God's Word.

Prov 11:2 Those who are truly wise are humble-minded. It is a contradiction of terms to speak of a wise man who is proud. "'I praise You, O Father, Lord of heaven and earth, that You have hidden these things from the wise and intelligent and have revealed them to infants. Yes, Father, for this way was well-pleasing in Your sight'" (Luke 10:21).

Prov. 16:21	*Discernment, ability to teach and persuade*
Prov. 29:20	*Considered counsel*
Acts 6:3	*Controlled by the Spirit and full of wisdom*
James 3:17, 18	*Peacemaker who is pure in motive, considerate, submissive, full of mercy and good fruit, impartial, sincere, producing righteousness*

16.   Is there any other quality, not listed in your answers above, that is important in counseling and resolving conflict? Explain why.

| *Able to teach* | *It is not enough for elders to decide an issue; they must also teach the congregation what Scripture says on the subject. Also, elders must confront conflicts in a timely manner. They must not fail to act out of fear or avoidance.* |

ASSIGNMENT:

Review your church's doctrinal statement. Discuss with your mentoring elder the church's doctrinal distinctives and any relevant history. Question him as to differences of opinion on doctrinal issues that will be tolerated by the elder council. Review any reservations you have concerning the doctrinal statement and devise a study plan to resolve them.

SCRIPTURE MEMORY ASSIGNMENT

"Be diligent to present yourself approved to God as a workman who does not need to be ashamed, accurately handling the word of truth."   2 Timothy 2:15

Prov. 16:21 This verse means that a wise man has a positive reputation and influence because of his keen discernment and ability to skillfully and graciously instruct others. People recognize and seek out such a person. "Those who lack judgment or who talk above their hearers' heads need not pine for recognition, only for wisdom."[10]

Prov. 29:20 This proverb refers to a person who always speaks his mind and opinion before he thinks or seeks counsel. He is impossible to correct or dissuade because he thinks he is always right, yet he is proud and ignorant of his true state. Since elders must hear doctrinal arguments or relational problems between people, they must "be quick to hear, slow to speak and slow to anger" (James 1:19).

James 3:17, 18 Note from the larger context the striking contrasts between earthly, demonic wisdom and the wisdom from above (James 3:14-18). A gardening metaphor is employed in v. 18 to emphasize the virtue of peaceableness: the wise, peacemaking gardeners carry out their work (leading or reconciling people) in a peaceful way. The fruit of their efforts is "righteousness," that is, all the beautiful virtues described in v. 17-purity, peaceableness, gentleness, reasonableness, mercy, etc. An example of v. 18 is James himself and the council in Jerusalem (Acts 15 and 21). The council consisted of wise, peacemaking men who proceeded to complete their work in a peaceful, reasonable manner. The fruit was peace-"righteousness," "the wisdom from above."

[1] Fenton J. A. Hort, *The Christian Ecclesia* (1897; repr. ed., London: Macmillan, 1914), pp. 81-83.

[2] P. T. Forsyth, *The Church and the Sacraments* (1917; repr. London: Independent, 1955), p. 9.

[3] Paul E. Little, *Know What You Believe: A Practical Discussion of the Fundamentals of the Christian Faith* (Wheaton: Victor Books, 1987).

[4] Paul E. Little, *Know Why You Believe* (Downers Grove: InterVarsity Press, 1988).

[5] Paul Enns, *The Moody Handbook of Theology* (Chicago: Moody Press, 1989). An additional resource is Charles C. Ryrie, *Basic Theology: A Popular Systematic Guide To Understanding Biblical Truth* (Wheaton: Victor Books, 1987).

[6] Gordon R. Lewis, *Decide for Yourself: A Theological Workbook* (Downers Grove: InterVarsity, 1970).

[7] Charles Swindoll, *Hand Me Another Brick* (Nashville: Thomas Nelson, 1978), p. 78.

[8] Charles Bridges, *A Modern Study in the Book of Proverbs: Charles Bridges' Classic Revised for Today's Reader*, by George F. Santa (Milford: Mott Media, 1978), p. 4.

[9] Derek Kidner, *The Proverbs, The Tyndale Old Testament Commentaries* (Downers Grove: InterVarsity, 1964), p. 67.

[10] Ibid., p.121.

Lesson 3
The First Elder Appointments
"Guard Yourselves"

LESSON OVERVIEW

In this lesson we will be confronted by the significance of Acts 14:23 to the New Testament doctrine of eldership and learn to think accurately about the Greek word for "appointed," which is frequently misinterpreted to mean church election or ordination.

Most of the lesson covers Acts 20:28*a*: "Be on guard for yourselves." Shepherds cannot guard others from Satan's many deceptions if they do not first guard their own souls. This lesson reinforces the Lord's call for us to be men of the Word and of prayer.

THE FIRST ELDER APPOINTMENTS

"When they had appointed elders for them in every church, having prayed with fasting, they commended them to the Lord in whom they had believed."   Acts 14:23

Read pages 133-140.

1.   What unique contributions does Acts 14:23 make to the subject of eldership?

    a.   *Acts 14:23 provides the historical background, establishing that on his first missionary journey Paul appointed elders in churches, even though his subsequent letters to those churches do not reflect this fact.*

---

1. Be sure your mentoree understands the unique and significant role Paul played in establishing the foundation of Christianity. Emphasize that Paul was the great apostle and teacher of the Gentiles (1 Tim. 2:7). He was directly chosen and specially gifted by the risen Christ (Acts 9:15, 16; Gal. 1:15, 16; 1 Cor. 3:10). Seventy percent of the NT was written by Paul or his close colleagues Luke and Mark. Paul's work of organizing the first churches is profoundly significant to all subsequent churches. Therefore, the fact that Paul believed eldership was necessary for these first churches cannot be brushed aside as irrelevant.

b.   *This is the first mention of elders in the Gentile churches.*

c.   *The apostles established the eldership structure of government for the churches.*

d.   *The apostles appointed multiple elders to be the leadership in each church.*

e.   *This verse proves that elders were appointed by the apostles, not elected by the congregation.*

2.   What errors are commonly made when translating the Greek verb cheirotoneō, which means "appointed"?

a.   *That it means to ordain, by the laying on of hands. This is incorrect; the verb* epitithēmi *means to "lay on hands."*

b.   *That it means to elect or vote by a show of hands. The verb cheirotoneō does not indicate the method of appointment. However, the context proves that the elders were appointed by the apostles. No mention is made of an election of the elders by the congregation or of its having a role in selecting elders.*

3.   Some scholars and denominations teach that Paul and Barnabas merely presided over each church's election of its elders. Carefully study the Greek word *cheirotoneō* and its context. In your own words, summarize the points made in *Biblical Eldership* for rejecting the view that Paul and Barnabas only supervised the congregation's election of elders. If you find it too difficult to understand some of these technical linguistic points, find someone to help you.

a.   *At the time, the term* **cheirotoneō** *was used to indicate either election or appointment. In each case, the context determined the intended meaning.*

b.   *The verb* **cheirotoneō** *indicates either appointment or choice, without reference to whether or not a vote was involved.*

c.   *In Acts 14:23, Paul and Barnabas, not the congregation, are the subjects of the verb* **cheirotoneō**.

d.   *In contrast to its secular use,* **cheirotoneō** *is never used in the Septuagint or NT for "elect"; it always means "appoint."*

2., 3. Be sensitive to the fact that many men have difficulty understanding technical, linguistic points of argument. Although you or your mentoree may struggle with the details of these two questions, stress the main point of the passage: *it is certain that Paul and Barnabas appointed the first Christian elders. This text does not suggest or prove congregational voting or congregational church government.*

e. *The pronoun "them," that follows "appoint," indicates that the elders were appointed* **for** *the church, not* **by** *the church.*

4. What fundamental spiritual lesson did Barnabas and Paul teach the new Galatian believers by their act of praying with fasting before they entrusted the elders to God's care in the apostles' absence? See pp. 153-156.

The apostles took so seriously the commending of the elders to God's care that they did so only after a period of prayer and fasting. This involved devoting a period of time to prayer without stopping for meals so that they might concentrate fully on prayer. This special effort in entrusting the elders to God's care demonstrated to the Galatian believers their imperative need for total dependence on God (Gal. 2:20).

"GUARD YOURSELVES"

"'Be on guard for yourselves.'"   Acts 20:28a

"Pay close attention to yourself and to your teaching; persevere in these things, for as you do this you will insure salvation both for yourself and for those who hear you."   1 Timothy 4:16

"'But we will devote ourselves to prayer and to the ministry of the word.'"   Acts 6:4

"A good servant of Christ Jesus [is] constantly nourished on the words of the faith and of the sound doctrine."   1 Timothy 4:6b

"Now He was telling them a parable to show that at all times they ought to pray and not to lose heart.   Luke 18:1

> ### Read pages 140-147.

Before a shepherd elder can guard God's flock from the enemy, *he must first be able to guard his own inner spiritual life.* In Paul's message to the Ephesian elders, he exhorts them to guard themselves from enemy attack first, then to guard the flock. To guard yourself spiritually–among other spiritual disciplines–you must cultivate a consistent life pattern of Bible reading, study, meditation, and prayer. This is especially important because elders are to dedicate themselves to prayer and the Word (Acts 6:4).

THE ELDER AND THE WORD

5.   Study how Paul instructs Timothy to guard himself in 2 Timothy 3:13-17. List what this
        passage teaches the shepherd of God's flock.

        a.   *Attempts to deceive the congregation with false teachings will always continue. This situa-*
                tion will not improve as time goes on (v. 13).

        b.   *The elder must function according to the teachings of Scripture, which are inspired by God*
                (v. 14).

        c.   *The elder should persistently build on the foundation of godly heritage; he should not*
                wander off on his own but should continue in the things he has learned (vv. 14, 15).

        d.   *Building one's knowledge of Scripture produces wisdom (vv. 14, 15).*

        e.   *God intends all Scripture to be understood so that it may be used in teaching, reproof,*
                correction, and training in righteousness (v. 16).

        f.   *The shepherd who does not know the Word is inadequate and not equipped for God's work*
                (v. 17).

God's Word will be your primary weapon for protecting the flock, so you must know it well and be
able to use it. It is also your personal source of incredible spiritual strength, wisdom, and encouragement. That is why, at the end of his farewell, Paul commended the Ephesian elders "to God and to the
word of His grace" (Acts 20:32). Only God and His living, breathing Word could sustain these elders
through the fierce storms that lay ahead. Therefore, a godly elder must be a *man of the Book!* He must
be a *Word-filled* and *Word-controlled* believer. With the Psalmist, a godly elder says, "O how I love Your
law! It is my meditation all the day" (Ps. 119:97).

Unfortunately, in our hyperactive, overly busy society, regular, meditative reading of the Bible is often
neglected. John Stott points out the paradox:

> This much purchased book is a much neglected book. Probably tens of thousands of people
> who buy the Bible never read it. Even in churches, knowledge of the Bible is abysmal. Few
> church members make a practice of daily Bible meditation.[1]

In a sermon to his congregation, S. Lewis Johnson remonstrates:

---

5. The main charge in this passage is to "continue in the things [doctrines based on Scripture] you have learned." False teachers do not
stand firmly on the truth or on God-breathed Scripture. Instead, they depart from biblical doctrines because they allow themselves to
become deceived. Timothy received the truth from impeccable sources: his esteemed mother and grandmother (2 Tim. 1:5) and Christ's
chosen apostle, Paul (2 Tim. 3:10, 11). Even more important, Timothy was assured of the truth by the ultimate source of his learning-
God-breathed, holy Scripture. Timothy was instructed to deal with false teachers by steadfastly adhering to God's Word.

> I have come to believe . . . that the great sin of Christians in evangelical churches is neglect of the Bible. It has been my observation, and I am including myself, that our greatest failure is that we don't read the Bible. We listen to people talk about the Bible. We listen to preachers like me, and we read books, but we do not read the Bible.[2]

As a spiritual guide to God's people, the elder must love God's infallible Word. This love for God's Book will be manifested primarily by the elder's desire to read the Bible regularly. A man who has no such desire for the Word is not called of the Spirit to be a shepherd elder. In fact, such a man is a danger to the church.

To become more consistent and productive in reading and meditating on God's precious Word, carefully consider the practical suggestions presented below. *If any of these suggestions will not work for you, state the reason and propose an alternative.*

Use an Accurate Translation of the Bible.

For your regular reading, study, and meditation of Scripture, use a sound, accurate translation of the Hebrew and Greek–not a paraphrase. A paraphrased Bible is good for comprehending the overall context of a passage, but it is not adequate for study and interpretation. In the translation process, choices are made between making the translation easy to read and retaining accuracy. When detailed interpretation is your objective, an accurate translation must be used.

The three most popular Bibles that are based on accurate Hebrew and Greek texts and are used for study and preaching are the New International Version, New American Standard Bible, and New King James Version. Your study Bible will be a useful tool for ten or twenty years. It will become the familiar repository for your own marginal notes, cross-references, and underlined passages. So invest in a high quality Bible with easy-to-read print and adequate margins for notes.

Only the Scripture that you have memorized or can easily find is truly useful to you in most ministry situations. It would be to your advantage to work out a system for indexing passages by theological or counseling subjects so that you can find them quickly at the moment of need.

6.   Record how you will use your study Bible:

   a.   What Bible is your main study Bible?

   b.   How do you mark key passages?

   c.   If you are keeping a doctrinal subject index, how do you key these passages? Show your mentor how you do this.

Use a Bible-reading Program to Guide You in Your Daily Bible Reading.

Bible reading is different in purpose from detailed Bible study in which we work through a theological issue or prepare to teach. We need to read through the entire Bible in order to understand the scope of redemptive history and learn where specific issues are addressed. Consistent reading of the whole Bible enables us to understand God's mind and is essential to understanding individual passages.

Without a clear plan of action, however, most of us seldom go beyond the good intention stage. Many Christians stumble along for years, reading the Bible haphazardly and inconsistently or not at all. If you believe that regular, disciplined Bible reading is indispensable to personal Christian growth, then you must spend time in the Word on a regular basis.

The secret to a consistent, Bible-reading lifestyle is to have a Bible reading plan that will enable you to realistically and accurately evaluate your time with God in the Word. If you cannot find a Bible reading plan that suits you well, develop your own. Your program should include reading through the New Testament epistles twice a year because the epistles are the heart and soul of the Christian faith; they interpret the rest of Scripture for us.

Meditate on your Scripture reading as an adjunct to prayer. Select a portion of what you have read and, using a 3x5 card to moderate your pace, focus on each word. Do not race through. It is better to read smaller portions of Scripture profitably than to read longer passages with little comprehension and spiritual interaction.

7.   *What Bible reading plan do you use, and why do you like it? If you do not employ one at present, what is your plan?*

Schedule Time for Your Bible Reading.

A Puritan preacher once declared, "The Bible is full of infinities and immensities." In truth, the Bible is an extensive document that presents a considerable challenge. If you desire to master God's Word, you must commit to sacrificially spend time reading and studying it. If you do not consciously allocate a portion of your busy day to quietly read and meditate on the Word, this responsibility will remain unmet. Consider the observations of Geoffrey Thomas, in his excellent booklet, *Reading the Bible:*

> For what can be done at any time may be done at no time. So we deliberately create a time to study the Word of God, choosing a part of the day which is set aside for that precious purpose. These moments will not appear as if by magic. Our whole pattern of life must be structured with this time in view.[3]

As to when to read the Scripture, Thomas says,

> Whatever time best suits you when your mind can be free of the clamor of the day and you can concentrate, that period must be guarded jealously. It will often come under attack and we shall

find ourselves almost automatically sacrificing it under pressures. Weakness there will mean weakness everywhere, while conversely, strength there brings a strength which will be present in other circumstances. The greatest battles we fight in our Christian lives do not change; we march that familiar terrain of our victories and our set-backs all the years of our pilgrimage. The self-denial required to create a daily time for God's Word is the continued duty of every Christian.[4]

8. Your Bible-reading schedule:

    a. Describe your current schedule:

    b. Do you intend to improve or change it? If so, how?

Read and Study in a Designated Place.

A very practical matter that is often neglected is finding a conducive place for reading and studying Scripture. Your regular place of study should include a desk, good lighting, pens, paper, highlighters, your Bible, and study tools. Again, listen to the practical advice of Geoffrey Thomas:

> You can take a Bible anywhere, and it is one of the great pleasures of the Christian life to be on a hilltop, or at the seaside, or by a river, reading the Word. But for regular, disciplined reading a place is needed as free from distraction and as conducive to study as possible. Our Saviour went to a garden, Peter had a rooftop and Elijah an upper room. There is an advantage of reading the Scriptures day after day in the place which is firmly associated in your mind with that activity. You can slip into the right frame of mind the moment you sit down, because you have established the habit of getting down to study once you are in that place. Make sure it is well lit. Good light is very important for reading the double columns of a Bible. It should also be properly ventilated and neither too hot nor too cold. The less you are aware of your surroundings while reading, the better.[5]

9. Evaluate your study place:

    a. Where do you study and/or read your Bible?

    b. Do you plan to improve your study environment? If so how?

Pray for the Desire and Self-discipline to Read and Study the Bible.

Regular Bible reading is like exercising: we all know we need to do it and we always feel better afterward, but we still neglect it. The reason we fail at regular Bible reading is that we lack self-discipline and strong desire. But discipline is a fruit of the Holy Spirit (Gal. 5:23), and God wants to develop this virtue in your life. Pray that your Father will help you become a more disciplined Christian.

One way to develop a self-disciplined lifestyle is to commit to specific, regular responsibilities that test our progress or failure. Establishing a daily Bible reading program will improve your self-discipline. Initially it is more important to establish regularity than to attempt a large block of time. Start small and increase your time as you succeed. On your days off, spend extra time in God's Word or catch up on your Bible reading program if you have missed a day or two (which happens to all of us).

Remember: disciplined reading and study requires setting priorities and putting family, work, leisure time, television, and sleep in their proper places. Spiritual success does not come without self-sacrifice and discipline.

10.   Listed below are some common hindrances to regular Bible reading:

- I have too many other books and magazines to read.
- I have no real desire to read the Bible in a regular, disciplined way.
- I react to Bible reading as a legalistic and mechanical requirement.
- I have a hard time doing anything consistently.
- I don't know how to get started.
- I can't seem to find time to read the Word.
- I find Bible reading unfulfilling and difficult.
- I spend too much time in front of television.

a.   Using this list as an aid, what keeps you from disciplined Bible reading?

b.   What do you propose to remedy or remove these hindrances?

Learn to Handle Accurately the Word of Truth.

The neglect of Scripture is not the only reason that false teachings infiltrate the church. All cults support their positions by misusing Scripture, so the shepherd elder must know how to accurately interpret Scripture and convincingly correct those who misrepresent the teachings of the Word.

A detailed study of *hermeneutics,* the science of interpretation, is beyond the scope of this Guide. However, the fundamental principles of hermeneutics are simple and, if applied, will enable the elder to be "a workman who does not need to be ashamed, accurately handling the word of truth" (2 Tim. 2:15). The proper interpretation of Scripture is based on the following principles:

a. The authors of Scripture, under the guidance of the Holy Spirit, wrote with the intention that their statements would be understood. Therefore, the natural interpretation that fits the intent or context of the overall passage is the most probable interpretation.

b. A foundational Protestant principle of biblical interpretation states that the Bible interprets the Bible:

> The infallible rule of interpretation of Scripture is the Scripture itself; and therefore, when there is a question about the true and full sense of any Scripture (which is not manifold, but one), it may be searched and known by other places that speak more clearly.[6]

c. God revealed Himself over an extended period of history. Therefore, we must use the most recent revelation to interpret the older.

Based on the fact that God has revealed Himself and His will progressively, Edward J. Carnell, in *The Case for Orthodox Theology,*[7] states five summary principles of hermeneutics:

1 The New Testament interprets the Old Testament.

2 The Epistles interpret the Gospels.

3 Systematic passages interpret the incidental.

4 Universal passages interpret the local.

5 Didactic passages interpret the symbolic.

A recommended book on hermeneutics is R. C. Sproul's *Knowing Scripture.*[8]

THE ELDER'S PRAYER LIFE

Prayer is a major part of the Lord's work, especially for those who lead His people. In fact, it would be more accurate to say, prayer is our work. The disciples made this very clear in Acts 6:4: "We will devote ourselves to prayer and to the ministry of the word." Elders often face perplexing and agonizing situations that cannot be addressed without the Lord's guidance, wisdom, and strength.

Prayer is also absolutely essential to the elder's relationship with Jesus Christ and his personal growth. In *Spiritual Disciplines for the Christian Life,* Donald Whitney points out: "Where there is

Godliness there is prayerfulness. Typically picturesque, Spurgeon said it this way: 'Even as the moon influences the tides of the sea, even so does prayer . . . influence the tides of godliness.'"[9]

As important as prayer is to the Christian life, however, few Christians have a consistent, meaningful prayer life. Consider carefully the following statements:

> During the 1980's, more than seventeen thousand members of a major evangelical denomination were surveyed about their prayer habits while attending seminars on prayer for spiritual awakening. Because they attended this kind of seminar, we can assume these people are above average in their interest in prayer. And yet, the surveys revealed that they pray an average of less than five minutes each day. There were two thousand pastors and wives at these same seminars. By their own admission, they pray less than seven minutes a day. It's very easy to make people feel guilty about failure in prayer. . . . But we must come to grips with the fact that to be like Jesus we must pray.
>
> Donald S. Whitney[10]

> What is both surprising and depressing is the sheer prayerlessness that characterizes so much of the Western church. It is surprising, because it is out of step with the Bible that portrays what Christian living should be; it is depressing, because it frequently coexists with abounding Christian activity that somehow seems hollow, frivolous, and superficial.   D. A. Carson[11]

> Jesus never taught his disciples how to preach, only how to pray. He did not speak much of what was needed to preach well, but much of praying well. To know how to speak to God is more than knowing how to speak to man. Not power with men, but power with God is the first thing. Jesus loves to teach us how to pray.
>
> Andrew Murray[12]

> When a man is speaking to God he is at his very acme. It is the highest activity of the human soul, and therefore it is at the same time the ultimate test of a man's true spiritual condition. There is nothing that tells the truth about us as Christian people so much as our prayer life. Everything we do in the Christian life is easier than prayer.
>
> D. Martyn Lloyd-Jones[13]

God's will for us is to pray. Prayer is not an option, it is a command. Consider these biblical imperatives:

- "Devote yourselves to prayer" (Col. 4:2a).
- "Pray without ceasing" (1 Thess. 5:17).
- "[You] ought to pray and not to lose heart" (Luke 18:1b).
- "[Be] devoted to prayer" (Rom. 12:12c).
- "Therefore, take up the full armor of God. . . . With all prayer and petition pray at all times in the Spirit, and with this in view, be on the alert with all perseverance and petition for all the saints" (Eph. 6:13a, 18).

Meditate on the Word to Motivate and Enrich Your Prayers.

Donald Whitney points out that meditation is the link between Scripture reading and prayer: "We learn to pray by meditating on Scripture for meditation is the missing link between Bible intake and prayer."[14]

Reflect upon this wise counsel from George Müller, one of the strongest men of prayer and faith ever to grace the church of God:

> Now what is the food for the inner man? Not prayer, but the Word of God; and here again, not the simple reading of the Word of God, so that it only passes through our minds, just as water passes through a pipe, but considering what we read, pondering over it and applying it to our hearts.

> When we pray we speak to God. Now prayer, in order to be continued for any length of time in any other than a formal manner, requires, generally speaking, a measure of strength of godly desire, and the season therefore when this exercise of the soul can be most effectually performed *is after the inner man has been nourished by meditation on the Word of God*, where we find our Father speaking to us, to encourage us, to comfort us, to instruct us, to humble us, to reprove us.[15]

11. Choose a short passage of Scripture that you have recently used in your meditation time. Write out several thoughts that you derived from the passage and which you were able to turn into prayer.

Planning Is Necessary.

John Piper reminds us of the simple fact that if we want a good prayer life, we must plan for it. Heed what he says:

> Unless I'm badly mistaken, one of the main reasons so many of God's children don't have a significant prayer life is not so much that we don't want to, *but that we don't plan to*. If you want to take a four-week vacation, you don't just get up one summer morning and say, "Hey, let's go today!" You won't have anything ready. You won't know where to go. Nothing has been planned. But that is how many of us treat prayer. We get up day after day and realize that significant times of prayer should be a part of our life, but nothing's ever ready. We don't know where to go. Nothing has been planned. No time. No place. No procedure. And we all know that the opposite of planning is not a wonderful flow of deep, spontaneous experiences in prayer. The opposite of planning is the rut. If you don't plan a vacation you will probably stay home and watch TV. The natural, unplanned flow of spiritual life sinks to the lowest ebb of vitality. There is a race to be run and a fight to be fought. If you want renewal in your life of prayer you must plan to see it.[16]

12.   As is true of your Bible reading, it is essential to set aside a specific time to meet with the Lord in prayer. What is your place and schedule for prayer?

Develop a Prayer Notebook.

People will give prayer requests to their shepherd elders. However, we all have short memories, especially when it comes to remembering prayer requests. If you do not write these requests down, you will often forget them as soon as the next urgent issue comes to your attention. If the shepherd elder takes prayer seriously and considers it part of his spiritual work, he will maintain a notebook. This will help him pray specifically and faithfully.

Revise your prayer notebook often. Reviewing past requests and seeing God's answers will be a great incentive to remain faithful in prayer. Next to your Bible, your prayer notebook is the most important book you have.

13.   If you do not already have a prayer notebook, start one. Show it to your mentor, or submit copies of enough pages so that your mentor can see how you organize your notebook, how you record what and who you need to pray for, when you pray about each item, and how you record God's answers.

Use Music to Aid Your Prayers.

For many, music is an excellent aid to prayer. Indeed, singing God's praises is praying. Before you pray, sing or read several hymns, or listen to a music tape. Praising the Lord in song will set the context for your praying.

Try Different Modes for Praying.

It is hard to separate our attitude from our posture. Hudson Taylor found that standing or walking during prayer was the best position for him because it kept his mind from wandering. You could kneel, lie face down, or sit. Or, you can pray out loud as Martin Luther did.

Find a Quiet Place to Pray.

14.   What do the following verses teach you about Jesus and prayer?

Mark 1:35   *Jesus chose a place and a time when he could be alone and free from distractions.*

Mark 6:45, 46 *Jesus made arrangements to be alone for prayer.*

Luke 5:16   *Jesus often sought an isolated place to pray alone.*

Luke 6:12   *Jesus went to an isolated place to pray for long periods.*

Luke 9:18   *Jesus prayed alone, even when with His disciples.*

Learn to Pray Spontaneously as the Spirit Prompts You.

Hear what D. Martyn Lloyd-Jones says about this matter:

> Always respond to every impulse to pray. The impulse to pray may come when you are read-ing or when you are battling with a text. I would make an absolute law of this–always obey such an impulse. Where does it come from? It is the work of the Holy Spirit; it is a part of the meaning of "Work out your own salvation with fear and trembling. For it is God which wor-keth in you both to will and to do of his good pleasure" (Phil. 2:12, 13). This often leads to some of the most remarkable experiences in the life of the minister. So never resist, never post-pone it, never push it aside because you are busy. Give yourself to it, yield to it.[17]

From this point on, begin your meetings with your mentor by reporting on your progress in becom-ing a disciplined, effective prayer warrior and Bible reader. Have your mentor hold you accountable for your progress in Bible reading and prayer.

15.   Read, then meditate on Luke 10:38-42.

    a.   How does this passage apply to you as a future shepherd among God's people?

    Time spent in conversation and fellowship with the Lord is important and not to be crowd-ed out by "the Lord's work."

15a. Throughout life, every Christian must learn and relearn the lesson that our personal relationship and fellowship with Jesus Christ is our supreme priority, not our work or service. When, like Martha, we become "distracted" from sitting at Jesus' feet because we "are worried and bothered about so many things," we become bitter with others and even with the Lord Himself. In v. 40, the phrase, "has left me," indicates that Mary had worked in the kitchen with Martha, but when the Lord sat down to speak, she ran to His feet to hear His words. This was the right response to Jesus' presence. We know that Mary did the right thing because Jesus commends her and mildly rebukes Martha. As David Gooding has said, "[Jesus] would have preferred Martha's fellowship to her service."[18] For another insight into Mary's deep love for Jesus, read John 12:1-8. Consider also William Kelly's remarks on this passage:

> How many there are who are fond of serving the Lord, but are much more full of their own doings for Him than of what He is to them! . . . This deceives many. They measure faith by their round of bustle and activity. But in truth this always has a great deal of self in it.[19]

b.   What is the "one thing" Mary chose, "the good part, which shall not be taken away from her" (v. 42)?

She chose to listen to the Lord's word and fellowship with Him.

SCRIPTURE MEMORY ASSIGNMENT:

"When they had appointed elders for them in every church, having prayed with fasting, they commended them to the Lord in whom they had believed."   Acts 14:23

"'Be on guard for yourselves and for all the flock, among which the Holy Spirit has made you overseers, to shepherd the church of God which He purchased with His own blood.'"   Acts 20:28

15b. Point out that Luke 10:42 is beautifully illustrated for us in Phil. 3:13, 14. Paul writes, "But one thing I do: forgetting what lies behind and reaching forward to what lies ahead, I press on toward the goal for the prize of the upward call of God in Christ Jesus" (italics added). The "prize" is knowing and intimately fellowshipping with Jesus Christ. D. L. Moody once said that when he got to heaven he wanted, like Paul, to be able to say, "this one thing I did," not "these forty things I dabbled in."

---

[1] John Stott, *You Can Trust The Bible: Our Foundation for Belief and Obedience* (Grand Rapids: Discovery House, 1982), pp. 9, 10.

[2] S. Lewis Johnson, "From Knowledge to Life Through Christ: Colossians 1:9-14," audio cassette (Dallas: Believers' Chapel, 1968).

[3] Geoffrey Thomas, *Reading the Bible* (Edinburgh: The Banner of Truth Trust, 1980), p. 11.

[4] Ibid., p. 13.

[5] Ibid.

[6] *The Westminster Confession of Faith*, I, 9.

[7] Edward J. Carnell, *The Case for Orthodox Theology* (Philadelphia: Westminster Press), 1959, pp. 51-65.

[8] R. C. Sproul, *Knowing Scripture* (Downers Grove: InterVarsity, 1977).

[9] Donald Whitney, *Spiritual Disciplines for the Christian Life* (Colorado Springs: NavPress), 1991, p. 82.

[10] Ibid., p. 62.

[11] D. A. Carson, *A Call to Spiritual Reformation* (Grand Rapids: Baker, 1992), p. 9.

[12] Andrew Murray, *With Christ in the School of Prayer* (1835; New York: Revell, n.d.), p. 6.

[13] D. Martyn Lloyd-Jones, *Studies in the Sermon on the Mount*, 2 vols. (Grand Rapids: Eerdmans, 1971), 2: 46.

[14] Whitney, *Spiritual Disciplines for the Christian Life*, p. 72.

[15] Roger Steer, *Spiritual Secrets of George Müller* (Wheaton: Harold Shaw, 1985), pp. 62, 63.

[16] John Piper, *Desiring God: Meditations of a Christian Hedonist* (Portland: Multnomah, 1986), pp. 150, 151.

[17] D. Martyn Lloyd-Jones, *The Preacher and Preaching* (Grand Rapids: Zondervan, 1971), p. 395.

[18] David Gooding, *According to Luke: A New Exposition of the Third Gospel* (Grand Rapids: Eerdmans, 1987), p. 216.

[19] William Kelly, *An Exposition of The Gospel of Luke* (Denver: Wilson Foundation, 1971), p. 175.

Lesson 4

Protecting the Flock from False Teachers
The Source of the Elder's Strength
The Pauline Model for Elders

LESSON OVERVIEW

Lesson 4 deals with the elders' solemn duty to protect their flock from "savage wolves," that is, false teachers. It covers Paul's farewell message to the Ephesian elders in Acts 20:18-35. An elder who desires to be a faithful guardian of Christ's Word and flock must become thoroughly familiar with this Scripture passage. It answers the question of who places elders in the local church as overseers and pastor shepherds, and establishes the inestimable worth of the body of Christ, which elders are called to guard from Satanic workers.

The second half of the lesson addresses the elders' need to trust in God and His Word for strength and guidance. It also explores Paul's example of self-employment and generosity to others.

PROTECTING THE FLOCK FROM FALSE TEACHERS

"'Be on guard for yourselves and for all the flock, among which the Holy Spirit has made you overseers, to shepherd the church of God which He purchased with His own blood. I know that after my departure savage wolves will come in among you, not sparing the flock; and from among your own selves men will arise, speaking perverse things, to draw away the disciples after them. Therefore be on the alert, remembering that night and day for a period of three years I did not cease to admonish each one with tears.'"

Acts 20:28-31

> Review pages 17-22, 27-29, 31-34, 109-115, 140-147. Read pages 147-159.

1. According to *Biblical Eldership* (pp. 19, 20), major failures on the part of local church leaders (shepherd elders) during the last century caused leading denominations and churches to abandon historic, biblical Christianity. What were these failures?

     a.   *Shepherd elders did not sufficiently educate themselves; therefore, they were not prepared to discern or confront false teachers. They rejected sound biblical doctrine in favor of what was popular and condoned immorality. They became preoccupied with their own comforts and self-interests, failing to act against false teachers.*

     b.   *Church leaders lost courage and became inattentive, prayerless, and blind watchmen. They did not stay alert to Satan's deceptive strategies.*

     c.   *Elders of local churches allowed their seminaries to decline and adopt these same attributes. They also invited young wolves in sheep's clothing into church leadership.*

2.   In the context of Acts 20:28-31, what does the Greek verb *prosechō* mean? (See p. 145.)

Pay strict attention; keep continual watch, especially for false teachers. The tense used indicates continuous action.

3.   The essence of Paul's final message to the Ephesian elders is: ***Guard the church, wolves are coming.*** Since protecting the church against false teachers is one of the elders' major duties, what qualifications are especially necessary and why?

1 Timothy 3:2-7	**Titus 1:6-9**	**1 Peter 5:1-3**
1. Above reproach	1. Above reproach	1. Not shepherding under compulsion, but voluntarily
2. The husband of one wife	2. The husband of one wife	2. Not shepherding for sordid gain, but with eagerness
3. Temperate [self-controlled, but balanced]	3. Having children who believe	3. Not lording it over the flock, proving to be an example
4. Prudent [sensible, good judgment]	4. Not self-willed	
5. Respectable [well-behaved, virtuous]	5. Not quick-tempered	
6. Hospitable	6. Not addicted to wine	
7. Able to teach	7. Not pugnacious	
8. Not addicted to wine	8. Not fond of sordid gain	
9. Not pugnacious [not belligerent]	9. Hospitable	
10. Gentle [forbearing]	10. Lover of what is good [kind, virtuous]	
11. Peaceable [uncontentious]	11. Sensible [see prudent]	
12. Free from the love of money	12. Just [righteous conduct, law-abiding]	
13. Manages his household well	13. Devout [holy, pleasing to God, loyal to His Word]	
14. Not a new convert	14. Self-controlled	
15. A good reputation with those outside the church	15. Holds fast the faithful [trustworthy NIV] Word, both to exhort and to refute	

     a.   ***Able to teach:*** *The elders must teach the flock the truth and how to discern false teachings. The elders cannot guard untaught sheep.*

b.   *Hold fast the faithful Word, both to exhort and refute: Elders must both know and be committed to the teachings of the Word if they are to confront false teachers effectively and protect the flock.*

c.   *Above reproach: In the struggle against false teachers, the elders' credibility is of utmost importance. The false teacher will attack the elders' vulnerabilities in order to divert attention away from the examination and exposure of his character and teachings.*

d.   *Prudent: Elders must be sensible and balanced, exercising discretion and good judgment in their dealings with false teachers.*

e.   *Devout: Elders must be devoted and pleasing to God. They must be loyal to His Word as they constantly watch over the flock.*

4.   What does the little word "all" in verse 28 teach about the work of the eldership?

The eldership is responsible for the entire congregation, not just for the church staff, leaders, or each elder's circle of personal friends.

5.   As a shepherd, you must know the condition and needs of the sheep you are responsible to guard. Jesus said that He knew His sheep and they knew His voice (John 10:2, 27). The spiritual care of the flock of God requires earnest prayer on the part of the shepherds for the sheep. Some have found it profitable to pray for two or three families in the congregation each day. Another way elders can begin to know the people more intimately is to visit each member's home and invite members into their homes.

a.   Discuss the above ideas. Do you have other suggestions or plans for getting to know the people?

b.   If the ratio of members to elders in your church is too large to permit individual attention by the elders, how do you propose the need to know the people be dealt with, so that the elders fulfill the scriptural mandates?

If the church is too large for the elders to protect all the members through close association, they must oversee a structure for doing so that involves others whom they train and oversee. The elders must also participate, caring for some of the flock personally.

6.   Why is it better to translate the Greek word *episkopos* as "overseer" rather than as "bishop"? What does the Greek term *episkopos* teach you about the work of an elder?

a. *In some denominations, the word "bishop" has become associated with a hierarchical position, a leader who presides over other churches or elders in a region. To the contrary, the Greek word means to oversee, supervise, manage, or be a guardian. It emphasizes the elders' function as that of overall supervision of the congregation.*

b. *The elder is charged with overseeing the congregation and all its functions. He is responsible for the church's safety and purity. He is to oversee, guard, protect, manage, and supervise.*

7. List several ways in which the knowledge that the Holy Spirit of God sovereignly placed you in the local church as an overseer should impact your work and thinking.

a. *Keep me humble, dependent upon the Lord*

b. *Give me strength, fortitude, courage, confidence in the Lord and His Word*

c. *Help me be obedient to the task the Lord has given me to do and keep me responsible and accountable to God, who appointed me*

"'Shepherd the church of God, which he bought with the blood of his Own' (20:28). With this we touch the mainspring of all true defense and shepherding of the church: the cost at which God bought it. That cost was the blood of his own, that is, of his own dear, loved, cherished Son. The story still has power to stagger imagination."

David Gooding[1]

---

8. Discouragement is a leading reason why many shepherd elders leave the work. Endless problems, battles, and criticisms cause every elder to question, at one time or another, *Is it worth all this frustration and stress?* When you experience discouragement and want to give up, remember Paul's words to the elders in Acts 20:28: "Shepherd the church of God which He purchased with His own blood."

a. What basic, fundamental Christian doctrines are expressed by the clause, "which He purchased with His own blood"?

Redemption, substitutionary atonement, adoption

b. When you are discouraged and tempted to quit, how do the words, "the church of God which He purchased with His own blood," encourage you to persevere in your shepherding work?

8b. Prepare your mentoree for the fact that being an elder can be extremely discouraging work. Its challenges can easily break a man emotionally and spiritually. It is not uncommon for an elder to become resentful and bitter with the people he is called to love and lead. People can be ruthless with their spiritual leaders. We will be tempted to think that the people are not worth our sacrifice and effort. We must remember the degree to which God values His people and the awesome price He paid for their salvation–the life of His own Son. The elder is motivated by his desire to please his Lord and to adhere to unfailing biblical truth, rather than being influenced by changeable feelings or the capricious gratitude of men.

These truths remind me of the immeasurable worth of the church to God. It is His Church— His most precious possession, His blood-bought children. When things are difficult, my belief in these truths, rather than my ever-changing feelings, sustains me.

c. How do the words, "the church of God which He purchased with His own blood," affect your thinking about the work of protecting the church from false doctrine?

It is a privilege to shepherd the church of God. If Christ was willing to shed His blood for the saints, I should be willing to work hard to protect them. These words inspire me to commit my all to the task. I will not neglect the flock, become inattentive to the dangers, or shirk the grave responsibility. Protection of the church is not an academic pursuit. We are defending God's truth and lives are at stake.

9. What do the following images teach you about the nature and people of "the church of God," which you are called by the Holy Spirit to protect from false teachers?

a. **"The bride,"** Rev. 21:9

Next to God, there is nothing in life that a man values more highly than his bride and his unique, intimate relationship with her. The image of "bride" expresses the supreme value Christ places on His church, which He bought with His blood and intends to present to the Father as spotless, holy, and blameless (Eph. 5:25-27). Woe to the man who takes lightly the task of protecting Christ's precious bride.

b. **"The household of God,"** 1 Tim. 3:15

The church is God's personal family. Elders must guard such a loved and valued possession at all costs.

10. What does Paul's example in Acts 20 teach about how you should guard your flock?

Acts 20:18, 19

Paul served with humility, never leaving the flock and even enduring persecution. The degree of his concern for them was evidenced by his tears. Elders should humbly and passionately serve the flock, enduring all trials.

Acts 20:20, 21

Both publicly and in their homes, Paul courageously taught the flock everything they needed to know about the gospel. Elders should make sure that the complete teachings and doctrines of Scripture are taught to their flock.

Acts 20:20, 21 Paul taught doctrine. It is critical that elders oversee the teaching of the full range of Christian doctrine to the local church. In too many churches, teaching the whole spectrum of biblical truth is intentionally avoided, placing the church's spiritual health at risk.

Acts 20:26, 27

Because Paul declared the whole purpose of God, he fully discharged his responsibility to the Ephesian church. Elders fulfill their responsibility only by being forthright truth-tellers.

Acts 20:31

Paul worked hard at staying alert and admonished his flock, but he did so with tears. Elders should be willing to gently and persistently admonish, and not just in the classroom or from the pulpit, even though it is costly.

Acts 20:33-35

Paul was solely interested in the church, not in monetary gain. He demonstrated that he was willing to work hard and to support himself while serving the church. Setting the example, the elders must work hard because "it is more blessed to give than to receive."

11. Elders have been given a divine mandate to guard the flock of God from false teachers. Thus, shepherds must know as much as possible about the crafty ways of their archenemies. During the past two thousand years of Christian history, false teachers have been enormously successful in ravishing churches and denominations.

Just as Satan does not call attention to himself, false teachers do not advertise their purpose. Initially they are hard to identify. In order to increase your ability to be a discerning elder, study the following passages. Using commentaries, list the characteristics of the false teacher.

a.   The **evil motives** of the false teacher:

Matt. 23:6-12; Gal. 6:12   *He pridefully seeks recognition, adulation, attention, titles, personal power, and success.*

---

11. All these texts teach, first and foremost, that the false teacher is concerned with himself, not God. An invaluable illustration of this consuming egotism is found in the writings of Charles Russell, the false teacher who founded Jehovah's Witnesses: Russell's appalling egotism is evident from a comment made by him about his *Scripture Studies* series:

> "Not only do we find that people cannot see the divine plan in studying the Bible by itself, but we see, also, that if anyone lays the 'Scripture Studies' aside, even after he has used them, after he has become familiar with them, after he has read them for ten years–if he then lays them aside and ignores them and goes to the Bible alone, . . . our experience shows that within two years he goes into darkness. On the other hand, if he had merely read, 'Scripture Studies,' with their references and had not read a page of the Bible as such, he would be in the light at the end of two years . . ." Russell, in other words, considered his books so indispensable for the proper understanding of Scripture that without them one would simply remain in spiritual darkness.

Russell's own wife divorced him "on the grounds of 'his conceit, egotism, domination, and improper conduct in relation to other women.'"[2]

Phil. 3:18, 19; 1 Tim. 6:5; Titus 1:11	*He is materialistic and greedy, seeking secular rewards and financial gain. He is preoccupied with his own comforts.*
1 Tim. 4:1-3	*He follows deceitful spirits and the doctrines of demons.*

b. The **subtlety** of the false teacher:

2 Tim. 3:13	*He is an impostor and deceiver.*

c. The **disguises** of the false teacher:

Matt. 7:15; 24:24; 2 Cor. 11:13-15	*He is a sly deceiver, hard to discern. Satan's servant disguises himself as a servant of righteousness. He may appear to be harmless, do good, and even perform miracles, but he remains an enemy of Christ.*

d. The **distinguishing marks** of the false teacher concerning:

Morality:

Jer. 23:14	*He commits adultery.*
2 Tim. 3:6	*He preys on women.*
2 Peter 2:2, 10 , 14, 18, 19	*He is a slave of corruption: with "eyes full of adultery," he follows his sensual desires, indulging the flesh. He appeals to worldly, sensual appetites, enticing the unstable.*
Jude 4, 18, 19	*He is worldly minded, licentious, and depraved; he follows his own ungodly lusts.*

Truth:

Jer. 23:14	*He walks in falsehood.*
2 Tim. 3:8, 13	*He opposes the truth, deceives, and is deceived.*
2 Peter 2: 2, 18	*He maligns the truth and uses arrogant words of vanity.*
Jude 18	*He is a mocker, has nothing of substance to say.*
1 Tim. 4:2	*He has a seared conscience and is a liar.*
Titus 1:10	*He is an empty talker.*

Authority:

Jude 8, 19	*He rejects biblical authority and truth, scholarship, factual evidence. He causes divisions.*
2 Peter 2:10	*He despises authority; he is self-willed.*
Titus 1:10	*He is rebellious.*

e.   The **teachings** of the false teacher:

Col. 2:4, 8, 18, 19	*He seduces with false humility and spirituality. He persuades by substituting humanistic philosophy, psychology, and sociology for the message of the Word.*
1 Tim. 6:3-5	*He introduces controversial questions and arguments over minutiae.*
Gal. 1:9; 1 Tim. 4:1-3; 2 Peter 2:1; 2 John 7	*He introduces heresies and deceptions. His teachings are harmful to people's basic needs (forbids marriage, foods).*
Deut. 13:1-3, 5, 6; Jer. 23:25, 26, 28, 30-32; Col. 2:18	*He professes to speak for God, claims direct revelation, and elevates his own revelations over the Word.*

f.   The **deeds** of the false teacher:

| Jer. 10:21; 23:1, 2; Acts 20:29, 30 | *He upsets, savages, steals, or scatters the sheep; he misleads even the elect.* |
| Rom. 16:17, 18; Gal. 1:6, 7; 1 Tim. 1:3-7; 6:3-5; Titus 3:10, 11; Jude 19 | *He causes confusion, meaningless discussions, controversies, and divisions.* |

12.   As a church leader, you must clearly recognize and persistently confront the false teacher's methods. According to *Biblical Eldership* (pp. 31-34), what key method does the false teacher consistently use to spread and maintain false doctrines?

The false teacher consistently redefines biblical terms in order to change their meaning, thereby blinding the listener to the truth of God's Word.

13. Describe the false teacher (as studied above) who would pose the greatest threat to your congregation. Explain why such a person would be a great threat.

   a.

   b.

14. What contemporary false doctrines (secular or religious) may possibly invade your church in the near future? What are you doing by way of study and teaching to protect your flock and defend the truth of the Word from these errors?

---

12. As to the crucial significance of the terminology battle, the late Walter Martin, world-renowned expert on cults and aberrant Christian doctrines, urges us to be alert to "scaling the language barrier:"

> The problem of semantics has always played an important part in human affairs, for by its use, or abuse, whichever the case may be, entire churches, thrones and even governments for that matter, have been erected, sustained or overthrown. . . . The communist dictatorship of China, which even the Russian theorists have rejected as incalculably brutal and inept, dares to call itself the People's Democratic Government. As history testifies, the people have very little, if any, say in the actual operation of communism. . . . Both the Chinese communists and the Russians have paid a terrible price for not defining terminology and for listening to the siren song of Marxism. . . . Applying this analogy to the field of cults, it is at once evident that a distinct parallel exists between the two systems. For cultism, like communism, plays a type of hypnotic music upon a semantic harp of terminological deception. And there are many who historically have followed these strains down the broad road to spiritual eternal judgment. There is a common denominator then, and it is inextricably connected with language and precise definition of terminology. It is what we might call the key to understanding cultism.[3]

Martin gives a superb example of the destructive impact caused by redefining biblical terminology, from an article written by Bernard Ramm concerning the liberal theologian Paul Tillich:

> Writing in *Eternity* Magazine, the noted theologian Dr. Bernard Ramm calls attention to this particular fact, when evaluating the theological system of Dr. Paul Tillich, leading theological luminary of our day and Professor of Theology at the University of Chicago's Divinity School. Dr. Ramm charges that Tillich has so radically redefined standard theological terms that the effect upon Christian theology is nothing short of cataclysmic. "Such Biblical notions of sin, guilt, damnation, justification, regeneration, etc., all come out retranslated into a language that is foreign to the meaning of these concepts in the Scriptures themselves."[4]

a.   Examples:

b.   Preparation:

Counterfeits in the Church

"What comes to mind when you hear the terms 'false prophets' and 'false teachers'? Many people tend to think of Eastern mystics and gurus, the spokespersons for nonbiblical religions, or dynamic cult leaders-people who are recognizably outside the boundaries of the Christian church. But the apostle Peter devoted an entire chapter in one of his letters to false prophets and teachers who operate within the church: 'But false prophets also arose among the people, just as there will be false teachers among you, who will secretly introduce destructive heresies, even denying the Master who bought them, bringing swift destruction upon themselves' (2 Peter 2:1). These people are in our churches right now, disguised as workers of righteousness.

"Notice that the lure of false teachers is not primarily their doctrine: 'And many will follow their sensuality, and because of them the way of the truth will be maligned' (v. 2). What does Peter mean by 'follow their sensuality'? He is talking about Christians who evaluate a ministry based on the outward appearance and charm of its leaders. We say, 'He's such a nice guy'; 'She's a very charismatic person'; 'He's a real dynamic speaker'; 'She's so sweet and sounds so sincere.' But is physical attractiveness a biblical criterion for validating a ministry or a teacher? Of course not! The issue is always truth and righteousness, and false teachers who appeal to the physical senses have maligned the way of the truth.

"Peter goes on to reveal two ways by which we can identify false prophets and false teachers who operate within the church. First, they will be involved in immorality of some kind, indulging 'the flesh in its corrupt desires' (v. 10). They may be discovered in illicit activities involving sex and/or money. They may be antinomian, claiming that God is all love and grace so we don't need to abide by any law. Their immorality may not be easy to spot, but it will eventually surface in their lives (2 Corinthians 11:15).

"Second, false prophets and teachers 'despise authority' and are 'daring, self-willed' (2 Peter 2:10). These people have an independent spirit. They do their own thing and won't answer to anybody. They either won't submit to the authority of a denomination or board, or they will pick their own board which will simply rubber-stamp anything they want to do.

"There are historic leadership roles in Scripture: prophet (preaching and teaching), priest (pastoring and shepherding), and king (administration). Only Jesus in His perfection is capable of occupying all three roles simultaneously. I believe we need the checks and balances of a plurality of elders in the church, distributing the three critical roles to more than one person. No one can survive his own unchallenged authority. Every true, committed Christian in a leadership role needs to submit himself and his ideas to other mature believers who will hold him accountable."

Neil Anderson[5]

THE SOURCE OF THE ELDERS' STRENGTH

"'And now I commend you to God and to the word of His grace, which is able to build you up and to give you the inheritance among all those who are sanctified. . . .' When he had said these things, he knelt down and prayed with them all. And they began to weep aloud and embraced Paul, and repeatedly kissed him, grieving especially over the word which he had spoken, that they would see his face no more. And they were accompanying him to the ship."   Acts 20:32, 36-38

Review pages 153-159.

15.   As Paul departed from Asia Minor, he entrusted the church elders to God and the Word of God. As spiritual leaders bereft of their founding father and mentor, the elders were to trust solely in God and the Word of God for help, strength, guidance, blessing, and wisdom. They were, therefore, to be models of faith in God and in the Word of God. Trusting God is not only absolutely fundamental to salvation but also to living for Christ (Gal. 2:20). As the Scripture says, "Man does not live by bread alone, but man lives by everything that proceeds out of the mouth of the Lord" (Deut. 8:3*b*).

Elders who do not trust in God and His Word have nothing more than their own feeble strength and wisdom to draw upon for help, and they inevitably mislead the flock of God into a desert of deadly false teachings. As a future pastor elder, what do each of the following Scripture texts teach you about faith, that is, *trust*, in God and His Word?

Jer. 17:5, 7 Thus says the Lord, "Cursed is the man who trusts in mankind and makes flesh his strength, and whose heart turns away from the Lord. . . . Blessed is the man who trusts in the Lord and whose trust is the Lord."

Self-confidence in his personal ability and secular experience is the elder's greatest temptation. Such pride, which is the same as turning away from the Lord, brings God's curse on the man. The elders who trust in the Lord, however, will be blessed.

Isa. 31:1 Woe to those who go down to Egypt for help and rely on horses, and trust in chariots because they are many and in horsemen because they are very strong, but they do not look to the Holy One of Israel, nor seek the Lord!

Elders who look to human power and circumstances, rather than seeking the Lord for sustaining energy, incur disaster.

Isa. 66:2*b* But to this one I will look, to him who is humble and contrite of spirit, and who trembles at My word.

God approves of and blesses the servant who is aware of his sinful propensities and is humbly ruled by God's Word.

Ps. 56:3, 4 When I am afraid, I will put my trust in You. In God, whose word I praise, in God I have put my trust; I shall not be afraid. What can mere man do to me?

When the elder is tempted to fear others' criticism and attacks, he must reaffirm his trust in God and His Word.

Prov. 3:5-7 Trust in the Lord with all your heart and do not lean on your own understanding. In all your ways acknowledge Him, and He will make your paths straight. Do not be wise in your own eyes; fear the Lord and turn away from evil.

Reliance on his personal experience and wisdom is, for the elder, prideful and evil. Elders must instead search for God's wisdom and guidance, trusting in the Lord and His Word.

Matt. 6:30-33 But if God so clothes the grass of the field, which is alive today and tomorrow is thrown into the furnace, will He not much more clothe you? You of little faith! Do not worry then, saying, "What will we eat?" or "What will we drink?" or "What will we wear for clothing?" For the Gentiles eagerly seek all these things; for your heavenly Father knows that you need all these things. But seek first His kingdom and His righteousness, and all these things will be added to you.

The elder who is armed with active faith, is not anxious, and is intent on Kingdom pursuits will lack nothing because his Father knows all his needs and will provide for him.

Heb. 10:35, 36, 38-11:2, 6 Therefore, do not throw away your confidence, which has a great reward. For you have need of endurance, so that when you have done the will of God, you may receive what was promised. . . . But My righteous one shall live by faith; and if he shrinks back, My soul has no pleasure in him. But we are not of those who shrink back to destruction, but of those who have faith to the preserving of the soul. Now faith is the assurance of things hoped for, the conviction of things not seen. For by it the men of old gained approval. . . . And without faith it is impossible to please Him, for he who comes to God must believe that He is and that He is a rewarder of those who seek Him.

Our courage and endurance flow from our faith in God. Such conviction is absolutely necessary if we are to please God and receive our rewards, including stamina, from Him.

2 Cor. 1:8, 9 For we do not want you to be unaware, brethren, of our affliction which came to us in Asia, that we were burdened excessively, beyond our strength, so that we despaired even of life; indeed, we had the sentence of death within ourselves so that we would not trust in ourselves, but in God who raises the dead.

God designs our weaknesses, afflictions, and burdens so we will keep our trust centered on Him.

Gal. 2:20 I have been crucified with Christ; and it is no longer I who live, but Christ lives in me; and the life which I now live in the flesh I live by faith in the Son of God, who loved me and gave Himself up for me.

The elder's life, powered by faith, will be sacrificial, and will resemble that of his Savior, who died for him.

Eph. 6:13, 16 Therefore, take up the full armor of God, so that you will be able to resist in the evil day, and having done everything, to stand firm. . . . In addition to all, taking up the shield of faith with which you will be able to extinguish all the flaming arrows of the evil one.

We are not to attempt to battle evil forces without faith, the armor provided by God. The elder's reliant faith in God will shield him and extinguish the enemy's doubt attacks, enabling him to stand firm.

THE PAULINE MODEL FOR ELDERS

"I have coveted no one's silver or gold or clothes. You yourselves know that these hands ministered to my own needs and to the men who were with me. In everything I showed you that by working hard in this manner you must help the weak and remember the words of the Lord Jesus, that He Himself said, 'It is more blessed to give than to receive.'"

Acts 20:33-35

> **Review pages 144-159.**

16.   Paul set a personal example of earning his own living while planting and shepherding the churches, a practice we now refer to as *tentmaking*. In 2 Thessalonians 3:7-11, 1 Corinthians 9:14-19, and 2 Corinthians 11:8-12, 30, Paul further comments on his practice.

   a.   What were Paul's reasons for tentmaking?

   Everything Paul did was for the sake of the gospel and winning people for Christ. He chose to be a loving, voluntary, selfless servant to the church, rather than to be a

---

16. If we want to understand Paul and his extraordinary lifestyle, we must grasp this one overriding principle: *He does everything for the sake of the gospel and to win as many people to Christ as he can.* "I do all things for the sake of the gospel, so that I may become a fellow partaker of it" (1 Cor. 9:23). The reason Paul did not accept money from the Corinthians for his teaching was to eliminate any possible speculation that he personally profited financially from his proclamation of the truth of Christ. "He made the gospel without cost to others, at all cost to himself,"[6] writes William Kelly. Commentator F. L. Godet succinctly explains Paul's reason for this practice:

> Paul had discerned how useful and even indispensable to the honour of the gospel this mode of acting was [self-supported teaching], especially in Greece. It was the one way of distinguishing the preaching of salvation from that venal eloquence and wisdom on which the rhetoricians lived.[7]

To apply 1 Cor. 9:1-14 today, consider Gordon Fee's summary:

> The whole reason for the argument is to assert that his giving up of these rights [financial support] does not mean that he is not entitled to them. In a day like ours such rights usually mean a salary and "benefits." On the other hand, the reason he feels compelled to make this kind of defense is that he has given up these rights. Contemporary ministers seldom feel compelled so to argue! *The key to everything must be for us what it was for Paul–"no hindrance to the gospel."* For every valid ministry in the church of Jesus Christ this must be the bottom line. All too often, one fears, the objective of this text is lost in concerns over "rights" that reflect bald professionalism rather than *a concern for the gospel itself* (italics added).[8]

financial burden to others. He demonstrated that one's motive in ministry should be giving rather than receiving. He did not accept financial help because he did not want to give false teachers any basis for criticism; no one could say he taught just for money. Paul also made it clear that ministry involves hard work, self-discipline, and sacrifice.

b.   How do we reconcile Paul's personal example with 1 Cor. 9:14?

It is acceptable for a man who is engaged in ministry to be supported by those he serves, but this is not a right to be demanded or abused.

c.   Why do you think churches give less honor to those who support themselves while at the same time ministering to the church than to those who are supported by the church and thus are deemed to be "in full-time service"?

This is a cultural distortion of the original order, due to pride in human authority. We have made an unbiblical distinction between the salaried clergy and the "lay" elders. We have become spiritually lazy, undisciplined, and selfish, choosing to pay others to do the work of ministry rather than doing it ourselves.

17.   What does the fact that the first churches were shepherded–that is pastored–by ordinary men, who earned their own bread, reveal about Christian ministry? (See heading, "Hard Work," pp. 27-29, and pp. 109-115; cf. lesson 5, question **10**.)

a.   *The ministry is to be a team effort by men who jointly shoulder the work. The eldership is not to be overly reliant on those who require full-time support.*

b.   *We are all called to "hard work" in the ministry, thus we should expect far more from tent-makers than has been the traditional culture in the church.*

c.   *Those who desire to be pastor elders must be willing to forego a comfortable lifestyle and commit to a life of sacrifice, long hours, and hard work.*

SCRIPTURE MEMORY ASSIGNMENT:

"I know that after my departure savage wolves will come in among you, not sparing the flock; and from among your own selves men will arise, speaking perverse things, to draw away the disciples after them. Therefore be on the alert, remembering that night and day for a period of three years I did not cease to admonish each one with tears. And now I commend you to God and to the word of His grace, which is able to build you up and to give you the inheritance among all those who are sanctified. I have coveted no one's silver or gold or clothes. You yourselves know that these hands ministered to my own needs and to the men who were with me. In everything I showed you that by working hard in this manner you must help the weak and remember the words of the Lord Jesus, that He Himself said, 'It is more blessed to give than to receive.'"

Acts 20:29-35

[1] David Gooding, *True to the Faith: A Fresh Approach to the Acts of the Apostles* (London: Hodder & Stoughton, 1990), p. 360.

[2] Anthony A. Hoekema, *The Four Major Cults* (Grand Rapids: Eerdmans, 1963), p. 227.

[3] Walter Martin, *The Kingdom of the Cults* (Minneapolis: Bethany, 1965), p. 19.

[4] Ibid., p. 18.

[5] Neil Anderson, *The Bondage Breaker* (Eugene: Harvest House, 1990), pp. 163, 164.

[6] William Kelly, *Notes on the First Epistle to the Corinthians* (Denver: Wilson Foundation, n.d.), p. 148.

[7] F. L. Godet, *Commentary on First Corinthians* (Grand Rapids: Kregel, 1977), p. 462.

[8] Gordon D. Fee, *The First Epistle to the Corinthians*, NICNT (Grand Rapids: Eerdmans, 1987), p. 414.

Lesson 5
Humble Servants and The Chief Shepherd
Hard-Working Men

LESSON OVERVIEW

Lesson 5 covers 1 Peter 5:1*a*, 3*b*-5 and 1 Thessalonians 5:12, 13. Peter exhorts elders to shepherd the flock through the power of personal example and encourages them with the promises of the glorious return of the "Chief Shepherd" and the "crown of glory." Finally, he calls on elders, as well as the flock, to clothe themselves with humility so that all may live together in peace.

Paul's exhortation to the congregation at Thessalonica reinforces the elders' task of leading and admonishing the congregation. In order to bear this great responsibility, pastor elders must be self-disciplined, highly committed disciples of the Master. Clearly, board elders cannot pastor a local church: only hard-working, self-disciplined, shepherd elders can.

Like Peter, Paul also calls the congregation and its leaders to work for peace and to love one another. Without humility, love, and peace there is little hope of experiencing the joys of Christlike community and effective pastoral leadership.

HUMBLE SERVANTS AND THE CHIEF SHEPHERD

Therefore, I exhort the elders among you, . . . be examples to the flock. And when the Chief Shepherd appears, you will receive the unfading crown of glory. You younger men, likewise, be subject to your elders; and all of you, clothe yourselves with humility toward one another, for God is opposed to the proud, but gives grace to the humble.   1 Peter 5:1*a*, 3*b*-5

> Read pages 249-252.

1. Why is a leader's personal example of godly character and conduct absolutely necessary to effective, long-term leadership within the local Christian church? (See also pp. 70-72, 78, 79.)

Since the elder is entrusted with God's most valued possession-His children-he must be a steward of the utmost integrity. An elder's personal example teaches more effectively than his words ever can. Our Lord taught in this way and encourages us to do so. The congregation seeks and will follow a godly example.

> "Sherwood Eddy, a missionary statesman and author, who knew [Amy Carmichael] well, was deeply impressed by the 'beauty of her character'; and character, according to Eddy, was the key to successful world evangelism. 'Here is the point where many a missionary breaks down. Every normal missionary sails with high purpose but as a very imperfect Christian . . . . His character is his weakest point . . . . It was just here that Miss Carmichael was a blessing to all who came into intimate and understanding contact with her radiant life . . . . Amy Wilson Carmichael was the most Christlike character I ever met, and . . . her life was the most fragrant, the most joyfully sacrificial, that I ever knew.'"
>
> Ruth A. Tucker[1]

2. In his book *Spiritual Leadership*, J. Oswald Sanders writes, "Leadership is influence, the ability of one person to influence others."[2] Ask your wife or a close friend to help you answer the following questions.

   a. Which traits in your spiritual life and service will make your leadership influential in the flock?

      Mentor: Does the answer correspond to your observations?

   b. Which traits may have an adverse effect on your leadership influence?

      Mentor: Does the answer display honesty, candor, and a good understanding of self?

3. Why was the promise of the Chief Shepherd's appearance significant to the Asian elders?

   They were experiencing persecution. The knowledge that the eternal outcome would be victory and reward upon the return of Christ, their Shepherd, encouraged them.

4. Evaluate the effect that your awareness of the Chief Shepherd's imminent return and His reward for faithful service has on your ministry. Choose the two statements below that best represent your thinking, and explain why you hold each view.

   __ I believe the doctrines, but they have little effect on my thinking.
   __ I rarely think about these matters.
   __ I have no idea what these promises mean.

___ I often think of His evaluation of my work when He returns; this motivates me to better service.

___ I am encouraged and comforted by the thought of His appearance; it keeps me going in the face of discouragement and setbacks.

___ My work as an elder is unaffected by the thought of future reward.

___ I am looking forward to the day of reward in the presence of Christ my Lord.

5.   Peter exhorts both the young men and elders of the churches of northwestern Asia Minor to "clothe yourselves with humility." Humility is central to the spirit of the Christian community, especially to the church eldership team. Write out a short definition of humility. It will be helpful to check both secular and theological dictionaries.

Humility is being lowly; of modest, unpretentious character and mind. It is the absence of pride or self-assertion; it is resting in the security that God will provide for me.

6.   The virtue of humility is absolutely indispensable for a team of elders who are called to work together in unity and peace. Summarize seven principles that explain why humility is essential. The following passages (as well as chapter 5, pp. 85-98) will help.

Obad. 3 The arrogance of your heart has deceived you, you who live in the clefts of the rock, in the loftiness of your dwelling place, who say in your heart, "Who will bring me down to earth?"

---

5. In his uniquely grandiose and theological style, eighteenth-century American pastor-theologian, Jonathan Edwards defines humility as the correct understanding of and response to our natural and fallen lowliness before an infinite, perfect, creator God:

> Man's natural [before the Fall] meanness [lowliness] consists in his being infinitely below God in natural perfection, and in God's being infinitely above him in greatness, power, wisdom, majesty, &c. And a truly humble man is sensible [aware] of the small extent of his own knowledge, and the great extent of his ignorance, and of the small extent of his understanding as compared with the understanding of God. He is sensible of his weakness, how little his strength is, and how little he is able to do. He is sensible of his natural distance from God; of his dependence on him; of the insufficiency of his own power and wisdom; and that it is by God's power that he is upheld and provided for, and that he needs God's wisdom to lead and guide him, and his might to enable him to do what he ought to do for him. He is sensible of his subjection to God, and that God's greatness does properly consist in his authority, whereby he is the sovereign Lord and King over all; and he is willing to be subject to that authority, as feeling that it becomes him to submit to the divine will, and yield in all things to God's authority....The truly humble man, since the fall, is also sensible of his moral meanness and vileness. This consists in his sinfulness. His natural meanness is his littleness as a creature; his moral meanness is his vileness and filthiness as a sinner.[3]

Obad. 3 Wilkinson and Boa write: "Obadiah offers one of the clearest biblical examples of pride going before a fall (1 Cor. 10:12)."[4] Because the Edomites gleefully supported the invading armies of the Philistines and Arabians who sought to destroy Judah (2 Chron. 21:16, 17), the prophet Obadiah prophesied the Edomite's (the descendants of Esau, Jacob's twin brother) utter destruction. The nation of Edom was exceedingly proud of its secure rock-fortified city. Its capital city, Petra (Sela), was enclosed and protected by a rugged wall of mountains. It was accessible only by a narrow canyon leading to it. Trusting in their mountain fortress, the Edomites claimed to be invincible to invading armies. As history demonstrates, their pride and security proved to be an illusion.

2 Chron. 26:3*a*, 16 Uzziah was sixteen years old when he became king, and he reigned fifty-two years in Jerusalem. . . . But when he became strong, his heart was so proud that he acted corruptly, and he was unfaithful to the Lord his God, for he entered the temple of the Lord to burn incense on the altar of incense.

2 Chron. 32:24-26 In those days Hezekiah became mortally ill; and he prayed to the Lord, and the Lord spoke to him and gave him a sign. But Hezekiah gave no return for the benefit he received, because his heart was proud; therefore wrath came on him and on Judah and Jerusalem. However, Hezekiah humbled the pride of his heart, both he and the inhabitants of Jerusalem, so that the wrath of the Lord did not come on them in the days of Hezekiah.

Prov. 11:2*b* With the humble is wisdom.

Prov. 13:10 Through presumption [insolence] comes nothing but strife, but with those who receive counsel is wisdom.

Prov. 16:18 Pride goes before destruction, and a haughty spirit before stumbling.

Prov. 26:12 Do you see a man wise in his own eyes? There is more hope for a fool than for him.

Isa. 66:2 "For My hand made all these things, thus all these things came into being," declares the Lord. "But to this one I will look, to him who is humble and contrite of spirit, and who trembles at My word."

Luke 14:10, 11 But when you are invited, go and recline at the last place, so that when the one who has invited you comes, he may say to you, "Friend, move up higher"; then you will have honor in the sight of all who are at the table with you. For everyone who exalts himself will be humbled, and he who humbles himself will be exalted.

Eph. 4:1, 2 Therefore I, the prisoner of the Lord, implore you to walk in a manner worthy of the calling with which you have been called, with all humility and gentleness, with patience, showing tolerance [forbearance] for one another in love.

Phil. 2:3-5 Do nothing from selfishness or empty conceit, but with humility of mind regard one another as more important than yourselves; do not merely look out for your own personal interests, but also for the interests of others. Have this attitude in yourselves which was also in Christ Jesus.

Col. 3:12 So, as those who have been chosen of God, holy and beloved, put on a heart of compassion, kindness, humility, gentleness and patience.

Prov. 13:10 The word "insolence" means "pride." Allen P. Ross comments on this term:

The idea of "pride". . . here describes contempt for other opinions, a clash of competing and unyielding personalities (Kidner, *Proverbs*, p. 102). This kind of conceited person creates strife, enflames passions, and wounds feelings (McKane, p. 454). Only strife . . . can come from him. But the wise are "those who take advice."[5]

a.   *Humility is the natural precursor of compassion, gentleness, patience, and forbearance, all of which are required for godly leadership (Col. 3:12; Eph. 4:1, 2).*

b.   *In order to follow Jesus and lead as He did, we must be humble (Phil. 2:3-5).*

c.   *Whereas arrogance or the lack of humility will cloud our reason (Obad. 3), wisdom comes from humility (Prov. 11:2b). Arrogance is actually foolishness (Prov. 26:12).*

d.   *Arrogance corrupts and robs one of his integrity (2 Chron. 26:3a, 16). It encourages evil.*

e.   *An arrogant leadership will cause strife in the congregation (Prov. 13:10).*

f.   *God will punish the proud and bring about his destruction (2 Chron. 32:24-26; Prov. 16:18). Those who are self-appointed will be humbled (Luke 14:10, 11).*

g.   *God searches for and chooses the humble to lead (Isa. 66:2).*

The admonition to be a peacemaker is sometimes misunderstood as meaning that we are to humbly maintain the peace. Peacemaking, however, does not mean that problems are not confronted. Rather, they are addressed in such a way, with humility and gentleness, that the outcome is peace within the congregation. In 2 Thessalonians 3:14-16, for example, Paul urges decisive action that will ultimately restore peace. The passive overlooking of sin for the purpose of maintaining peace is never taught in Scripture.

HARD-WORKING MEN

"But we request of you, brethren, that you appreciate those who diligently labor among you, and have charge over [Greek, *prohistēmi*] you in the Lord and give you instruction [admonish NIV; Greek, *noutheteō*], and that you esteem them very highly in love because of their work. Live in peace with one another."   1 Thessalonians 5:12, 13

Read pages 161-174.

7.   In his letters to the churches, why did Paul *not* call on the elders (or any other leaders) to handle problems or difficulties within the church (see also pp. 291-295)? How does this fact affect your thinking toward the congregation and your leadership over the congregation?

a.   *Paul addressed the church rather than the elders because church problems were to be solved in the open, not in secret board meetings. The church belongs to Christ, not to the elders. They may not be authoritarian, aloof, secretive, or independent.*

b.   *Led by its elders, the congregation needs to be taught God's ways and truth in the midst of dealing with difficult circumstances.*

c. *Every member must share in responsibility for the church. Elders should view church problems as opportunities to teach and protect the flock, not as matters to be hidden or controlled by a few.*

d. *Paul had a high view of the congregation; the body is a royal priesthood, a holy people, and God speaks through them. Elderships that neglect listening to their congregations cut themselves off from the very voice of the Lord, which is expressed through the great diversity and wisdom of the body.*

8. What is meant by the statement on p. 27 of *Biblical Eldership*: "Biblical eldership, however, cannot exist in an atmosphere of nominal Christianity"? Review pp. 27-29.

   Biblical eldership can be sustained only in a church where there is biblical Christianity: men who seek first God's kingdom and righteousness (Matt. 6:33) and live committed, sacrificial lives (Rom. 12:1, 2).

9. How does Luke 14:25-33 apply to a prospective elder?

   In the same way that a tower builder or king going into battle counts the cost of his endeavor, a prospective elder must evaluate what will be expected of him. Christ's disciple must commit his life, his all; the half-hearted efforts of a spiritually lazy Christian will not suffice.

"I defy you to read the life of any saint that has ever adorned the life of the Church without seeing at once that the greatest characteristic in the life of that saint was discipline and order. Invariably it is the universal characteristic of all the outstanding men and women of God . . . Obviously it is something that is thoroughly scriptural and absolutely essential."

                                                                      D. Martyn Lloyd-Jones[6]

"It has been well said that the future is with the disciplined and that quality has been placed first on our list, for without it the other gifts, however great, will never realize their maximum potential. Only the disciplined person will rise to his highest powers. He is able to lead because he has conquered himself."

                                                                      J. Oswald Sanders[7]

8., 9. Emphasize for your mentoree that Christ's requirements of personal discipleship and allegiance to His Lordship lie at the heart of biblical eldership. A biblical elder is a mature disciple of Jesus Christ, an obedient servant of the Lord Christ and His Word. Board elders can function even if they are not mature disciples or servants of the Word, but "biblical eldership is dependent on men who seek first the kingdom of God and His righteousness (Matt. 6:33), men who have presented themselves as living sacrifices to God and slaves of the Lord Jesus Christ (Rom. 12:1, 2)" *Biblical Eldership*, pp. 27, 28. The truth is, a small group of sacrificial, dedicated shepherd elders who are committed to obedience to the Lord Christ can accomplish more for the spiritual life of the local church than a roomful of spiritually nominal board elders.

10.   As our text states, elders *work hard* at leading and admonishing the church. Elders must be disciplined men who keep their priorities straight and wisely manage their time and responsibilities. What do the following Scripture texts teach about the necessity of self-discipline in a spiritual leader's life?

Gal. 5:22*a*, 23*a* But the fruit of the Spirit is love, joy, . . . self-control.

The indwelling Holy Spirit is the source of the virtue of self-control, or discipline, in the believer's life. When a man is not self-disciplined, it is a sign that the Holy Spirit is not controlling his life.

Titus 1:7*a*, 8 For the overseer must be above reproach as God's steward, . . . hospitable, loving what is good, sensible, just, devout, self-controlled [disciplined].

God's steward must be self-disciplined (having the inner strength of the Holy Spirit to control his desires and behaviors) in order to oversee well.

1 Tim. 4:7*b* Discipline yourself for the purpose of godliness.

Godliness does not come naturally, but requires purposeful training.

1 Cor. 9:25-27 Everyone who competes in the games exercises self-control in all things. They then do it to receive a perishable wreath, but we an imperishable. Therefore I run in such a way, as not without aim; I box in such a way, as not beating the air; but I beat [discipline] my body and make it my slave, so that, after I have preached to others, I myself will not be disqualified.

---

10. Underscore the need for continual development in self-control because *it is a virtue that affects every area of life*. Our personal character is shaped and defined by our exercise of self-control. Many of our personal problems and failures are due directly to a lack of self-discipline. "Perverted values, wasted time, dulled thinking, flabby bodies, and distorted emotions provide ample evidence," writes D. G. Kehl, of our undisciplined lives.[8] Since discipline is a fruit of the Holy Spirit, we can pray daily for its development in our lives. An undisciplined elder will not only struggle with spiritual disciplines in his personal life, such as Bible reading, study, and prayer, but will mismanage and neglect the flock.

Gal. 5:23*a* The Greek term for "self-control" is *enkrateia*, formed from *eg*, "I," and *kratos*, "strength." The word conveys the idea of self-strength, self-restraint, or self-mastery-what we call willpower. Larry Richards defines *enkrateia* as, "to have power over oneself and thus to be able to hold oneself in."[9] Although "self-discipline" and "self-control" are used interchangeably in English, "self-control" communicates the biblical concept more fully.

1 Tim. 4:7*b* In this verse the Greek word for "discipline" is *gymnazō*, used to describe an athlete's training. Larry Richards says "*gymnazō* means, 'to exercise,' that is, to train and discipline one's body."[10] So "train," "exercise," or "discipline" are good translations of this Greek term. In fact, in v. 8, the related noun is used literally: "bodily discipline" or "bodily exercise" (Greek, *gymnasia*; the derivation of our English word gymnasium). Training for a sport always involves personal commitment, concentration, self-discipline, hard work, pain, sacrifice, and a specific plan. Paul is using athletic imagery to emphasize that training in godliness results from personal commitment and self-discipline.

1 Cor. 9:25-27 This passage teaches that a spiritual leader can be disqualified from office or service. To protect himself from being disqualified by sin or personal failure, Paul practiced rigorous self-denial and self-discipline. These virtues are essential for finishing life and ministry well for God. Consider John H. Armstrong's exposition of this often controversial passage:

> The word for disqualified, or rejected, refers to something/someone who fails the test and is rejected, or cast off, i.e., "disqualified from the prize." Debates about the nature of this disqualification swirl around the issue of salvation, the security of the believer, and the grace of God. As we will see, though, whatever interpretation you accept, a strong argument is made from the greater moral danger to the lesser one: if a minister can live in a manner that brings "disqualification" in the life to come-whether this is understood as loss of spiritual reward or spiritual salvation-then he can engage in certain immoral behavior that could disqualify him from preaching to others during his earthly life.[11]

Paul trains like a competitor in the games, controlling his mind and body for his Lord's service so that he will receive the crown that lasts forever. Discipline characterizes those godly men who succeed in God's work (Phil. 3:14). Paul saw self-denial and self-discipline as the means of protecting himself from being disqualified in the ministry.

Prov. 25:28 Like a city that is broken into and without walls is a man who has no control over his spirit.

The undisciplined man is defenseless against passions, irritation, temper, and the like. He is like a city with broken, breached walls.

Prov. 16:32 He who is slow to anger is better than the mighty, and he who rules his spirit, than he who captures a city.

The man who patiently controls his anger, his emotions, and his spirit, accomplishes more than the man who is acclaimed for capturing a city. Self-discipline makes him a strong, effective leader.

11.   Of the following elder qualifications, choose those that relate to self-discipline and explain how they apply.

1 Timothy 3:2-7

1.   Above reproach
2.   The husband of one wife
3.   Temperate [self-controlled, balanced]
4.   Prudent [sensible, good judgment]
5.   Respectable [well-behaved, virtuous]
6.   Hospitable
7.   Able to teach

Titus 1:6-9

1.   Above reproach
2.   The husband of one wife
3.   Having children who believe
4.   Not self-willed
5.   Not quick-tempered
6.   Not addicted to wine
7.   Not pugnacious

1 Peter 5:1-3

1.   Not shepherding under compulsion, but voluntarily
2.   Not shepherding for sordid gain, but with eagerness
3.   Not lording it over the flock, but proving to be an example

---

Prov. 25:28 Charles Bridges writes:

Certainly the noblest conquests are gained or lost over ourselves. *Anyone who has no control over his own spirit* is an easy prey to the invader. Anyone can irritate and torment him. He yields himself to the first assault of his uncontrolled passions, offering no resistance; *like a city that is broken into and without walls,* he becomes the object of contempt. Unable to discipline himself, any temptation leads to sin and causes him to do things he never dreamed of.... Every outbreaking of irritation, every spark of pride kindling in the heart, before it ever shows itself in the face or on the tongue, must be attacked, and determinably resisted. It is the beginning of a breakdown in the walls of the city. Without instant attention, it will widen to ruin the whole city.[12]

Prov. 16:32 The spiritual leader should memorize this exceptionally significant verse. The real battle for control of our spirits is inside ourselves,. The undisciplined man is a captive of his passions; the disciplined man is the mighty one, the conqueror. James 1:19, 20 builds on this proverb: "This you know, my beloved brethren. But everyone must be quick to hear, slow to speak and slow to anger; for the anger of man does not achieve the righteousness of God."

11. Read George Knight's quotation on p. 188. Note that many of the qualifications for elder require self-discipline. An elder must be under the control of the Holy Spirit (Eph. 5:18), not of fleshly passions and ambitions. Furthermore, to be a student of the Word, man of prayer, teacher, and skilled manager of people, the elder must have strong self-discipline.

1 Timothy 3:2-7	Titus 1:6-9	1 Peter 5:1-3
8. Not addicted to wine	8. Not fond of sordid gain	
9. Not pugnacious [not belligerent]	9. Hospitable	
10. Gentle [forbearing]	10. Lover of what is good [kind, virtuous]	
11. Peaceable [uncontentious]	11. Sensible [see prudent]	
12. Free from the love of money	12. Just [righteous conduct, law-abiding]	
13. Manages his household well	13. Devout [holy, pleasing to God, loyal to His Word]	
14. Not a new convert	14. Self-controlled	
15. A good reputation with those outside the church	15. Holds fast the faithful [trustworthy NIV] Word, both to exhort and to refute	

a.   *Above reproach: Only the self-disciplined man is above reproach.*

b.   *Temperate: This calls for discipline in maintaining a sober mind and remaining emotionally balanced. Temperate also means that the elder is moderate in his habits and is never under the influence of alcohol or any drug.*

c.   *Prudent, sensible: These are aspects of self-discipline. The elder must restrain impulsive and spontaneous reactions, allowing reason and good sense to prevail.*

d.   *Gentle: A man's power has to be controlled and restrained in accordance with Christ's example.*

e.   *Not self-willed: The elder's personal agenda, desires, and ambitions are to be set aside.*

f.   *Self-controlled: The elder must be under the control of the Holy Spirit.*

12.   Read the quote by R. Paul Stevens on pp. 28, 29. What does Stevens mean by his statement that "tentmakers must live a pruned life and literally find leisure and rest in the rhythm of serving Christ" (Matt. 11:28)?

In order to be a responsible employee or self-employed person and at the same time minister to his family and the church, the elder must adopt a sacrificial lifestyle. This means living a "pruned life" that is centered on the important, which requires eliminating many of the activities our culture demands. The tentmaking elder will find refreshment in the alternating of duties and in his partnering with God. In the joy of service, the elder will find God's compensations.

13.   To be effective as a shepherd elder, you must clearly understand the elders' identity and function in the church. Define the Greek term *prohistēmi*. How does this term clarify the position and work of the elders (see pp. 167, 168)?

a.   *The word* **prohistēmi** *means to have charge over, lead, preside, govern, manage, support, care for in spiritual matters.*

b.   *The authority of the elder is to be used for the well-being of the congregation. He is to diligently lead in spiritual matters. The word* **prohistēmi** *always includes the concept of caring for those over whom you have authority.*

14.   To gain an accurate picture of the elders' work, you must also understand the meaning of the Greek term *noutheteō.*

a.   What does *noutheteō* entail?

Noutheteō *means to counsel in the sense of warning, advising, or exerting a corrective influence. It means to offer appropriate corrective instruction that results in understanding.*

b.   Why is the ministry of admonition vitally important to a Christian congregation (see pp. 151-153, 165-169)?

Vigilant care and protection of the flock requires that the elders continuously and decisively equip and warn each believer.

15.   A shepherd must be very concerned about the peace of the flock, and it should weigh heavily in all the elders' discussions or decisions. From the above lists of elder qualifications, which qualifications relate to peacemaking? Explain the role each plays.

a.   *Gentle: The elder's gracious, understanding forbearance will generate peace and healing in the body.*

b.   *Not **pugnacious**, **peaceable** [uncontentious]: The elder must not cause or aggravate dissension within the church.*

c.   *Not quick-tempered: The elder must expect controversy, criticism, and even attack. However, he must respond in a way that encourages calm consideration that is informed by biblical teaching.*

d.   *Not self-willed, self-controlled: The elder's own history must not deter him from being an impartial judge in disputes.*

e.   *Not **lording it over the flock** but **proving to be an example**: The elder's personal, visible example in dealing with dissension in the church can be a powerful force for peace.*

16.   Among the qualifications you have just listed, *gentle* stands out for making peace amidst disagreement and failure.

    a.   Define this excellent character quality.

        Gentle means loving, tender, kindly, mild, forbearing, yielding, and not harmful.

    b.   Explain how gentleness establishes peace among the Lord's people.

        If the elders are gentle and Christlike, they will be wise and controlled. They will not harm the flock by their use of strength and authority, even when handling the most contentious difficulties. This active, corporate, humble self-control will make peace in the body (Matt. 5:9).

"Self-sacrificing love is thus made the essence of the self-sacrificing love of Christ himself: Christ's followers are to 'have the same mind in them which was also in Christ Jesus.' The possessive pronouns throughout this passage [John 15]-'abide in *my* love,' 'in *my* love,' 'in *his* (the Father's) love'-are all subjective: so that throughout the whole, it is the love which Christ bears his people which is kept in prominent view as the impulse and standard of the love he asks."

B. B. Warfield[13]

---

17.   Paul E. Billheimer says the local church is a "laboratory" of love (p. 171).[14] If this is so, explain how serving on the eldership team would be a far greater testing ground of love?

    Elder councils must handle difficult situations within the church and must strive for consensus decisions among highly principled men. This increased opportunity for conflict that arises during the course of church leadership will gravely test men's love for each other. Thus elders are under greater pressure to exercise and manifest patience, gentleness, and forbearance.

---

16. Highlight this qualification, *gentle*. Without doubt it is one of the most important qualities. The church leader constantly deals with troubled people and tense situations. Without forbearing gentleness, he will hurt many people and undermine his efforts.

17. Warn your mentoree that, should he become an elder, his relationships with his fellow elders will undergo great stress. He may risk good friendships with brothers because of the intense nature of the conflicts and issues they will be called upon to decide. The pressures and battles of ministry will expose weaknesses and flaws in his character and judgment that his friends may not appreciate, and he may not prefer what he discerns in them as a result of the strains of disagreement. Sometimes elders who were once close friends become distant. In addition, because they are engaged in God's work, they will experience Satan's attack upon their relationships as he attempts to undermine God's work.

SCRIPTURE MEMORY ASSIGNMENT:

"But we request of you, brethren, that you appreciate those who diligently labor among you, and have charge over you in the Lord and give you instruction, and that you esteem them very highly in love because of their work. Live in peace with one another."   1 Thessalonians 5:12, 13

[1] Ruth A. Tucker, *From Jerusalem to Irian Jaya: A Biographical History of Christian Missions* (Grand Rapids: Zondervan, 1983), p. 239.

[2] J. Oswald Sanders, *Spiritual Leadership* (Chicago: Moody, 1967, 1980), p. 35.

[3] Jonathan Edwards, *Charity and Its Fruits* (1852; Carlisle: The Banner of Truth Trust, 1969), pp. 133, 134.

[4] Bruce Wilkinson and Kenneth Boa, *Talk Thru the Bible* (Nashville: Thomas Nelson, 1983), p. 253.

[5] Allen P. Ross, "Proverbs," in *The Expositor's Bible Commentary*, 12 vols., ed. Frank E. Gaebelein (Grand Rapids: Zondervan, 1991), 5:977.

[6] D. Martyn Lloyd-Jones, *Spiritual Depression* (Grand Rapids: Eerdmans, 1965), p. 210.

[7] Sanders, *Spiritual Leadership*, p. 67.

[8] D. G. Kehl, "The Forgotten Fruit of the Spirit," *Christianity Today*, (October 7, 1983), p. 33.

[9] Lawrence O. Richards, *Expository Dictionary of Bible Words* (Grand Rapids: Zondervan, 1985), p. 546.

[10] Ibid., p. 601.

[11] John H. Armstrong, *Can Fallen Pastors Be Restored? The Church's Response to Sexual Misconduct* (Chicago: Moody, 1995), p. 101.

[12] Charles Bridges, *A Modern Study in the Book of Proverbs: Charles Bridges' Classic Revised for Today's Reader*, by George F. Santa (Milford: Mott Media, 1978), pp. 571, 572.

[13] B. B. Warfield, "The Emotional Life of Our Lord," in *The Person and Work of Christ* (Philadelphia: Presbyterian and Reformed, 1950), p. 104.

[14] Paul E. Billheimer, *Love Covers* (Fort Washington: Christian Literature Crusade, 1981), p. 34.

Lesson 6
Team Leadership

LESSON OVERVIEW

Lesson 6 examines the plurality of overseers mentioned in Philippians 1:1, the equating of overseers with elders, the significance of church leadership terminology, the importance and practice of team leadership, and the principle of "first among equals."

The major focus of the lesson is on learning how to work with fellow elders in Christian harmony, which is not an easy task. Becoming a good team player takes years of effort and commitment. The key to team leadership is *agapē* love.

ELDER: THE OFFICE AND THE TITLE

"Paul and Timothy, bond-servants of Christ Jesus, to all the saints in Christ Jesus who are in Philippi, including the overseers and deacons."   Philippians 1:1

Review pages 31-34. Read pages 174-180.

1.   According to *Biblical Eldership*, "Paul's brief mention of overseers and deacons provides a wealth of valuable information for our study on eldership" (p. 174). What special contributions to our understanding of the New Testament concept of eldership are made by Philippians 1:1?

   a.   *This verse confirms that elders were established in the churches founded by Paul in Macedonia (Europe), and not just in Asia Minor and Palestine as recorded in Acts.*

   b.   *In the Greek culture, the term **overseer** was always associated with an official position. Therefore, the use of the term **overseers** to designate elders proves that the office of elder was generally recognized as an official church leadership position.*

   c.   *Paul's usage of the plural, **overseers**, indicates that there was a plurality of elders governing the church.*

2.   What biblical evidence do we have to prove the assertion that the "overseers" mentioned in Philippians 1:1 are the same group of leaders who are called *elders* elsewhere? List the biblical arguments equating "overseers" with elders, in order of decreasing significance for you.

      a.   *Acts 20:17, 28 refers to the same group of leaders as elders and overseers.*

      b.   *In Titus 1:5-7, Paul uses the term* **overseer** *in the middle of a passage that describes the qualifications of elders.*

      c.   *In 1 Tim. 3:1-13, Paul lists the qualifications for overseers. Later in the same letter he refers to them as elders (5:17).*

      d.   *In 1 Peter 5:1, 2, Peter tells the elders to oversee the church.*

3.   Why should the terminology (or titles) we use to describe our church leaders be a matter of critical importance to the local church?

      a.   *The titles define the function of the offices. If the titles are incorrect, then the function will be incorrect also.*

      b.   *If we are to be biblical, we must be faithful to the biblical usage. The technique of the false teacher is to redefine the meaning of biblical terms. We must protect the church from such false teachings by using correct terms, and by defining their meanings in a way that is consistent with NT usage.*

4.   What titles does your church use for its leaders? In what ways do these accurately represent (or misrepresent) the language and concepts of the New Testament church?

---

2. Remind your mentoree that the singular term *overseer* in 1 Tim. 3:2 and Titus 1:7 is a generic singular, that is, a singular noun representing an entire class or type. Because of the common assumption that the *overseer* is different from the elders, meaning that he is the senior pastor, this point must be continually reinforced. Some of these technical points of biblical exegesis have to be repeated again and again before the mentoree truly grasps the meaning. Do not hesitate to have your mentoree reiterate the arguments for supporting these key positions. We all learn by review, review, review.

3. Refer again to Walter Martin's quotation on "scaling the language barrier" in lesson 4, note on question 12. Urge your mentoree to learn to read more critically and to observe how an author uses his terminology. It is shocking how many authors employ such basic terms as "church," "pastor," "ordination," "minister," "ministerial," "discipleship," "love," "law," "faith," etc., in an unscriptural manner, that subverts their biblical meanings.

ASSIGNMENT:

In Philippians 1:1, deacons are closely associated with elders (overseers). To help you know who deacons are and what they do, consider reading *Ministers of Mercy: The New Testament Deacon.*[1] It would also be profitable to observe the deacons at work in your church.

PLURALITY OF ELDERS AND OVERSEERS

Review pages 35-45, 101-117.

5. According to *Biblical Eldership* (p. 35), "The New Testament provides *conclusive evidence* that the pastoral oversight of the apostolic churches was a team effort-not the sole responsibility of one person." What evidence does *Biblical Eldership* present to justify this strong statement?

   a. *Collective leadership was displayed in the Jerusalem conference, recorded in Acts 15.*

   b. *James instructed the sick to "call for the elders [plural] of the church [singular]" (James 5:14).*

   c. *Paul and Barnabas appointed elders (plural) in each newly founded church (Acts 14:23).*

   d. *When leaving Ephesus, Paul summoned the elders (plural) of the church to meet with him (Acts 20:17, 28).*

   e. *Paul greeted the leaders of the church at Philippi as overseers (plural, Phil. 1:1).*

   f. *Paul did not consider a church to be fully developed until qualified, functioning elders had been appointed (Titus 1:5).*

   g. *When writing to churches in Asia Minor, Peter exhorted the elders (plural) to pastor the flock (1 Peter 5:1).*

   h. *An examination of all the Scripture passages that mention church leadership overwhelmingly indicates plural leadership of individual congregations.*

---

5. The point to emphasize with your trainee is this: according to Acts and the epistles, the call to shepherd the local church is *always* made to a group of men, never to one man.

6.   In what ways does church government by a plurality of elders preserve the true, biblical nature of the local church as designed by God?

    a.   *It preserves the intimate family nature of the church. It allows any brother in the community who desires and qualifies to share fully in the leadership (pp. 109-111).*

    b.   *It preserves the non-clerical nature of the leadership of the local church. The church is not to be governed by a professional clergy (pp. 111-114).*

    c.   *It preserves the nature and purpose of the local church as a humble-servant community in which elders humbly submit to each other in the exercise of collegial leadership (p. 114).*

    d.   *It preserves the supreme headship and leadership of Christ in each congregation, which was its intended structure. A council of elders is responsible to Christ rather than to a senior pastor (p. 115).*

7.   One of the significant benefits of team leadership is that it provides genuine accountability for leaders (pp. 42-44). In what ways is mutual *accountability* both a practical benefit to the elders and an important theological reason for plurality of leadership?

    a.   Practical benefits:

Accountability shields the individuals involved from the corrupting effects of pride and power. It also compensates for our sinfulness by providing close connections and the best setting for encouragement and admonishment. If the team is accountable to build and honor each man (with his unique gifts), and to shield him from unscriptural criticism for not having all the gifts, the benefits derived from the diversity of gifts will be enhanced.

    b.   Theological reason:

Personal accountability is necessary because we are all sinful and all power tends to corrupt. The accountability of being one among equals in a shared leadership role prevents such corruption.

8.   How would you answer those who say that James was the senior pastor of the church in Jerusalem (pp. 104-106)?

6., 7. These two questions deal with the doctrinal necessity for plural eldership. They are important because they will prompt your mentoree's thinking about eldership as it relates to fundamental theology: the doctrines of the nature of the church and of fallen man. Although there are practical reasons for implementing plural eldership, the biblical-theological reasons are far more important. Help your mentoree progress in his thinking about eldership on a theological as well as an exegetical level.

8. Make sure your mentoree thoroughly understands what the NT *actually does and does not state* about James, our Lord's brother. This is necessary because James is one of the chief examples people employ to substantiate the senior pastor model.

*James was an apostle and a leading man among the brothers, but he was considered to be **a** pillar, not **the** pillar, of the church (Gal. 2:9). The NT does not identify James as **the** pastor of the Jerusalem church.*

9. From the elder qualification lists below, which character traits are necessary for working in close Christian harmony with others on the eldership team? List the characteristics in decreasing order of importance and explain why each is important.

1 Timothy 3:2-7

1. Above reproach
2. The husband of one wife
3. Temperate [self-controlled, balanced]
4. Prudent [sensible, good judgment]
5. Respectable [well-behaved, virtuous]
6. Hospitable
7. Able to teach
8. Not addicted to wine
9. Not pugnacious [not belligerent]
10. Gentle [forbearing]
11. Peaceable [uncontentious]
12. Free from the love of money
13. Manages his household well
14. Not a new convert
15. A good reputation with those outside the church

Titus 1:6-9

1. Above reproach
2. The husband of one wife
3. Having children who believe
4. Not self-willed
5. Not quick-tempered
6. Not addicted to wine
7. Not pugnacious
8. Not fond of sordid gain
9. Hospitable
10. Lover of what is good [kind, virtuous]
11. Sensible [see prudent]
12. Just [righteous conduct, law-abiding]
13. Devout [holy, pleasing to God, loyal to His Word]
14. Self-controlled
15. Holds fast the faithful [trustworthy NIV] Word, both to exhort and to refute

1 Peter 5:1-3

1. Not shepherding under compulsion, but voluntarily
2. Not shepherding for sordid gain, but with eagerness
3. Not lording it over the flock, but proving to be an example

a. *Gentle, lover of what is good: The elder must maintain a close relationship with other elders and handle conflicts and problems with loving kindness.*

b. *Prudent, sensible: The elder must be able to be objective in the midst of controversy and conflict and not prone to make quick judgments. Good judgment is essential in achieving consensus.*

c. *Temperate, not quick-tempered, self-controlled: Since decisions must be made by consensus, discussions should be free of accusations or displays of temper.*

d. *Not pugnacious, peaceable [uncontentious]: The elder must be a peacemaker on the council, not a man given to belligerence or obstinance.*

e.   *Respectable: Each elder should be worthy of the respect of the other members of the council.*

f.   *Not self-willed: Each elder must be free of self-interest in the proposals that he brings to the council.*

g.   *Above reproach: A team effort depends on mutual trust. Nothing in the elder's life should detract from the positions he takes on issues in the council. When an elder speaks to the congregation on behalf of the council, he must be trusted to faithfully represent its position.*

10. From your past experience in working with committees or groups, indicate whether the following statements apply: use **T** for true, or **F** for false. Take time to honestly evaluate yourself before God. Ask your wife or a close friend to help you answer objectively.

T†   I act impulsively and dislike waiting for others to make decisions.

F├   I generally trust the collective judgment of my fellow team members.

T   I feel genuine concern for the interests and plans of my fellow workers.

F   I often act independently of the leadership body.

T   I make myself accountable to my fellow team members.

T†   I work hard to cooperate with my partners in ministry.

F├   I share my burdens, fears, and problems with my brothers.

F   I am inclined to carry a grudge.

F   I am easily frustrated by disagreement.

F   I am afraid to speak honestly in a group.

T   I feel free to correct and direct my fellow team members.

T   I actively contribute to discussions and decisions.

T   I tend to be bossy.

F   I am too sensitive.

F   I tend to dominate discussions.

F   I have a hard time apologizing or admitting I am wrong.

T   I love my fellow colleagues.

T   I consciously try to be humble and serve my brothers.

T   I pray for my team members regularly.

With your mentor's help, identify your areas of weakness as a team member. Give these weaknesses special prayer attention and peer accountability. Together, focus on how the profound quotation by Paul E. Billheimer (*Biblical Eldership*, p. 171) applies to you.

11.   The secret to unity and cooperation among elders is *agapē* love. Read the following verses and list the characteristics of *agapē* love that enable elders to work together in unity and peace and to handle the many hurts and disagreements leaders regularly encounter.

John 13:1, 4, 5, 14 Now before the Feast of the Passover, Jesus knowing that His hour had come that He would depart out of this world to the Father, having loved His own who were in the world, He loved them to the end. . . . [He] got up from supper, and laid aside His garments; and taking a towel, He girded Himself. Then He poured water into the basin, and began to wash the disciples' feet and to wipe them with the towel with which He was girded. . . . "If I then, the Lord and the Teacher, washed your feet, you also ought to wash one another's feet."

Agapē love models a humble, selfless, servant attitude toward one's colleagues.

Rom. 12:9a Let love be without hypocrisy. Abhor what is evil.

Agapē love is genuine, sincere, of good motive.

Rom. 12:10 Be devoted to one another in brotherly love; give preference to one another in honor.

Agapē love is brotherly devotion; it is preferring and honoring one another above one's self.

Rom. 14:15 For if because of food your brother is hurt, you are no longer walking according to love. Do not destroy with your food him for whom Christ died.

Agapē love is considerate of a brother's sensitivities and weaknesses and will not insist on using knowledge of the truth. Love for the brother for whom Christ died is to be the motive.

1 Cor. 8:1 Now concerning things sacrificed to idols, we know that we all have knowledge. Knowledge makes arrogant, but love edifies.

Agapē love deters pride, tempers knowledge, and builds up the brother. The pride of knowledge divides.

1 Cor. 13:4 Love is patient [suffers long], love is kind and is not jealous; love does not brag and is not arrogant.

---

11. Of *agapē* love, Michael Green writes:

> This word *agapē* is one which Christians to all intents and purposes coined, to denote the attitude which God has shown Himself to have to us, and requires from us towards Himself. . . . God's *agapē* is evoked not by what we are, but by what He is. It has its origin in the agent, not in the object. It is not that we are lovable, but that He is love. This *agapē* might be defined as a deliberate desire for the highest good of the one loved, which shows itself in sacrificial action for that person's good. That is what God did for us (John 3:16). That is what He wants us to do (1 John 3:16).[2]

Review pp. 92, 96, 114 to prepare for reinforcing the truth that without *agapē* love, elders cannot work together in Christian unity and peace. Read the last paragraph on p. 98 to your mentoree. Also read John 13:34, 35 as it applies to the church leadership team.

Agapē love is kind (not easily provoked), forbearing, selfless, and Christlike. It is not proud, boastful, envious. Agapē love is the result of deciding to obey God's command.

1 Cor. 13:5 [Love] does not act unbecomingly; it does not seek its own, is not provoked, does not take into account a wrong suffered.

Agapē love is not rude, irritable, touchy, self-seeking, or easily angered. It never allows hurt suffered at the hands of another to affect his conduct toward that person.

1 Cor. 13:8 Love never fails; but if there are gifts of prophecy, they will be done away; if there are tongues, they will cease; if there is knowledge, it will be done away.

The consequences of agapē *love are eternal.*

Eph. 4:2 With all humility and gentleness, with patience, showing tolerance [forbearance] for one another in love.

Agapē love is humble; it puts aside its own rights for the sake of gently and patiently dealing with another.

Philem. 8, 9 Therefore, though I have enough confidence in Christ to order you to do what is proper, yet for love's sake I rather appeal to you—since I am such a person as Paul, the aged, and now also a prisoner of Christ Jesus.

Agapē love does not command, but persuades, brothers. It responds to relationships.

1 Peter 4:8 Above all, keep fervent in your love for one another, because love covers a multitude of sins.

We are to be so intensely devoted to our brothers in Christ that our agapē *love for them allows us to freely forgive their sins toward us.*

1 John 3:16 We know love by this, that He laid down His life for us; and we ought to lay down our lives for the brethren.

We must be willing to sacrifice anything for the sake of a brother in Christ, even our own life. Agapē love is defined by Christlike self-sacrifice.

12.   Which biblical concept above is God encouraging you to nurture and adopt?

FIRST AMONG A COUNCIL OF EQUALS: LEADERS AMONG LEADERS

"The elders who rule well are to be considered worthy of double honor, especially those who work hard at preaching and teaching. For the Scripture says, 'You shall not muzzle the ox while he is threshing,' and 'The laborer is worthy of his wages.'"   1 Timothy 5:17, 18

> **Review pages 45-50.**

13. List examples from Peter's life and ministry that demonstrate the principle of "first among equals."

   a. *Peter was usually the spokesman for the disciples (Acts 2:14; 5:3; etc.).*

   b. *Peter was among the three (Peter, James, and John) whom Jesus often selected from the rest of His disciples (Mark 14:33; Luke 8:51; 9:28).*

   c. *Jesus instructed Peter to "strengthen your brothers" (Luke 22:32). Jesus recognized Peter as a leader among the men, one who could strengthen and encourage them.*

   d. *Peter never exercised authority over the other disciples and was never given a separate title. The other eleven never acted as a staff to Peter, or took a subservient role.*

14. Which traits characterize an elder who is first among his equals?

   a. *Leadership ability, as evidenced by a concern for the whole church, not just a particular ministry, the ability to clearly articulate concepts orally and in writing, and the ability to encourage and articulate a consensus decision of the council*

   b. *The ability to effectively teach the Word*

---

13. The principle of "first among equals" describes a reality: in a group of leaders facing a certain set of circumstances, the man with the gifts most appropriate to the situation will come to the fore, and will have the principal influence. For example, in the OT, Judah and Ephraim were *first among equals*, the twelve tribes of Israel, with Judah eventually becoming the leading tribe. A NT example can be found in Peter among the twelve apostles.

   In some elder councils there may be an exceptional, multi-talented man. The principle of "first among equals," if recognized, allows such a man to use his talents without fear of intimidating the others. It is tragic when highly talented individuals are excluded from participating in leadership because they threaten the other elders. It is crucial that your mentoree grasp this principle, understanding both its benefits and pitfalls.

c.   *The desire and willingness to devote much of his energy to the ministry of the church*

15.   How does the principle of "first among equals" help protect and sharpen an exceptionally gifted teacher and/or leader?

a.   *The accountability inherent in being an equal in a group of elders prevents the exceptionally gifted man from being corrupted by the temptations of imperialism.*

b.   *If the exceptional leader is immersed in a group of equals, the other gifted men will foster his development and protect him by admonishing his pride and flaws. "Iron sharpens iron, so one man sharpens another" (Prov. 27:17).*

c.   *The exceptional teacher of the Word may be encouraged by being specially honored as such, and that may include the congregation's financial support of his full-time effort.*

16.   What is wrong with calling one elder "pastor" and the other men "elders"?

a.   *The use of separate titles for the same biblical function creates an unbiblical status distinction between these groups. It invariably disparages the role of the tentmaker who sacrificially supports himself in ministry.*

b.   *When one or more men are set apart as "pastors," they are denied the accountability that is available from a group of mutually accountable equals.*

c.   *There is no biblical precedent for such a practice.*

17.   Plurality of leadership has inherent risks that may lead to weaknesses and frustrations in team ministry. In parallel columns, describe the inherent risks of shared leadership and the corresponding remedies.

---

17. Some men naively assume that plurality of leadership will solve all the church's problems. This is not the case! Eldership creates its own problems, and these must be understood and continually addressed. However, when properly implemented, biblical eldership best allows the church to be what God designed it to be, protects the church from dangerous extremes, and fosters the spiritual development of the leading men of the church family.

   It is appropriate to consider Jon Zens's three warnings, especially the first, about our attitudes toward the doctrine of eldership: "(1.) We must not idolize the subject of eldership; (2.) we must not polarize over this subject; (3.) we must not minimize this subject."[3] Concerning his first point, Zens writes:

   As men grow in the truth it is quite often the case that a newly-found biblical concept can be magnified out of proportion . . . It is possible to have the eldership doctrine straight, and somewhat implemented on the local level, and still be far from the overall New Testament pattern for church order. It is shameful if a church blessed with elders manifests a superior attitude and looks down their nose at other churches who are not "straight" in this area. . . . Having an eldership certainly will not cure all church problems. The realization of an eldership in a church may create some difficulties, and churches with an eldership have had to go through some of the thorniest problems imaginable. The real point before us is that if oversight by elders is biblical, then it will indeed provide a Christ-ordained way of handling general order and special problems. But in no way must it be regarded as a panacea for all the problems churches face today.[4]

Inherent Risks	Remedies
Elders relinquish their responsibility to one or two exceptionally gifted men, out of laziness or exhaustion on the elders' part and selfishness on the leaders' part.	*The elders should exercise more care in the selection of elders. Both those who are unwilling to serve and those who desire to lord it over others must not be appointed elders.*
The elder council lacks direction and purpose. Progress in making decisions is slow.	*The elders should choose from among themselves an elder to moderate/manage consensus, based on his gifts.*

SCRIPTURE MEMORY ASSIGNMENT:

"The elders who rule well are to be considered worthy of double honor, especially those who work hard at preaching and teaching. For the Scripture says, 'You shall not muzzle the ox while he is threshing,' and 'The laborer is worthy of his wages.'"   1 Timothy 5:17, 18

---

[1] Alexander Strauch, *Ministers of Mercy: The New Testament Deacon* (Littleton: Lewis and Roth, 1992).

[2] Michael Green, *The Second Epistle of Peter and the Epistle of Jude* (Grand Rapids: Eerdmans, 1968), p. 71.

[3] Jon Zens, "The Major Concepts of Eldership in the New Testament," *Baptist Reformation* 7 (Summer 1978): 26.

[4] Ibid.

Lesson 7
Qualified Leaders

LESSON OVERVIEW

The major emphasis of lesson 7 is the necessity of church elders being "above reproach." The lesson also reviews Paul's purpose in writing 1 Timothy, the Ephesian elders' failure to protect the church from false teaching, the faithful saying of 1 Timothy 3:1, and the qualifications for overseers.

THE BOOK OF FIRST TIMOTHY

"I am writing these things to you, hoping to come to you before long; but in case I am delayed, I write so that you will know how one ought to conduct himself in the household of God, which is the church of the living God, the pillar and support of the truth."　　　　　1 Timothy 3:14, 15

> **Read pages 181-186.**

1.　　According to 1 Timothy 3:14, 15:

　　a.　　What was Paul's purpose in writing 1 Timothy?

　　To establish the standard and give instructions for proper Christian conduct within the church.

　　b.　　Why is eldership a vital part of that purpose?

The elders must lead in teaching the standards for proper conduct to the church, and in setting personal examples of Christlike behavior. The proper ordering of God's house and its leadership is essential to the well-being of its members. The elders are to see that the leadership exhibit godly conduct. If the elders display reproachful conduct, the entire household of God will suffer.

2.   The church in Ephesus was thoroughly disrupted by false teachers who most likely came from within, just as Paul had predicted. *Biblical Eldership* suggests that the Ephesian elders made mistakes that you, as a future elder, can learn from and avoid repeating. What were these mistakes?

   a.   *The elders did not heed Paul's warning (Acts 20:28 ff.) to guard against the very things that occurred.*

   b.   *They had appointed unqualified men to be elders, thereby allowing false teachers (who most likely came from within) to arise and acquire official status.*

   c.   *The novice elders lacked the maturity and strength to successfully guard the truth and counter false teachers.*

   d.   *The elders did not deal with sin as it emerged from within their ranks.*

   e.   *The elders did not properly teach and equip the flock to resist false teaching.*

ASSIGNMENTS:

Since "1 Timothy is the most important letter of the New Testament for the study of biblical eldership" (p. 181), you should own a number of sound commentaries on the Pastoral Epistles. Invest in any good commentary on the Pastoral Epistles.

You should also make use of expository preaching series on 1 Timothy and Titus.[1] Do not be limited to one favorite preacher. We can learn from all of God's servants, even those who are not part of our familiar circle (1 Cor. 3:21-23).

As soon as you are able, undertake an in-depth study of 1 Timothy and Titus. An excellent way to learn these books is to teach them to others, since you learn best when you teach.

A FAITHFUL SAYING

"It is a trustworthy statement: if any man aspires to the office of overseer, it is a fine work he desires to do. An overseer, then, must be above reproach."   1 Timothy 3:1, 2a

---

2. Validate the correlation between the Ephesian elders' failure to protect the church from false teachers and Paul's earlier warning for them to guard God's flock from "savage wolves" (Acts 20:28-31). The Ephesian elders became slack and apparently allowed the wrong men into leadership or did not discipline sinning elders (1 Tim. 1:19, 20; 5:19-25). False teachers are always aggressive, indomitable people who will push their agendas until we either tire and give in, or demonstrate that we will stand firm on the truth at all costs (Acts 15:1, 2). The point is, being vigilant and protecting the church from false teachers is exhausting work, and many church elders have failed to stand their ground. Be sure to read the second paragraph on p. 186.
ASSIGNMENTS As stated earlier in this *Guide*, maximize the training of men for eldership by encouraging them to listen to expository Bible tapes. If your church does not have a tape library, consider starting one.

Review pages 186-188.

3.   Write out your own paraphrase of 1 Timothy 3:1. Be creative, using a number of sentences. For an example, see F. F. Bruce's paraphrase of Titus 1:5-7, on pp. 227, 228.

It should be emphasized that it is correct and honorable for a man to desire to serve God by being an elder who oversees the affairs of the church. The aspiration is not sinful or self-promoting. In fact, this desire is commendable because the man is choosing a worthy, noble, and excellent work—that of shepherding the church for whom Christ died. It should be known in the congregation that a qualified man who is bearing responsibility in the church by leading and teaching is to be encouraged and helped to prepare for eldership.

4.   To the best of your recollection:

   a.   When did you first desire to be a shepherd elder?

   b.   What sparked your initial desire to be a shepherd elder?

   c.   Describe an event or problem that has caused you to doubt your desire to be a shepherd elder.

   d.   How intense is your desire to be a shepherd elder?

   e.   In what ways do you think an intense desire is appropriate or inappropriate?

   f.   Do you ever doubt your qualifications to be an elder? If so, how seriously?

   g.   If, at this time, you are not appointed to be a shepherd elder, what should be your response?

5. Many people try to prove the senior pastor theory by the singular use of the word "overseer" in 1 Timothy 3:2 and Titus 1:7. How does *Biblical Eldership* explain the singular use of "overseer" in these two passages?

    Here Paul is using the generic singular, as he has elsewhere when referring to an entire class or type of individuals. In both cases, "overseer" is preceded by the generic singular construction, "if any man." Other examples of the generic singular are "woman," "widow," "elder," and "the Lord's bond-servant" (1 Tim. 2:11-14; 5:5, 19; 2 Tim. 2:24). The same Ephesian overseers are referred to in the plural in Acts 20:17, 28.

APOSTOLIC QUALIFICATIONS FOR ELDERSHIP

"An overseer, then, must be above reproach, the husband of one wife, temperate, prudent, respectable, hospitable, able to teach, not addicted to wine or pugnacious, but gentle, peaceable, free from the love of money. He must be one who manages his own household well, keeping his children under control with all dignity (but if a man does not know how to manage his own household, how will he take care of the church of God?), and not a new convert, so that he will not become conceited and fall into the condemnation incurred by the devil. And he must have a good reputation with those outside the church, so that he may not fall into reproach and the snare of the devil."   1 Timothy 3:2-7

Review pages 67-83, 186-202.

6. "Above reproach" is the "general, overarching, all-embracing" qualification for a church elder. How would you answer the critic who asserts: "No one is above reproach!" "No one meets all the biblical qualifications for eldership, so you cannot insist upon elders meeting all these qualifications." (Also see pp. 228, 229.)

    There is a significant difference between being above reproach and being perfect or without fault. Being above reproach means that the elder's reputation has not been marred by moral or ethical disgrace. We must insist that elders meet the biblical requirements because: (1) they are stewards of God's household, (2) they are to be examples to the congregation, and (3) they are to protect the church from incompetent or morally corrupt leaders. Only elders who meet the biblical standards can fulfill these responsibilities.

7. Some elders earn their living in the business community. List the specific implications of being "above reproach" for this elder.

    The elder must be above reproach in his business ethics. He must be a respected businessman in the community's eyes. This includes being known for his financial integrity and for being an ethical employer. If he is involved in sales, the elder must offer a quality product at a fair price. The elder must not be involved in deceptive business practices or in the selfish use of wealth.

8.   A good deal of debate occurs over the qualification "the husband of one wife." Which interpretation of this qualification do you favor and why?

At the time of consideration of his appointment as elder, and for the entire period that he is an elder, a man must be absolutely and exclusively committed to one woman for life. All of his behavior should communicate that he is a one-woman man. If he is single, he must also be committed to this principle. A single man, a widower, or a divorced man who has had a biblically sanctioned divorce is not disqualified for eldership. This interpretation is consistent with the context of the passage and does not contradict other teachings of Scripture.

Before you answer the next three questions, read the quotations below from John H. Armstrong's book, *Can Fallen Pastors Be Restored? The Church's Response to Sexual Misconduct*:

In 1988 *Leadership*, a journal read mostly by ministers, conducted a poll on the sexual practices of clergymen and printed the staggering results in an article titled, "How Common Is Pastoral Indiscretion?" Based on more than three hundred responses from its readership, their survey revealed the existence of a growing moral breakdown in pastors' lives. . . .

Twelve percent answered yes to the question: "Have you ever had sexual intercourse with someone other than your spouse since you have been in local-church ministry?". . . If these statistics are not frightening enough, 18 percent responded that they had engaged in "other forms of sexual contact with someone other than your spouse, i.e., passionate kissing, fondling/mutual masturbation," while in local-church ministry.

Similar research done by the Fuller Institute of Church Growth indicates that 37 percent of ministers "have been involved in inappropriate behavior with someone in the church." Harry W. Schaumburg, a therapist who works with problems of sexual misconduct and sexual addiction, adds . . . the following observation: "Evidence indicates that this shocking and disturbing statistic is true. I frequently receive calls for counseling from Christian leaders around the country who have 'fallen,' who are sexually addicted or have been involved in sexual misconduct. . . ."

The *Leadership* survey of pastors found that more than two-thirds of the pastors had become sexually involved with people from within the congregation, often serving in leadership roles within the local church. Asked for the major reason for this illicit relationship, respondents most often replied, "physical and emotional attraction." After reviewing these results, one prominent counseling professor at a major seminary said, "We're living in a Corinthian age, but we're preparing students for the Victorian age."

---

8. The application of the phrase, "husband of one wife," has resulted in much controversy. Describe to your mentoree the dangers of basing marital requirements for elders on this inconclusive, three-word phrase, for example, teaching that an elder or deacon can only be married once in his lifetime. It is very important to understand that this three-word phrase does not deal with all the complex issues related to sexual infidelity, restoration, divorce, and remarriage of a church leader. The last paragraph on p. 192 and the first full paragraph on p. 193 will provide resources for your discussion.

One religion editor, who devoted considerable study to this problem, recently wrote: "Experts who have studied clergy members' sexual misconduct believe at least one-third of all ministers have committed some type of sexual abuse on members of their congregations--and the rate could be higher."[2]

Sexual sin need not directly involve another person. An impure thought life of vicarious sex with real or imaginary partners can be equally damaging. Robertson McQuilkin maintains that "pornography destroys spiritually all who involve themselves in producing or using it, and its corrupting influence spills over into the entire life of the society that tolerates it."[3]

9.   Why is it absolutely essential to the inner spiritual life and the external witness of the church that an elder's marital and sexual life be "above reproach"?

Both the Old and New Testaments emphasize sexual purity because the relationship of a man to his wife is to model the covenant relationship of God to his people, particularly that of Christ's relationship to the church. The elders' failure to be above reproach in their marital and sexual lives will produce moral decay in the church and will incur the watching world's condemnation.

10.   According to Proverbs 6:27-35, what are the consequences of committing adultery? Be thorough in listing and understanding adultery's devastating consequences.

a.   *A man cannot isolate the action and escape unharmed (vv. 27, 28).*

b.   *The man will inevitably be scarred, disgraced, and punished (vv. 29, 33).*

c.   *Adultery is far more serious than the theft of material items; it is stealing a person. The adulterer risks destruction (vv. 30-32).*

---

9. Carefully review pp. 74, 75. Because a church leader has regular interaction with many women, the opportunity for inappropriate intimacy is increased. Refresh your trainee's memory of Paul's personal example of self-discipline and self-denial (1 Cor. 9:25-27); he feared disqualification because of sin and failure (lesson 5, question 10.). Also mention Job's covenant with his eyes, which is a principle to follow in avoiding the temptations of lust (Job 31:1). Warn your mentoree of the dangers of pornography or flirtatious relationships with women. When we play with sin, we *always* lose.

10. It is self-evident that an adulterer will be shamefully and severely burned by his sin. Inevitably, he will be punished (vv. 27, 28). "Touches her" is a figure of speech (euphemism) for sexual intercourse (v. 29b). Allen P. Ross remarks, "The rest of the passage then reasons that there is no restitution acceptable for adultery as there might be with thievery. The thief, when caught, has to pay dearly (v. 31). But the adulterer will be humiliated and ruined. Nothing will satisfy the husband but revenge."[4]

Note that v. 32 says that the adulterer destroys himself. Under Mosaic law, the adulterer could be put to death (Deut. 22:22); at the least he was ruined socially and spiritually. On the phrase, "his reproach will not be blotted out" (v. 33), John Armstrong says:

Like few other sins, adultery destroys personal reputation. . . It is a frightful thing to contemplate a reproach that will never be wiped away in this life. Watson warns, in a manner rarely heard in modern discussion, "Wounds of reputation no physician can heal. When the adulterer dies, his shame lives. When his body rots underground, his name rots above ground."[5]

    d.   *Because what is his alone has been stolen, the husband of the woman is also involved. He will not easily forgive and may pursue revenge (vv. 33, 35).*

    e.   *The stain of this sin and its consequences will never be erased (vv. 33, 35).*

Church leaders are committing sexual sins and divorcing at epidemic rates. You can be certain that Satan will do everything in his power to ruin your marriage relationship and defile your sexual purity. Discuss with your mentor the problems and stresses you are experiencing in your marriage. Prior to this discussion, ask your wife for her viewpoint so that you can share her perspective.

Do not be afraid to talk about your marital frustrations; we all have them! What matters is how you handle your problems. People who have problems and solve them can help and comfort others. People who hide their marital sins and abuses, however, experience the deepest problems and bring disgrace to the Lord's name.

For elders, sexual sin usually does not begin as sexual temptation. Instead, it starts by our allowing intimacy to develop outside our marriage relationships. The man who puts his work ahead of his wife and, as a consequence, incurs her resentment of his ministry involvement, is the most vulnerable. The temptation to step across the line with another woman who appreciates him then becomes enormous.

Men need to receive respect and to believe that their work is significant. If their wives resent or belittle their ministries, men are tempted to look elsewhere for affirmation. If you are seeking appreciation or companionship from women other than your wife, you must step out of ministry and resolve your marital difficulties as your first priority. If you anticipate that the work of being an elder could lead to this temptation, you should not proceed until you have your wife's full and unreserved support.

To prevent the occurrence of inappropriate intimacy, elderships should have in place a strong accountability system. Randy Alcorn, in his booklet, *Sexual Temptation: How Christian Workers Can Win the Battle,* presents a plan for anticipating and preventing sexual temptations. It involves repeatedly reminding one's self and one's fellow brothers of the horrific consequences and costs of immorality.

Counting the Cost

"In 1850 Nathaniel Hawthorne published *The Scarlet Letter,* a powerful novel centered around the adulterous relationship of Hester Prynne and the highly respected minister, the Reverend Mr. Arthur Dimmesdale. The fallen pastor, remorseful but not ready to face the consequences, asks the question, 'What can a ruined soul, like mine, effect towards the redemption of other souls?-or a polluted soul, towards their purification?' He describes the misery of standing in his pulpit and seeing the admiration of his people, and having to 'then look inward, and discern the black reality of what they idolize.' Finally he says, 'I have laughed, in bitterness and agony of heart, at the contrast between what I seem and what I am! And Satan laughs at it!'

"[I asked] . . . a man who had been a leader in a Christian organization until he committed adultery, . . . 'What could have been done to prevent this?' He . . . said with haunting pain, 'If only I had really known, really thought through what it would cost me, my family and my Lord, I honestly believe I never would have done it.'

"Some years ago my copastor and friend Alan Hlavka and I each developed a list of all the specific consequences we could think of that would result from our immorality. The lists were devastating, and to us they spoke more powerfully than any sermon or article on the subject.

"Periodically . . . we read through this list. In a personal and tangible way it brings home God's inviolate law of choice and consequence. It cuts through the fog of rationalization and fills our hearts with the healthy, motivating fear of God. We find that when we begin to think unclearly, reviewing this list yanks us back to reality and the need both to fear God and the consequences of sin.

"What follows is an edited version of our combined lists. I've included the actual names of my wife and daughters to emphasize the personal nature of this exercise. I recommend that you use this as the basis for your own list, adding those other consequences that would be uniquely yours. The idea, of course, is to not focus on sin, but on the consequences of sin, thereby encouraging us to refocus on the Lord and take steps of wisdom and purity that can keep us from falling.

☐ Dragging Christ's reputation into the mud.
☐ Having to one day look Jesus in the face at the judgment seat and tell why I did it.
☐ Untold hurt to Nanci, my best friend and loyal wife. . . Loss of Nanci's respect and trust.
☐ The possibility that I could lose my wife and my children forever.
☐ Hurt to and loss of credibility with my beloved daughters, Karina and Angie. ('Why listen to a man who betrayed Mom and us?')
☐ Shame to my family. ('Why isn't Daddy a pastor anymore?' The cruel comments of others who would invariably find out.)
☐ Shame and hurt to my church and friends, and especially those I've led to Christ and discipled. (List names.)
☐ An irretrievable loss of years of witnessing to my father.
☐ Bringing great pleasure to Satan, God's enemy.
☐ Possibly contracting a sexually transmitted disease . . . [or causing] pregnancy, . . . (a lifelong reminder of sin to me and my family).
☐ Loss of self-respect, discrediting my own name, and invoking shame and lifelong embarrassment upon myself.

"This is less than half of the items from my list. If only we would rehearse in advance the ugly and overwhelming consequences of immorality, we would be far more prone to avoid it."

Randy C. Alcorn[6]

ASSIGNMENT:

Have a joint session with your mentor and your wife to talk about your shepherding ministry and its inevitable effect on your marriage. Be realistic about the fact that the pressures of being an elder will put your family at risk. Answer the following questions:

   a.   Can you be an exemplary husband and also serve as an elder?

   b.   Can your wife wholeheartedly support your ministry?

11.   Before you become an elder, you must clearly understand the biblical teaching on divorce and remarriage. You must be prepared to answer tough questions on these issues, and you must answer them biblically.

   a.   Under what conditions is divorce permitted in your church?

   b.   Under what conditions is remarriage permitted?

   c.   Are you in agreement with the church elders on these issues? If not, how will you work together and counsel others?

ASSIGNMENT:

If you have not already completed an in-depth study of the biblical teaching on divorce and remarriage, begin studying this subject as soon as possible. Ask your elders to recommend a book or two that represent their view on divorce. This is a subject you must understand well in order to counsel others wisely.

12.   The following five character qualities mentioned in 1 Timothy 3:2, 3 require careful attention. See pp. 193, 196-198.

---

11. Can your mentoree locate and discuss the following key passages on divorce and remarriage: Deut. 24:1-4; Mal. 2:16; Matt. 19:1-12; Rom. 7:1-3; 1 Cor. 7:10-16? If not, direct him to study this issue immediately. An elder must be able to counsel people and explain the biblical teaching on this topic.

a.   In your own words define the following qualities.

Temperate: *Self-controlled, stable, mentally sober, circumspect; able to consistently think clearly, with balanced judgment*

Prudent: *Sound-minded, sensible, objective; exercises common sense, discretion; makes careful, thoughtful, constructive comments in discussions. Both temperate and prudent are related to overall self-control.*

Respectable: *Well-behaved, orderly, self-controlled, virtuous*

Not pugnacious: *Not a fighter, bad-tempered, irritable, out of control, or assaulting people verbally*

Peaceable: *Uncontentious, considerate; not fighting, quarrelsome, or divisive*

b.   What do these qualities have in common?

A person who is under the control of the Holy Spirit will exhibit these qualities of self-control. These qualities enable the elder to teach and gently correct, to be a peacemaker who calms disputes, and to lead others in lovingly resolving difficulties.

13.   What are the New Testament standards for a father that are required of a church elder? Check Titus 1:6 and pp. 229, 230.

The elder must demonstrate his ability to manage the household of God by managing his own household well. This ability is demonstrated primarily by his children's respect and obedience while they are under his authority.

"The Western world stands at a great crossroads in its history. It is my opinion that our very survival as a people will depend upon the presence or absence of masculine leadership in millions of homes. . . I believe, with everything within me, that husbands hold the keys to the preservation of the family."

James Dobson[7]

12b. Remind your mentoree of lesson 5, questions **10.** and **11.** Reinforce the teaching that an elder must be under the control of the Holy Spirit. If he is not, anger, impatience, bitterness, paranoia, and contentiousness will characterize his response to the endless pressures and conflicts involved in leading a congregation.

13.-15. Elders need accountability regarding their conduct as fathers. Fathering is an area in which Satan is winning stunning victories by destroying men for future church leadership.

14.   Eli was the priest over the house of the Lord at Shiloh. His two sons, Hophni and Phinehas, were also priests, but they were evil, lawless men. Eli made serious errors as a father that not only destroyed his sons, but destroyed his priestly ministry and the spiritual life of the nation. What were his errors in fathering? Read 1 Samuel 2:12-17, 22-36; 3:13.

   a.   *Eli allowed his sons to serve as priests when they did not know the Lord or their responsibilities.*

   b.   *Eli allowed sin and immorality to persist within his household and jurisdiction.*

   c.   *Eli chided his sons but did not rebuke, punish, or remove them from office.*

   d.   *When he had to choose between obeying and honoring God or deferring to his sons, Eli chose to protect his sons.*

15.   After first addressing the question with your wife, discuss with your mentor the quality of your relationship with your children and where it needs improvement. Ask your children to honestly express their feelings about your fathering skills.

---

14. The account of Eli's choice to honor his evil sons above God and the nation of Israel deserves attention by all church leaders. Reflect on W. G. Blaikie's comments on Eli's failure as a father from his classic commentary on 1 Samuel:

And how did the high priest deal with this state of things? In the worst possible way. He spoke against it but he did not act against it. He showed that he knew of it, he owned it to be very wicked; but he contented himself with words of remonstrance, which in the case of such hardened transgression were of no more avail than a child's breath against a brazen wall. At the end of the day, it is true that Eli was a decrepit old man, from whom much vigour of action could not have been expected. But the evil began before he was so old and decrepit, and his fault was that he did not restrain his sons at the time when he ought and might have restrained them. . . The men who had so dishonoured their office should have been driven from the place, and the very remembrance of the crime they had committed should have been obliterated by the holy lives and holy service of better men. It was inexcusable in Eli to allow them to remain. If he had had a right sense of his office he would never for one moment have allowed the interest of his family to outweigh the claims of God.

For what were the interests of his sons compared with the credit of the national worship? What mattered it that the sudden stroke would fall on them with startling violence? If it did not lead to their repentance and salvation it would at least save the national religion from degradation, and it would thus bring benefit to tens of thousands in the land. All this Eli did not regard. He could not bring himself to be harsh to his own sons. He could not bear that they should be disgraced and degraded. He would satisfy himself with a mild remonstrance, notwithstanding that every day new disgrace was heaped on the sanctuary, and new encouragement given to others to practice wickedness, by the very men who should have been foremost in honouring God, and sensitive to every breath that would tarnish His name.[8]

"Important as daily work may be, in the experience of the ordinary human being, the life of his family is far more important. His pride and his ambition may be involved in his professional advancement, but far more than pride and ambition are involved in his relationship to his *home*."[9]

"No matter how much a man may be concerned with his work in the world, he cannot normally *care* about it as much as he cares about his family. This is because we have, in the life of the family, a bigger stake than most of us can ever have in our employment. We can change business associates, if we need to, and we can leave a poor job for a better one, but we cannot change *sons*. If we lose the struggle in our occupational interests, we can try again, but if we lose with our children our loss is terribly and frighteningly *final*. A man who cares more for his work than he cares for his family is generally accounted abnormal or perverse and justifiably so. He is one who has not succeeded in getting his values straight; he fails to recognize what the true priorities are."

Elton Trueblood[10]

16.   Evaluate yourself in each of the following qualifications specified in 1 Timothy 3:2-7. Ask your wife or a close friend to make an independent evaluation of you as well.

  a.   A one-woman kind of man:

Needs Improvement

_____7_____6_____5_____4_____3_____2_____1_____

Exemplary   Discredited

  b.   Temperate: a self-controlled, balanced man:

Needs Improvement

_____7_____6_____5_____4_____3_____2_____1_____

Exemplary   Discredited

  c.   Prudent: a sensible man, of good judgment and discretion:

Needs Improvement

_____7_____6_____5_____4_____3_____2_____1_____

Exemplary   Discredited

  d.   Respectable: an orderly, disciplined, honorable man:

Needs Improvement

_____7_____6_____5_____4_____3_____2_____1_____

Exemplary   Discredited

e.   Hospitable:

Needs Improvement
_____7_____6_____5_____4_____3_____2_____1_____
Exemplary   Discredited

f.   Able to teach: meaning a man who is able to instruct others from the Bible:

Needs Improvement
_____7_____6_____5_____4_____3_____2_____1_____
Exemplary   Discredited

g.   Not addicted to wine: a man whose habits and lifestyle do not damage his testimony:

Needs Improvement
_____7_____6_____5_____4_____3_____2_____1_____
Exemplary   Discredited

h.   Not pugnacious: a man whose temper and emotions are in check:

Needs Improvement
_____7_____6_____5_____4_____3_____2_____1_____
Exemplary   Discredited

i.   Gentle: a forbearing, gracious, conciliatory man:

Needs Improvement
_____7_____6_____5_____4_____3_____2_____1_____
Exemplary   Discredited

j.   Peaceable: an uncontentious man, one who is not quarrelsome:

Needs Improvement
_____7_____6_____5_____4_____3_____2_____1_____
Exemplary   Discredited

k.   Free from the love of money: meaning a man who is not materialistic:

Needs Improvement
_____7_____6_____5_____4_____3_____2_____1_____
Exemplary   Discredited

l.   A man who manages his household well: a responsible Christian father, husband, and household manager:

Needs Improvement

_____7_____6_____5_____4_____3_____2_____1_____
Exemplary   Discredited

m.   Not a new convert: a man who is spiritually mature, tested:

Needs Improvement

_____7_____6_____5_____4_____3_____2_____1_____
Exemplary   Discredited

n.   A man with a good reputation outside the Christian community:

Needs Improvement

_____7_____6_____5_____4_____3_____2_____1_____
Exemplary   Discredited

SCRIPTURE MEMORY ASSIGNMENT:

"It is a trustworthy statement: if any man aspires to the office of overseer, it is a fine work he desires to do. An overseer, then, must be above reproach, the husband of one wife, temperate, prudent, respectable, hospitable, able to teach, not addicted to wine or pugnacious, but gentle, peaceable, free from the love of money. He must be one who manages his own household well, keeping his children under control with all dignity (but if a man does not know how to manage his own household, how will he take care of the church of God?), and not a new convert, so that he will not become conceited and fall into the condemnation incurred by the devil. And he must have a good reputation with those outside the church, so that he may not fall into reproach and the snare of the devil."   1 Timothy 3:1-7

---

[1] An excellent example is John MacArthur's series on 1 Timothy which may be ordered from Grace to You, P.O. Box 4000, Panorama City, California, 91412. Call 1-800-554-7223.

[2] John H. Armstrong, *Can Fallen Pastors Be Restored? The Church's Response to Sexual Misconduct* (Chicago: Moody, 1995), p. 20.

[3] Robertson McQuilkin, *An Introduction to Biblical Ethics* (Wheaton: Tyndale, 1989), p. 237. We encourage all elders to purchase and read McQuilkin's book. It interacts with all the major contemporary ethical issues. Wise men need to read books like this one to help them think critically and biblically and to be able to answer questions about ethical issues.

[4] Allen P. Ross, "Proverbs," in *The Expositor's Bible Commentary*, 12 vols., ed., Frank E. Gaebelein (Grand Rapids: Zondervan, 1991) 5: 938.

[5] Armstrong, *Can Fallen Pastors Be Restored?* p. 52.

[6] Randy C. Alcorn, *Sexual Temptation: How Christian Workers Can Win the Battle* (Gresham: Eternal Perspective Ministries, 1995), pp. 28-30.

[7] James C. Dobson, *Straight Talk to Men and Their Wives* (Waco: Word, 1980), p. 21.

[8] W. G. Blaikie, *The First Book of Samuel* (1887; Minneapolis: Klock and Klock, 1978), pp. 41-43.

[9] Elton Trueblood, *Your Other Vocation* (New York: Harper and Row, 1952), p. 80.

[10] Ibid., p. 82.

Lesson 8
Honoring and Discipling Elders

LESSON OVERVIEW

Lesson 8 surveys 1 Timothy 5:17-25, one of the most significant New Testament passages on the doctrine of Christian eldership. It focuses on elders who deserve double honor because of their capable leadership and diligent labor in the Word and explains the necessity of evaluating each elder's gifts.

The passage also addresses the difficult issue of disciplining elders who have been proved guilty of sin. The lesson emphasizes the need for leaders to be courageous in exposing sin, to judge justly, and to follow the New Testament precautions in appointing elders.

ELDERS DESERVING DOUBLE HONOR

"The elders who rule well are to be considered worthy of double honor, especially those who work hard at preaching and teaching. For the Scripture says, 'You shall not muzzle the ox while he is threshing,' and 'The laborer is worthy of his wages.'" 1 Timothy 5:17, 18

Read pages 206-215.

1. What unique, significant contributions does 1 Timothy 5:17, 18 make to our understanding of the New Testament doctrine of eldership?

---

1. Point out to your mentoree that 1 Tim. 5:17, 18 is a disturbing and perplexing text for most scholars and church leaders. The implications of this text simply do not fit the current paradigm for eldership or church leadership. Most books on church leadership and policy never mention it! The majority of Christians do not think of church elders laboring diligently in the Word or receiving financial support. Most Christians do not realize this text even exists. Yet it certainly exposes the erroneous distortion of the contemporary board-elder concept. The elders of 1 Tim. 5:17 are clearly pastor elders *and* teaching elders. Make sure your mentoree masters this biblical perspective.

Note that the passage refers to "those who work hard," not "those who desire employment." Men should equip themselves for ministry at their own expense, and involve themselves in ministry at their own expense. The eldership should then decide if it would benefit the church to support these elders financially (in full or in part) so that they would have more time for ministry.

This is a prime example of the principle of "first among equals" being used of the elder council. Some elders are specifically gifted to preach (exhort and evangelize) or teach (instruct from God's Word), and they work hard, exercising these gifts for the benefit of the church. Other elders use their exceptional gifts to lead and manage the flock, and they rule well. **All** *such elders deserve the church's financial support. Furthermore, this passage brings out the preeminence of the elders' teaching ministry.*

2. Since all elders are involved in leading the local church, what distinguishes those elders who "rule well"?

    They are those who exercise effective pastoral oversight. They are natural leaders, planners, organizers, and motivators.

3. How does *Biblical Eldership* explain the fact that all elders must be able to teach, but some elders labor at teaching and thus are entitled to financial support?

    Each elder has different spiritual gifts. All elders must be competent to teach and instruct, but not all elders are gifted teachers. Gifted teachers "work hard," that is, they concentrate their energy on teaching and should be financially supported by the body.

4. Note the close connection between leading and teaching that is made in 1 Timothy 5:17. In what sense does one who teaches the Word also lead?

    The teaching ministry lays out God's agenda for the church and His criteria for evaluating all activities. Christians are to be knowledgeable followers of Christ. The church must be moved by a thorough understanding of Scripture and its implications rather than by emotion or in response to a leader's charisma.

5. Ephesians 4:11 mentions the spiritual gift of "pastor" ("shepherd"). Describe this gift and explain why it is important to the eldership.

    Since the eldership's overall ministry is shepherding the flock, an elder with the shepherding gift increases the entire eldership's effectiveness in its primary role. The shepherding gift uniquely combines teaching and governance. The shepherd's teaching ministry is shaped by his intimate understanding of the congregation's needs. He teaches in order to benefit the congregation and contribute to their general health.

---

3. In 1 Tim. 5:17, "those who work hard at preaching and teaching" is plural, not singular. The assumption here and throughout the NT is that the local church will have multiple teachers (Acts 13:1-3; 15:22, 32, 35). Thus the eldership is not only a plurality of leaders who lead together, but it is a plurality of gifted teachers. A plurality of teachers is crucial for maintaining balance and protecting the teaching ministry of the local church. Emphasize to your mentoree that church-supported teachers are not given a special title or separate office from the other elders (p. 211).

4. In God's church, shepherds are to lead, protect, and grow the flock, which is done primarily by teaching God's Word. Contrast this mandate with many contemporary churches that are built on music ministry or innovative programs rather than on a Bible-based teaching ministry.

Below is a list of spiritual gifts that are particularly helpful in making the eldership team effective in shepherding.

- **"Administrations"** (1 Cor. 12:28): A much better translation of the Greek (*kybernēsis*) would be "acts of guidance," that is, able to provide wise counsel and direction for the congregation. Look up Proverbs 11:14 and 24:6, where this same term is translated as "guidance."

- **Leading** (Rom. 12:8): This is the Greek word *prohistēmi*, which we have noted several times. Refer to the exposition of 1 Thessalonians 5:12, 13 for an explanation of this term (pp. 167, 168, and lesson 5).

- **Exhorting** (Rom. 12:8): Exhorting could also mean "consoling" or "encouraging." Quoting Martin Luther, Leon Morris writes, "The teacher transmits knowledge; the exhorter stimulates."[1]

- **Shepherding** (Eph. 4:11): In this verse the Greek noun for "pastors" is *poimenas*, which means "shepherds." The noun *poimenas* is used only this once in Scripture to describe Christian leaders. The English word *pastor*, which is now erroneously used as a title, comes from the Latin translation of *poimenas*. *Pastor* is a spiritual gift; it is not an office separate from or superior to the office of elder. The elders are given the mandate to jointly pastor God's flock, and some elders have the spiritual gift of shepherding (pp. 149, 210, 211, *Biblical Eldership*). We have no scriptural precedent for calling some men in the local church "pastors" in distinction from the elders.

- **Teaching** (Eph. 4:11)

- **Evangelizing** (Eph. 4:11)

- **Showing mercy** (Rom. 12:8)

6.   How do we know that the word *honor* (Greek, *timē*) in 1 Timothy 5:17 includes the sense of financial maintenance?

   a.   *The next verse (18) specifically refers to wages.*

   b.   *In 1 Tim. 5:3, the word "honor" is used in reference to widows and the verse that follows includes instructions for providing for their livelihood.*

7.   In light of past problems at Ephesus, why is Paul particularly concerned that the elders who labor in the Word be financially supported by the church?

> *The Ephesian congregation needed the full-time watchful care of elders to protect it against false teachers by the sound and consistent teaching of the Word.*

ASSIGNMENTS:

An important question that an elder must continually ask regarding full- or part-time service is: how does he view himself in relation to the other elders, and how do the other elders view him? If your church has salaried elders and tentmaking elders, ask the different parties the above questions. Request scriptural support for their answers.

Also ask about the tensions and problems that naturally emerge between salaried elders who serve full or part time and tentmaking elders. Discuss this issue with your mentor.

Complete the Gifts Analysis Questionnaire, *"Discover Your Gifts,"* at the end of this lesson.

a.   What special contribution do you think your gift or gifts can make to the eldership team?

Mentor: Compare your mentoree's answer to his scores on the spiritual gifts analysis.

b.   What are you presently doing to distinguish, develop, and employ your spiritual gift(s)?

PROTECTING AND DISCIPLINING ELDERS

"Do not receive an accusation against an elder except on the basis of two or three witnesses. Those who continue in sin, rebuke in the presence of all, so that the rest also may be fearful of sinning. I solemnly charge you in the presence of God and of Christ Jesus and of His chosen angels, to maintain these principles without bias, doing nothing in a spirit of partiality. Do not lay hands upon anyone too hastily and thereby share responsibility for the sins of others; keep yourself free from sin. No longer drink water exclusively, but use a little wine for the sake of your stomach and your frequent ailments. The sins of some men are quite evident, going before them to judgment; for others, their sins follow after. Likewise also, deeds that are good are quite evident, and those which are otherwise cannot be concealed."   1 Timothy 5:19-25

---

7. We spend our money on what we think is important and valuable. If we value Bible teaching, we will be pleased to financially assist those who teach us. There is no higher priority for the church's resources than to support those who teach the Word and those who spread the Word. Ask your mentoree if he is aware of Paul's teaching that "the Lord directed those who proclaim the gospel to get their living from the gospel" (1 Cor. 9:14). See pp. 211-215.
ASSIGNMENT If your mentoree thinks he has the gift of teaching, encourage him to teach a Sunday school class or Bible study. The development of this spiritual gift warrants years of maturing in knowledge, skill, and effectiveness. One measure of the candidate's teaching ability and effectiveness is the fruit produced by his teaching.

Read pages 215-224.

8. Why does Paul require that elders receive specific protection from unsubstantiated accusations?

   Throughout history, God's leaders have been Satan's primary target. Satan is the master deceiver, and false accusation is one of his primary weapons against the church.

9. It is important that elders understand the legal principle, "on the evidence of two or three witnesses:"

   a. What is the origin of this principle?

      It is based on Deut. 19:15, "A single witness shall not rise up against a man on account of any iniquity or any sin which he has committed; on the evidence of two or three witnesses a matter shall be confirmed."

   b. Explain the principle.

      Because of the possibility of false accusation or distorted perception, the testimony of a single witness is not to be given greater credence than the elder's word. An accusation must be confirmed by two or more witnesses of the actual offense or sin, or by two or more persons who can verify the facts. Even multiple bearers of gossip are to be ignored because they are not witnesses.

   c. Why is it essential that elders follow this legal principle?

      Elders must be protected from the inevitable and false accusations of Satan and those he uses. The proper governance of the church depends on its elders being above reproach. Therefore, elders' reputations must be protected from false and unsubstantiated charges.

10. What is the main point of Paul's instruction concerning an elder who has sinned?

---

8. These essential verses for protecting the eldership and the flock from sin (1 Tim. 5:19-25) are *virtually unknown and unused by most Christians and churches.* Make sure your mentoree grasps their full implication.

9. The harsh reality is that people in spiritual authority will be targets of people's anger, rebellion, frustration, and accusations. Spiritual leaders will be both idolized and crucified. Throughout *Biblical Eldership*, the examples of Moses and David have been presented so that elders may identify with these great leaders when they, too, face false accusations.

10.-13. Ninety-five percent of our churches neglect these biblical injunctions. There is nothing more arduous than dealing with a colleague's sin. Question your trainee as to his intentions concerning these instructions and his understanding of why they are essential to the spiritual health and life of the local church. A thought-provoking book that deals with the controversial issue of restoring sexually fallen pastors is John H. Armstrong's *Can Fallen Pastors be Restored? The Church's Response to Sexual Misconduct* (Chicago: Moody, 1995).

Since the elder's personal example is crucial to his leadership, the sinning elder's confirmed offense (one that brings reproach on his personal reputation as an elder or on the eldership) must be exposed. The other elders must publicly reprove the sinning elder, thereby teaching God's standards to the congregation and allowing the elder to publicly repent of his sin.

11.   Note Paul's charge to Timothy:

   a.   What does Paul say to show his serious intentions about openness and fairness when judging an accusation of sin, or the actual sin, of a church elder?

   With the introductory phrase, "I solemnly charge you," Paul evokes God the Father, Christ, and the chosen angels as witnesses of the church's obedience in carrying out fair and impartial discipline of elders.

   b.   What is implied by the intensity of Paul's language?

   Paul considers this imperative to be a very high priority for the church.

12.   What will be the consequence for us if we disobey Paul's charge to judge other elders openly and fairly?

   We will be judged by how faithfully we carry out this instruction and responsibility. Paul's charge is stated in terms of our final judgment.

13.   What are the consequences for the elder council if they are too hasty in restoring an elder or in appointing an unqualified or untested elder?

   If he fails, the elders share in his sin. The elders bear the burden of responsibility.

"The faculty of keeping an open mind until all the facts and circumstances bearing upon a question have been ascertained is by no means common, and yet for the right guidance and management of complex affairs, it is obviously essential. I have had occasion repeatedly to observe that individuals gifted in some respects are sadly lacking in the quality mentioned; and yet unless the one in a central position is careful to hear and weigh all that has to be said touching the different aspect of a given affair, he will not be in a position either to reach a sound conclusion or to carry with him the consent and confidence of those affected by that conclusion."

D. E. Hoste[2]

14.   As a spiritual leader, you will be called upon to make judgments about people and their circumstances. In a sinful, unjust world, this is a difficult job. When dealing with relatives and close friends, even the most reputable Christians can be guilty of bias or of believing only one side of a story. Read the following verses and list the biblical principles that will help you judge people fairly and objectively.

Prov. 18:13 He who gives an answer before he hears, it is folly and shame to him.

Prov. 18:17 The first to plead his case seems just [right], until another comes and examines him.

Lev. 19:15 You shall do no injustice in judgment; you shall not be partial to the poor nor defer to the great, but you are to judge your neighbor fairly.

2 Chron. 19:6, 7 He [King Jehoshaphat] said to the judges, "Consider what you are doing, for you do not judge for man but for the Lord who is with you when you render judgment. Now then let the fear of the Lord be upon you; be very careful what you do, for the Lord our God will have no part in unrighteousness or partiality or the taking of a bribe."

Job 29:16 I was a father to the needy, and I investigated the case which I did not know.

Isa. 61:8a For I, the Lord, love justice, I hate robbery in the burnt offering; and I will faithfully give them their recompense.

---

14. In light of the fact that an elder is to be a wise counselor, a man of sound judgment and integrity (lesson 2, question **15.**), consider the above significant quotation by D. E. Hoste, successor to Hudson Taylor of the China Inland Mission. Hoste was one of the most godly and skilled people managers to grace the church of Jesus Christ. He exercised spiritual leadership over more than a thousand missionaries who faced dangerous and impossible circumstances. A number of this wise shepherd's insightful writings appear in this *Guide*.

Prov. 18:13 Our natural propensity is to jump to conclusions before we listen to all the facts or hear a person out. The tendency to rush to judgment or opinion must be trained out of us.

Prov. 18:17 This is a key principle for counselors. In Prov. 18 we are warned three times not to make hasty judgments (vv. 2, 13, 17), and in v. 17 we are told to hear both sides of a story. "Examine" means "investigate," but the context requires what is called cross-examination. "The proverb reminds us that there are two sides in any dispute (legal, domestic, or religious) and that all sides in a dispute must be given a hearing."[3] Charles Bridges advises us to "cultivate the spirit of self-distrust" when judging others:

> How often has the tale of wrongs from a hard-hearted overseer, landlord, or creditor roused our indignation, and perhaps provoked our protest. But a close look at the other side of the story has shown us the wrongness of a hasty, one-sided judgment. . . . Yet the true rule of justice would be to judge neither one to be right, till both sides have been heard. Let all the evidence be sifted; and often the plausible cover is swept away by a more searching investigation. . . . Cultivate the spirit of self-distrust.[4]

Lev. 19:15 John E. Hartley gives this counsel:

> Judges and councils, being human, are open to influence from factors other than the merits of a case. But in rendering a judicial decision no favoritism is to be shown to anyone, regardless of status (cf. Jas. 2:1, 9). The command not to favor the poor is surprising in light of the concern throughout the OT for the widow, the orphan, and the poor. . . . This prohibition seeks to prevent that concern from causing the elders to lean a judgment in favor of the unfortunate solely because that person is poor (Exod. 23:3). Justice may not be perverted even for the disadvantaged. Next it states that "the great" are not to be . . . "honored" or "favored," by allowing their position to influence a judgment. The people are to judge a close associate (cf. v. 11) righteously. . . . Since God is just, his people must establish justice in their courts as the foundation of their covenant relationship with him. The inner strength of a nation resides in the integrity of its judicial system.[5]

2 Chron. 19:6, 7 This passage records King Jehoshaphat's judicial reforms in Judah. The implementation of justice is based solidly on God's law and character and the judges are agents of Jehovah, not of men. Whenever we act as judges, executors of the Lord God who loves and demands justice, we must likewise fear and honor Him, not men.

John 7:51 Our Law does not judge a man unless it first hears from him and knows what he is doing, does it?

a. *The elder must hear both sides, including the accused's, and listen to all the evidence before forming a conclusion. The biases and distortions of each individual's testimony must be corrected by multiple witnesses and corroborating evidence.*

b. *The righteous need not fear true justice. It is the elders' God-given responsibility to see that all receive true justice.*

c. *In administering justice, the elder must be totally impartial, not showing favoritism to friends and those of similar status. All political and pragmatic considerations must be excluded. God will judge the elder if he shows partiality. He must pursue the cause of the weak and unpopular with vigor.*

Let us share some sound advice: keep records whenever you are involved in delicate matters, disputes, or judging cases of church discipline. We tend to avoid recording unpleasant facts, but that can prove unwise. Many elders have been saved from serious misunderstandings and false accusations by having accurate records of phone conversations, meetings, and events. On several occasions, we have been able to produce facts and records for people who questioned how our churches handled the discipline of members who later accused us of mishandling their situation (a charge unrepentant sinners make against those who confront and deal with their sin).

In sensitive, painful situations that require the judgment and wise counsel of the elders, it is easy to forget what was said and what was decided. All decisions and judgments made by the elders should be accurately recorded so that valuable time is not wasted in recalling past decisions.

15. What qualifications enable an elder to judge sinning members fairly and objectively? Explain your answers.

1 Timothy 3:2-7	Titus 1:6-9	1 Peter 5:1-3
1. Above reproach	1. Above reproach	1. Not shepherding under compulsion, but voluntarily
2. The husband of one wife	2. The husband of one wife	2. Not shepherding for sordid gain, but with eagerness
3. Temperate [self-controlled, balanced]	3. Having children who believe	3. Not lording it over the flock, but proving to be an example
4. Prudent [sensible, good judgment]	4. Not self-willed	
5. Respectable [well-behaved, virtuous]	5. Not quick-tempered	

John 7:51 The accused has the right to speak in his own defense before a verdict is reached (Deut. 1:16, 17). Speaking to King Agrippa, Festus set forth the Roman version of this law: "It is not the custom of the Romans to hand over any man before the accused meets his accusers face to face and has an opportunity to make his defense against the charges" (Acts 25:16).

1 Timothy 3:2-7	Titus 1:6-9	1 Peter 5:1-3
6. Hospitable	6. Not addicted to wine	
7. Able to teach	7. Not pugnacious	
8. Not addicted to wine	8. Not fond of sordid gain	
9. Not pugnacious [not belligerent]	9. Hospitable	
10. Gentle [forbearing]	10. Lover of what is good [kind, virtuous]	
11. Peaceable [uncontentious]	11. Sensible [see prudent]	
12. Free from the love of money	12. Just [righteous conduct, law-abiding]	
13. Manages his household well	13. Devout [holy, pleasing to God, loyal to His Word]	
14. Not a new convert	14. Self-controlled	
15. A good reputation with those outside the church	15. Holds fast the faithful [trustworthy NIV] Word, both to exhort and to refute	

a.   *Above reproach: The elder's personal character must be unassailable.*

b.   *Temperate, prudent, self-controlled: The elder must be able to dispassionately sift through the evidence and remain free of personal bias.*

c.   *Peaceable [uncontentious],* **not pugnacious, not quick tempered:** *The elder who is judging a matter must not cause attention to shift from the accused to himself because of his own imprudent behavior.*

16.   Confronting and rebuking a fellow elder (or anyone else) who is sinning requires a fearless spirit. If you, like most of us, lack the courage to exercise church discipline, read the following Scripture texts in their context and explain what you learn about this important leadership virtue. Discover the importance of courage on pp. 20-22.

Josh. 1:6-9   *Prosperity and strength result from knowing and following God's Word and commands.*

2 Sam. 10:12   *When leaders demonstrate courage, God's people are blessed and protected.*

1 Chron. 28:20   *We are not to be afraid because God is with us as we undertake godly efforts. He will be with us until our task is finished.*

Ezra 10:4   *When their leaders take responsibility and courageous action, the people will support and obey them.*

Ezek. 2:6, 7   *God's leaders are to fearlessly deliver His Word, whether or not the rebellious people listen and repent—even if they mock or threaten their leaders.*

Amos 7:10-17   *The man of God must be willing to deliver God's message despite attempts by those in secular or ecclesiastical power to intimidate him.*

John 2:13-22   *Godly leaders must bravely confront and discipline sin.*

Acts 15:1, 2   *Godly leaders must fearlessly stand up to false teachers.*

Gal. 2:11-14   *Godly leaders must dare to oppose false doctrine, deal with internal strife, and be dauntless in teaching the truth.*

17.   One unfit elder can cause untold trouble for a church and bring havoc on the eldership. In order to prevent unqualified and unworthy men from becoming elders, the Spirit of God gives invaluable counsel to the church family on selecting and examining a prospective elder.

a.   Since the warning, "Do not lay hands upon anyone too hastily," comes after instruction on rebuking an elder who has been found guilty of sin, what does 1 Tim. 5:22 imply about the restoration of such an elder?

We are to be cautious in the restoration process. The elder should not be restored to his position until he has removed the reproach of his sin by repentance and has established a fresh testimony of righteousness. A careful examination of his walk is necessary to discover his eligibility for office. Elders and deacons must be formally examined in light of the biblical qualifications and then they may serve.

b.   Write an expanded paraphrase and explanation of 1 Tim. 3:10. (See pp. 76, 77, 202-204.)

Deacons and elders must prove their integrity and devotion to ministry before they are appointed. They must have demonstrated over a considerable period of time and in the context of the life of the church that they meet the requirements that are stated in vv. 2-7.

c.   Explain how each of the following statements from 1 Tim. 5:24, 25 encourages and guides the local church and its elders in examining potential elders.

"The sins of some men are quite evident, going before them to judgment," v. 24*a*.

On even casual examination, some men's reputations disqualify them from eldership. Their lack of qualification is well-known to the church.

"For others, their sins follow after," v. 24*b*.

Some men will be found to be unqualified when the eldership closely examines their lives and track records in the church.

"Likewise also, deeds that are good are quite evident," v. 25a.

The qualified and tested candidate's deeds of service and ministry will be self-evident to the church, thus proving his qualifications to be an elder.

"And those which are otherwise [not evident] cannot be concealed," v. 25b.

Some men's good deeds are apparent only upon examination. God will not allow the qualified man's deeds to remain hidden if the elders are prayerful and diligent in their examination.

ASSIGNMENT:

Since you must someday be examined by the church and its elders as to your lifestyle, abilities, and doctrine (1 Tim. 3:10), ask the elders now for a list of questions and issues they will cover at that time.

18.   Here are key questions you should answer personally in order to prepare yourself for examination:

a.   How long have you been in your present local church?

b.   Do you agree with the church's doctrinal positions?

c.   How well do the congregation and elders know you?

d.   How do you know they have confidence in you?

e.   Is there anything in your past or present moral lifestyle that, if it became known, would bring reproach on the church or the eldership?

f.   In what ministries have you exercised your giftedness?

g.   What have you done to train for eldership?

SCRIPTURE MEMORY ASSIGNMENT:

"Do not receive an accusation against an elder except on the basis of two or three witnesses. Those who continue in sin, rebuke in the presence of all, so that the rest also may be fearful of sinning. I solemnly charge you in the presence of God and of Christ Jesus and of His chosen angels, to maintain these principles without bias, doing nothing in a spirit of partiality." 1 Timothy 5:19-21

[1] Leon Morris, *The Epistle to the Romans* (Grand Rapids: Eerdmans, 1988), pp. 441, 442.

[2] D. E. Hoste, *If I Am to Lead* (London: Overseas Missionary Fellowship, 1968), p. 7.

[3] Allen P. Ross, "Proverbs," *The Expositor's Bible Commentary*, 12 vols. ed. Frank E. Gaebelein (Grand Rapids: Zondervan, 1991), 5: 1027.

[4] Charles Bridges, *A Modern Study in the Book of Proverbs: Charles Bridges' Classic Revised for Today's Reader*, by George F. Santa (Milford: Mott Media, 1978), pp. 352-353.

[5] John E. Hartley, *Leviticus*, *Word Biblical Commentary* (Dallas: Word Books, 1992), pp. 315, 316.

DISCOVER YOUR GIFTS — GIFTS ANALYSIS QUESTIONNAIRE

Each statement in the following questionnaire has five response spaces following it: very little, little, some, much, very much. These represent percentages on a scale of 1-100%, as follows:

Very little	=	0 -	20%
Little	=	20 -	40%
Some	=	40 -	60%
Much	=	60 -	80%
Very much	=	80 -	100%

Read each statement. Decide to what extent the statement is true of you. Check the appropriate column. Your first impressions are usually correct. If most of your checks are placed toward the right or toward the left, don't worry about that. Each person has his own style with questionnaires. The questionnaire will help you discover your gifts. The results of this questionnaire will be only tentative, however.

THE FOLLOWING IS TRUE OF ME	1 Very Little	2 Little	3 Some	4 Much	5 Very Much
1. I am able to organize ideas, tasks, people, and time, for Christian service.	☐	☐	☐	☐	☐
2. I have used a particular creative ability (writing, painting, drama, etc.) to benefit the body of Christ.	☐	☐	☐	☐	☐
3. I am able to distinguish between spiritual truth and error.	☐	☐	☐	☐	☐
4. I have been used to encourage people to live Christlike lives.	☐	☐	☐	☐	☐
5. I like to talk about Jesus to those who don't know him.	☐	☐	☐	☐	☐
6. I have had the experience of knowing God's will with certainty in a specific situation even when concrete evidence was missing.	☐	☐	☐	☐	☐
7. I assume responsibility for meeting financial needs in church and community.	☐	☐	☐	☐	☐
8. I enjoy providing a haven for guests and do not feel put upon by unexpected visitors.	☐	☐	☐	☐	☐
9. I take prayer requests of others seriously and continue to pray for them.	☐	☐	☐	☐	☐
10. I motivate groups toward specific biblical objectives.	☐	☐	☐	☐	☐
11. I have a knack for turning compassion into cheerful deeds of kindness.	☐	☐	☐	☐	☐
12. I have pleaded the cause of God to the people of the church and/or world.	☐	☐	☐	☐	☐
13. I enjoy doing tasks that help others minister effectively.	☐	☐	☐	☐	☐

THE FOLLOWING IS TRUE OF ME	1 Very Little	2 Little	3 Some	4 Much	5 Very Much
14. I have been responsible for the spiritual lives of Christians with good results.	☐	☐	☐	☐	☐
15. Content "comes alive" for students (children or adults) when I teach.	☐	☐	☐	☐	☐
16. I like to plan things in which people are involved.	☐	☐	☐	☐	☐
17. I would enjoy expressing myself creatively for God through artistic expression (music, drama, poetry, etc.).	☐	☐	☐	☐	☐
18. I see a serious danger when false teachings and false practices creep into the church.	☐	☐	☐	☐	☐
19. I am sensitive to suffering, troubled, and discouraged people, and want to help them see God's answers to life's problems.	☐	☐	☐	☐	☐
20. I would like to be able to share the gospel freely and effectively with unbelieving persons.	☐	☐	☐	☐	☐
21. I find myself accepting God's promises at face value and applying them to given situations without doubt.	☐	☐	☐	☐	☐
22. I feel moved to give when confronted with financial needs in God's kingdom.	☐	☐	☐	☐	☐
23. I am sensitive to the acts of kindness which make such a difference for guests or strangers.	☐	☐	☐	☐	☐
24. I am sensitive to the prayer needs of others and concerned to give the needed prayer support.	☐	☐	☐	☐	☐
25. I have a desire to help, lead, guide, and direct people in an important church ministry.	☐	☐	☐	☐	☐
26. I would like to minister to those who have physical or mental problems.	☐	☐	☐	☐	☐
27. I have spiritual insights from the Scriptures relating to people and issues which make me want to speak out.	☐	☐	☐	☐	☐
28. I sense when others need a helping hand and am ready to give it.	☐	☐	☐	☐	☐
29. I desire to see the spiritual needs of believers met and I am willing to be personally involved in nurturing and discipling ministries.	☐	☐	☐	☐	☐
30. I like to help people understand things.	☐	☐	☐	☐	☐
31. I am able to make effective plans to accomplish goals.	☐	☐	☐	☐	☐
32. I have significant artistic ability (music, drama, writing, painting, sculpting, etc.) which I have put to good use in God's kingdom.	☐	☐	☐	☐	☐

THE FOLLOWING IS TRUE OF ME	1 Very Little	2 Little	3 Some	4 Much	5 Very Much
33. I have detected phony or manipulative persons and teachings when others have not.	☐	☐	☐	☐	☐
34. People in the Christian community have been stirred up to love and good works by my counsel and encouragement.	☐	☐	☐	☐	☐
35. I have been instrumental in leading others to believe in Christ as their Savior.	☐	☐	☐	☐	☐
36. In specific cases God has given me assurance that he would do what seemed unlikely.	☐	☐	☐	☐	☐
37. I give cheerfully and liberally in support of the Lord's work.	☐	☐	☐	☐	☐
38. I have a knack for making strangers feel at ease in my home and at church.	☐	☐	☐	☐	☐
39. I pray for others, recognizing that their effectiveness depends upon it.	☐	☐	☐	☐	☐
40. I enjoy leading and directing others toward goals and caring for them for the sake of Christ.	☐	☐	☐	☐	☐
41. I enjoy working with people who suffer physical, mental or emotional problems.	☐	☐	☐	☐	☐
42. I have proclaimed timely and urgent messages from God's Word.	☐	☐	☐	☐	☐
43. I like to work at little things that help build the body of Christ.	☐	☐	☐	☐	☐
44. I assume responsibility when I see a Christian being led astray.	☐	☐	☐	☐	☐
45. I am able to clarify things for learners (children or adults).	☐	☐	☐	☐	☐
46. I would enjoy giving oversight to an important church ministry.	☐	☐	☐	☐	☐
47. I have the potential to be very creative in an area that could be used in building up the church.	☐	☐	☐	☐	☐
48. I tend to look beneath the surface and perceive people's motives.	☐	☐	☐	☐	☐
49. I believe that people will grow to spiritual maturity through counsel and instruction from the Word.	☐	☐	☐	☐	☐
50. I have a burden for friends and acquaintances who do not believe in Christ.	☐	☐	☐	☐	☐
51. I have a sense for moments when the "prayer of faith" is needed.	☐	☐	☐	☐	☐

THE FOLLOWING IS TRUE OF ME	1 Very Little	2 Little	3 Some	4 Much	5 Very Much
52. I am willing to maintain a lower standard of living in order to benefit God's work with my financial support.	☐	☐	☐	☐	☐
53. I tend to be more aware of the needs of guests than of my own.	☐	☐	☐	☐	☐
54. I have an inner conviction that God works in response to prayer, and I want to be used to help others through prayer.	☐	☐	☐	☐	☐
55. If I had the opportunity, I would enjoy leading, directing, and motivating others in some aspect of the Lord's work.	☐	☐	☐	☐	☐
56. The sight of misery makes me want to find a way to express God's love to hurting persons.	☐	☐	☐	☐	☐
57. Given the opportunity, I would like to be an expository preacher of God's Word.	☐	☐	☐	☐	☐
58. It is my nature to like to do work that helps others do theirs.	☐	☐	☐	☐	☐
59. I sense in myself a shepherd's instinct when I know of Christians who need spiritual counsel.	☐	☐	☐	☐	☐
60. I quickly sense when people (children or adults) are unclear in their thinking.	☐	☐	☐	☐	☐
61. I have a sense for delegating important tasks to the right people at the right time.	☐	☐	☐	☐	☐
62. I am aware that people have been blessed through my creative or artistic ability.	☐	☐	☐	☐	☐
63. I have developed an ability to discriminate between good and evil in today's world.	☐	☐	☐	☐	☐
64. I am glad when people who need comfort, consolation, encouragement, and counsel seek my help.	☐	☐	☐	☐	☐
65. I am able to share the gospel in a way that makes it clear and meaningful to non-believers.	☐	☐	☐	☐	☐
66. I am able to go on believing God will act in a situation in spite of evidence to the contrary.	☐	☐	☐	☐	☐
67. I help people and the Lord's work through generous and timely contributions.	☐	☐	☐	☐	☐
68. My home is available to those in need of hospitality.	☐	☐	☐	☐	☐
69. I am conscious of ministering to others as I pray for them.	☐	☐	☐	☐	☐
70. I have accepted leadership responsibilities and have succeeded in helping a group work toward a goal.	☐	☐	☐	☐	☐

THE FOLLOWING IS TRUE OF ME	1 Very Little	2 Little	3 Some	4 Much	5 Very Much
71. Sick, helpless, and shut-in persons are helped when I minister to them.	☐	☐	☐	☐	☐
72. God uses me to build up, encourage, and comfort other Christians by speaking to them of spiritual things.	☐	☐	☐	☐	☐
73. I find practical ways of helping others and gain satisfaction from doing this.	☐	☐	☐	☐	☐
74. The Lord has used me to watch over, guide, and nurture other believers toward spiritual maturity.	☐	☐	☐	☐	☐
75. I hold the interest of those I teach.	☐	☐	☐	☐	☐
76. I have a sense for how and when projects or ministries need to be better organized.	☐	☐	☐	☐	☐
77. I sense a latent creative ability (in drawing, writing, music, etc.) which I would like to use for the kingdom of God.	☐	☐	☐	☐	☐
78. I am usually aware of people who pretend to be what they are not.	☐	☐	☐	☐	☐
79. I would be willing to spend some time each week in a counseling ministry.	☐	☐	☐	☐	☐
80. I am able to sense when a person doesn't know Jesus Christ, and I hurt for him or her.	☐	☐	☐	☐	☐
81. I inwardly sense what Jesus meant when he said mountains could be moved by faith.	☐	☐	☐	☐	☐
82. I have a conviction that all I have belongs to God, and I want to be a good steward.	☐	☐	☐	☐	☐
83. I have a genuine appreciation for each guest to whom I minister.	☐	☐	☐	☐	☐
84. I would be pleased if asked to be a prayer partner to someone involved in a ministry.	☐	☐	☐	☐	☐
85. I am usually quick to sense when a group I am a part of is "spinning its wheels," and I want to do something about it.	☐	☐	☐	☐	☐
86. I sense when people are hurting in some way.	☐	☐	☐	☐	☐
87. I think more Christians should speak out on the moral issues of the day, such as abortion, easy sex, racism, and so on.	☐	☐	☐	☐	☐
88. I wish I had more opportunity to assist others in their ministries.	☐	☐	☐	☐	☐
89. I would love to be in a position to equip saints for the work of ministry.	☐	☐	☐	☐	☐
90. I get excited about discovering new ideas I can share with others.	☐	☐	☐	☐	☐

When you have finished the Key Chart on page 133, continue by reading the following questions and answers.

1.   **Do I actually have the spiritual gifts I have identified?**

Some people are surprised by the gifts which their questionnaire reveals; others are not. Whichever category you fall into, two things must be said. First, congratulations! To be aware of gifts which the Holy Spirit gives is an exciting experience, and very significant.

Second, be cautious. You may not actually have the spiritual gifts you identify by taking this questionnaire. Or you may have other gifts not identified here. Two more things should happen before you will be sure what your gifts really are:

a.   Others should observe your gifts and tell you what you do well.

b.   You should actually use your gifts in ministries and experience a degree of success.

2.   **What is the difference between a working gift and a waiting gift?**

A working gift is a gift you are already using in some way. You may not have recognized it as a spiritual gift, but you were using it nonetheless. You were able to identify working gifts by answering questions aimed at your activities in the kingdom.

A waiting gift, on the other hand, is a gift which remains to a large extent undeveloped. There may be hints of it in your activities, but for the most part you haven't used it. However, you do have potential in this area. You cannot identify such a gift simply by looking at activities. Instead you must look at interests, inclinations, sensitivities, attitudes, and concerns. These often reveal a gift *waiting* to be developed.

3.   **What am I to do in those areas where I don't have gifts?**

Don't think less of yourself because of those gifts which appear in box C, which for you are not gifts but roles. Remember that others have been given gifts in these areas for your sake. Thank God for these gifts and those who have them. In addition, you should encourage and pray for those who have these gifts: they are important to God and his cause. They need the support which you, with *your* gifts, can give them. Finally, you have a responsibility to be diligent in each of these areas as a member of the church. For example, if evangelism is last on your list, you should recognize that while God may not expect you to be involved in door-to-door visitation, you still have a responsibility to witness.

Discover Your Gifts - Gifts Analysis Questionnaire
Church Development Resources ™
A Ministry of CRC Publications
2850 Kalamazoo Ave. SE
Grand Rapids, MI 49560
Copyright © 1989

HOW TO USE THE KEY CHART

Complete the Key Chart on your own. Begin by reading the instructions carefully.

1. Place the numerical value (1-5) for each statement of the questionnaire (1-90) next to the corresponding number in the Key Chart.

2. In Chart A, add each row of three numbers, and write the total in the adjoining box in the "totals A" column. Do the same in "totals B" column for Chart B, adding to the left.

3. Circle the highest scores in the "totals A" column. Circle three or four, but not more than five. Write the names of those gifts in box A, "Working Gifts," with the highest-scored gift first, the next highest second. (In case of ties, it doesn't matter which one is listed first.)

4. Now in the "totals B" column circle the high scores which were not circled in step 3. Write these gifts in box B, "Waiting Gifts," beginning with the highest.

5. Place in box C any gifts not listed in boxes A and B. These are not likely to be your spiritual gifts, but you have, of course, a responsibility (role) in each of them.

6. Note the gifts in which your "totals B" score is significantly (two or more) higher than your "totals A" score. This may indicate a gift you should develop and use.

CHART A			Totals A	Totals B	CHART B		
1	31	61	Administration		16	46	76
2	32	62	Creative Ability		17	47	77
3	33	63	Discernment		18	48	78
4	34	64	Encouragement		19	49	79
5	35	65	Evangelism		20	50	80
6	36	66	Faith		21	51	81
7	37	67	Giving		22	52	82
8	38	68	Hospitality		23	53	83
9	39	69	Intercession		24	54	84
10	40	70	Leadership		25	55	85
11	41	71	Mercy		26	56	86
12	42	72	Prophecy		27	57	87
13	43	73	Service		28	58	88
14	44	74	Shepherding		29	59	89
15	45	75	Teaching		30	60	90

Box A Working Gifts
(Highest scored gifts)
1st _____
2nd _____
3rd _____
4th _____
5th _____

Box B Waiting Gifts
(Highest scored gifts, not in Box A)
1st _____
2nd _____
3rd _____
4th _____
5th _____

Box C Not a gift but a role (responsibility)

_____ _____ _____ _____

_____ _____ _____ _____

Lesson 9
Appoint Only Qualified Men

LESSON OVERVIEW

Lesson 9 reviews Paul's instructions to Titus and the underdeveloped churches on the Island of Crete that were facing attack from false teachers. Paul sets forth the qualifications for elders: church elders must control personal anger, be hospitable, be faithful to Christian doctrine, and be able to exhort in sound doctrine and refute false teachers. The lesson also examines the terms "ordination" and "appointment," and the unbiblical division between clergy and laity.

PAUL'S INSTRUCTIONS TO TITUS

"For this reason I left you in Crete, that you would set in order what remains and appoint elders in every city as I directed you." Titus 1:5

Review pages 104-106. Read pages 202-205, 225-228.

1.   One cannot grasp the significance of Paul's teaching on elders without first understanding the reasons why he wrote to Timothy and Titus.

   a.   What evidence is there that these letters were not strictly personal correspondence, but that they conveyed teachings that applied to all the churches?

   These letters authorized Timothy and Titus to act with apostolic authority. They were directed to the churches in which Timothy and Titus served and were to provide permanent directives for the churches to follow after Timothy and Titus left. Paul expected the churches to obey both his personal envoys and his letters.

   b.   What is the purpose of these letters?

   They were a significant part of Paul's missionary work and strategy. In addition to conveying apostolic authority, they gave instructions as to how the churches' organizational and leadership structures were to be developed and strengthened.

135

The letters also explained how to deal with false doctrines that might upset or uproot churches.

2.   Describe Titus's and Timothy's position and mission (pp. 104, 105, 204, 205).

They were apostolic delegates (legates) and Paul's partners in ministry. They were evangelists who planted and established churches. They were not permanent pastors of individual churches.

3.   Paul's choice of terminology in Titus 1:5-9 reveals important information about elder appointment. Consider the meaning and significance of Paul's terms.

    a.   What is the meaning of the verb *kathistēmi,* translated "appoint"?

        To appoint to an official position, as in to appoint a judge or governor. It is the common, ordinary word for appoint. It does not convey any special religious or ecclesiastical status, nor does it warrant the connotation of ordination.

    b.   What is the meaning of the verb *diatassō,* translated "directed"?

        To command, order, or charge.

    c.   What is the essence of Paul's instruction to Titus in Titus 1:5-9?

        Titus was to finish organizing and teaching the churches. Paul gave Titus explicit instructions on appointing elders, of specific qualifications, to oversee God's work in the churches. Titus was to appoint men who met the strict guidelines that Paul prescribed, thus establishing a council of qualified elders in each church who were responsible for its protection and proper ordering.

ELDER QUALIFICATIONS

"Namely, if any man is above reproach, the husband of one wife, having children who believe, not accused of dissipation or rebellion. For the overseer must be above reproach as God's steward, not self-willed, not quick-tempered, not addicted to wine, not pugnacious, not fond of sordid gain, but hospitable, loving what is good, sensible, just, devout, self-controlled, holding fast the faithful word

---

3b. The significance of the term *diatassō* should be emphasized. Some scholars maintain that eldership is not a biblical precept and is not an apostolic injunction. Rex A. Koivsto expresses this best:

    Were the congregations of the New Testament plural in their eldership? Of course. There is abundant evidence for that. But the question is whether this *pattern* is to be a *precept* for all the congregations at all times in the church of Christ. Quite simply, although there is evidence for a plural pattern, there is no evidence that this is a divine precept.[1]

However, qualified eldership *is* an apostolic directive. It *is* a Pauline precept. Paul uses the verb *diatassō,* meaning "command," to indicate the necessity of appointing qualified, plural elders for the local church. Review pp. 116, 117.

which is in accordance with the teaching, so that he will be able both to exhort in sound doctrine and to refute those who contradict. For there are many rebellious men, empty talkers and deceivers, especially those of the circumcision, who must be silenced because they are upsetting whole families, teaching things they should not teach for the sake of sordid gain." Titus 1:6-11

> **Review pages 228-238.**

4.   There is disagreement over the meaning of the Greek term *pistos*, "having children who believe," in Titus 1:6. Describe the opposing viewpoints and indicate the one you prefer and why.

   a.   *Translated actively as "believing" (1 Tim. 6:2), meaning children who have a personal faith in Christ*

   b.   *Translated passively as "faithful," "trustworthy," or "dutiful" (2 Tim. 2:2), meaning children who are obedient, respectful, controlled, and submissive to their father*

   c.   *The second meaning is preferred for three reasons:*

      1   *It is consistent with the parallel passage in 1 Tim. 3:4, which states that the prospective elder must keep "his children under control with all dignity."*

      2   *A father can be held responsible for his children's behavior in the home, but not for their personal faith because salvation is a supernatural act of God, not the guaranteed outcome of a faithful father's efforts.*

      3   *The strong contrast in the passage is between the lawless child and the controlled child.*

5.   Paul uses the Greek noun *oikonomos* ("steward") to identify the elder's function in the church.

   a.   What does *oikonomos* mean?

   House manager: the administrator or trustee of someone else's household, property, or business.

---

5. The biblical concept of *steward* is not familiar to most Christians. Few elders think of themselves as stewards of God's family or of apostolic doctrine, so be sure your mentoree is able to apply this concept to his future identity as an elder. Read Gen. 39:4-9. Many present-day churches wisely make their elders the legal trustees of the church corporation. This practical application of elders as God's stewards avoids the conflicts that arise when a competing board, especially a tightfisted one that is focused on conserving the property, buildings, etc., must function alongside an eldership that desires to expand God's kingdom. Since elders are God's stewards who are responsible for God's household, the local church, they should be its legal trustees.

b.   What does an *oikonomos* do (p. 70)?

He acts on behalf of another's interest or possessions. He is accountable and responsible to another for whatever is entrusted to his care.

c.   What does the term *oikonomos* tell you about an elder's identity and work?

An elder must be the most trusted servant of all because he has been chosen to be God's steward and is charged with managing His household (1 Tim. 3:15).

d.   What does the fact that elders are God's *oikonomoi* teach you about elders?

The emphasis is on God, *the steward's Master and owner. Therefore, the elders are* God's *household managers, not the church's.*

e.   Explain how the term *oikonomos* bolsters Paul's major point that the elder has to be qualified for office.

God demands that those to whom He entrusts His precious children must be morally and spiritually fit. He will not countenance unfit, untrustworthy stewards caring for His children and His truth.

"God has revealed to us that one of His own attributes is that He is slow to anger. A calm and patient spirit in the presence of wrong and injustice should be cultivated by every Christian man; but it is specially needful in the case of those entrusted with the high honour of preaching the Gospel or exercising oversight amongst the Lord's people. 'The beginning of strife is like the letting out of water.' It is of vital importance, therefore, if at any time we find ourselves tempted to enter into contention, that we should seek for grace to be kept from doing so, and give ourselves to quiet waiting upon the Lord for His power and guidance. In no other way can we be fitted to deal with the faults and disputes of others without ourselves becoming infected with the spirit of strife and partisanship."

D. E. Hoste[2]

---

6.   Uncontrolled anger ruins relationships, crushes the spirit, and divides churches and eldership teams. Unsanctified anger is a grave evil, especially in a leader (1 Sam. 20:30-34). Anger must always be controlled and channeled properly.

---

6. Teaching men the necessity of controlling their anger is a matter of utmost importance when training them for spiritual leadership in a team effort. Your mentoree *must* understand the destructive nature of uncontrolled anger. The work of pastoring people has a way of stirring up the temper of even the calmest person, but the Spirit-controlled elder will control expression of his anger. "The anger of man does not achieve the righteousness of God" (James 1:20).

a.   According to the following Scripture passages, what are the character traits of a man who controls his anger?

Prov. 14:17*a* **A quick-tempered man acts foolishly.**

Wise

Prov. 14:29 He who is slow to anger has great understanding, but he who is quick-tempered exalts folly.

Sensible, wise, patient

Prov. 15:18 A hot-tempered man stirs up strife, but the slow to anger pacifies a contention.

Peacemaking, patient, loving

Prov. 19:11 A man's discretion makes him slow to anger, and it is his glory to overlook a transgression.

Patient, sensible, prudent, wise

Prov. 29:11 A fool always loses his temper, but a wise man holds it back.

Self-controlled, self-disciplined

Eph. 4:26, 27 Be angry, and yet do not sin; do not let the sun go down on your anger, and do not give the devil an opportunity.

Self-disciplined, loving, forgiving, wise

James 1:19, 20 This you know, my beloved brethren. But everyone must be quick to hear, slow to speak and slow to anger; for the anger of man does not achieve the righteousness of God.

Prov. 14:29 "Patience is the evidence of understanding."[3]

Prov. 15:18 "The point here is that quarrels depend on *people* far more than on subject matter; *cf.* . . R. T. Archibald's characterization of the 'peacemakers' in the Beatitudes, 'who carry about with them an atmosphere in which quarrels die a natural death.'"[4]

Prov. 19:11 "The first line declares that 'prudence' or 'wisdom' [NASB *discretion*] causes patience. This *sēkel* ['discretion'] is good sense; it makes man even tempered."[5] Consider William McKane's comment:

It is evident that an even temper is an aspect of a disciplined person; it amounts to a toughness of intellectual and temperamental make-up which enables one to remain calm and unflurried even when subject to intense pressure or provocation. . . . Associated with tranquillity and coolness as a crowning achievement is magnanimity. The virtue which is indicated here is more than a forgiving temper; it includes also the ability to shrug off insults and the absence of a brooding hypersensitivity. It is the ability to deny to an adversary the pleasure of hearing a yelp of pain even when his words have inflicted a wound, of making large allowances for human frailties and keeping the lines of communication open. It contains elements of toughness and self-discipline; it is the capacity to stifle hot, emotional rejoinder and to sleep on an insult.[6]

Gentle, patient, self-controlled, self-disciplined, just, righteous

b.   Using what you have gleaned from *Biblical Eldership* (pp. 232, 233) and the verses above, explain why a quick-tempered, angry man does not qualify to be an elder.

God's leaders are required to be gentle and self-controlled, especially in response to opposition. They are to be peacemakers who bring calm, biblical reason to disagreements and disputes rather than feeding strife within the congregation.

7.   To deliver yourself from much unnecessary conflict and emotional stress, memorize and practice Proverbs 15:1:

**A gentle answer turns away wrath,
But a harsh word stirs up anger.**

a.   What does "a gentle answer turns away wrath" mean? Give an example from your own experience with people that illustrates this principle.

Meaning:

In response to a gentle answer, an angry person is inclined to lower his defenses and calmly examine the logic and truth of your statements.

Example:

Prov. 15:1 When shepherding contentious, complaining, unstable people, a Christlike shepherd must never respond in kind to the anger and attacks of others. A controlled, gentle response offers the only hope for maintaining peace and unity in the flock so that conflicts can be resolved. Of this crucial practice, Allen P. Ross writes:

> This antithetical proverb stresses that it is wise to use a gentle answer to turn away wrath. More than merely gentle or soft, the idea seems to be conciliatory, i.e., an answer that restores good temper and reasonableness. . . . To use a "harsh" word is to cause pain (same Hebrew word) and bring an angry response. . . . Gideon in Judges 8:1-3 is a classic example of the soft answer that brings peace, whereas Jephthah illustrates the harsh answer that leads to war (Judg. 12:1-6).[7]

This verse must be applied even in the heat of confrontations. Answering gently must become a way of life for the elder. As Charles Bridges advises:

> Let's think about this valuable rule for self-discipline, family peace, and church unity. . . . *The gentle answer* is the water to quench. *Harsh words* are the oil to *stir up* the fire. And this is, alas! man's natural tendency, to feed rather than to quench, the *angry* flame. We yield to irritation; reply in kind to our neighbor; have recourse to self-justification; insist upon the last word; say all that we could say; and think we "have good reason to be angry." Neither party gives up the smallest part of the will. Pride and passion on both sides strike together like two flints.[8]

b.   What does "a harsh word stirs up anger" mean? Give an example from your own experience with people that illustrates this principle.

Meaning:

In contrast to a gentle answer, a harsh answer—no matter how cogent—puts the other person on the defensive and tempts him to be resentful and combative.

Example:

> "The biblical shepherd is a shepherd of people–God's precious, blood-bought people. And like Christ, the Chief Shepherd, the church shepherd must give himself lovingly and sacrificially for the care of God's people (1 Thess. 2:8). This cannot be done from a distance, with a smile and a handshake on Sunday morning or through a superficial visit. Giving oneself to the care of God's people means sharing one's life and home with others. An open home is a sign of an open heart and a loving, sacrificial, serving spirit.
>
> "In my work as a church shepherd, I have found that the home is one of the most important tools for reaching and caring for people. Although the shepherd's ministry of hospitality may seem like a small thing, it has great impact on people. If you doubt this, ask those to whom a shepherd has shown hospitality. Invariably they will say that it is one of the most important, pleasant, and memorable aspects of the shepherd's ministry. In His own mysterious ways, God works through the guest-host relationship to encourage and instruct His people. If the local church's shepherds are inhospitable, the local church will be inhospitable. So we must never underestimate the power of hospitality in ministering to people's needs. Those who love hospitality love people and are concerned about them."
>
>   Alexander Strauch[9]

8.   The free, open exercise of hospitality is required of elders. Carefully consider the New Testament teaching on hospitality (pp. 194, 195)

a.   What do the following verses teach about hospitality?

---

8. The larger context in which these verses on hospitality appear is love. Hospitality is a practical, concrete expression of *agapē* love and the new commandment (John 13:34, 35). When you entertain in your home, include your mentoree. Modeling hospitality is the most effective way to teach it.

Rom. 12:10, 13

We are to be devoted to one another in brotherly love, preferring our brothers in Christ. As true servants, we are to put the needs of others ahead of our own and thereby serve Christ. We are to give liberally to the saints.

1 Peter 4:8-10

Hospitality demonstrates our love, thus we are to show our fervent love for our brothers in Christ through willing acts of hospitality. We are to be good stewards of the special gifts God has given us, using our gifts to serve one another. All Christians are commanded to show hospitality.

Heb. 13:1, 2

To demonstrate our love of the brethren, our hospitality should extend to all brothers in Christ, even to those who are initially strangers to us.

b.   Why is hospitality required of church elders?

Elders are to love and sacrificially care for others like Christ does. Love cannot be generic; it must have a specific object. Showing hospitality is a concrete way of loving the brethren and demonstrating a serving spirit.

c.   What does this requirement reveal about the nature of the local church?

The local church is to be an intimate, loving family. All must be welcome in any gathering, and all must be cared for. Exclusive cliques, especially among the leadership, cannot be tolerated. A church that is not hospitable is evidence of a selfish, lifeless, loveless Christianity.

ASSIGNMENT:

The biblical importance of hospitality is explained in Alexander Strauch's booklet, *The Hospitality Commands: Building Loving Christian Community, Building Bridges to Friends and Neighbors*. In addition, Edith Schaeffer's *L'Abri* (French for shelter) is an inspiring book on the power of hospitality in demonstrating the love of Christ and the reality of the gospel.

9.   Define the following elder qualifications:

---

9. These three elder qualifications, which emphasize personal, godly character, are not as well-known as other qualifica-tions. Your mentoree should recall that Job's life demonstrated these virtues.

a.   **Loving what is good:** *Taking those actions that are virtuous, beneficial, generous, and kind. Those who seek to help people and to live as Christlike examples must exhibit this virtue, which involves self-denying loving and compassion.*

b.   **Just:** *Being righteous or upright, living according to God's standards. This quality is needed so that the elder can be trusted to make fair, principled decisions for God's people and the church.*

c.   **Devout:** *Pleasing to God, separated from the world's demands, and dedicated to God and His Word. The devout elder will model godly commitment, character, and conduct. He will lead people into righteousness and devotion to God.*

10.   Paul was very specific in requiring that elders be able to teach the Word. He describes this elder qualification as **"holding fast the faithful word which is in accordance with the teaching."**

a.   What is the meaning of this qualification (see pp. 79, 80, 195)?

The elder must know and firmly adhere to the orthodox, historic, biblical teaching.

b.   According to Titus 1:10-16, why does Paul insist that this qualification is particularly necessary for an elder on the Island of Crete?

The church was under attack by those of the circumcision party who were motivated by monetary gain. They committed detestable deeds, rebelled against church leadership, and through false teachings attempted to lead members of the congregation away from the truth of the gospel.

11.   Elders are expected to prepare for exhorting the believers and refuting false teachers.

a.   What does being prepared **"to exhort in sound doctrine"** imply about preparation for eldership?

The elder must know the Word through self-study and training. He must be able to apply its teachings to the life situations the congregation faces and do so in an understandable

---

10. If there is any question concerning your mentoree's commitment to the absolute authority of Scripture in determining Christian doctrine, he should not be allowed to become a steward of God's people and the gospel. Many seminaries have departed from the historic Christian faith by permitting those who are not wholeheartedly committed to apostolic doctrine to teach. Instead of defending biblical doctrine, many seminary professors have adopted the methods of the liberal academics and have assumed contemporary cultural values. Some have even attacked the apostolic doctrine and cast doubt upon its credibility and truthfulness in conjunction with disparaging the authority of Scripture.

11. This is further proof that elders must assume the full responsibility of pastoral eldership, in contrast to simply being board elders.

and convincing way. The elder should prepare to be God's instrument for bringing about life change through His truth.

b.   What does being prepared **"to refute"** false teachers imply about preparation for elder-ship?

The elder is to have sufficient scriptural knowledge and experience to discern false teaching and to biblically and convincingly refute the teachings of the false teacher. The elder must be alert and have the courage to oppose false teachers by exposing their intent and motivations, as well as their doctrinal errors.

ASSIGNMENTS:

To prepare for defending the gospel against false teachers, make it your goal over the next several years to master the books of Romans and Galatians. These books deal with the heart of the gospel and Christian living. They are the centerpiece books of the New Testament and of biblical theology. It is prudent to use a number of sound commentaries on Romans and Galatians and to listen to the expository preaching of several teachers on them. When you are able, confirm your mastery of Romans and Galatians by teaching them to others.

12.   Evaluate yourself in each of the following qualifications, specified in Titus 1:6-9. Ask your wife or a close friend to make an independent evaluation of you as well.

a.   Not self-willed: a gentle, forbearing man:

Needs Improvement

_____7_____6_____5_____4_____3_____2_____1_____
Exemplary   Discredited

b.   Not quick-tempered:

Needs Improvement

_____7_____6_____5_____4_____3_____2_____1_____
Exemplary   Discredited

c.   Loving what is good: a kind, virtuous man:

Needs Improvement

_____7_____6_____5_____4_____3_____2_____1_____
Exemplary   Discredited

d.   Just: a righteous, law-abiding man:

Needs Improvement
_____7_____6_____5_____4_____3_____2_____1_____
Exemplary   Discredited

e.   Devout: a holy man, pleasing to God, loyal to His Word:

Needs Improvement
_____7_____6_____5_____4_____3_____2_____1_____
Exemplary   Discredited

f.   Self-controlled: a man controlled by the Holy Spirit:

Needs Improvement
_____7_____6_____5_____4_____3_____2_____1_____
Exemplary   Discredited

g.   Committed to the Word of God: a man who holds fast the trustworthy Word:

Needs Improvement
_____7_____6_____5_____4_____3_____2_____1_____
Exemplary   Discredited

h.   A man who is able to exhort in sound doctrine:

Needs Improvement
_____7_____6_____5_____4_____3_____2_____1_____
Exemplary   Discredited

i.   A man who is able to reprove and refute those who contradict sound doctrine:

Needs Improvement
_____7_____6_____5_____4_____3_____2_____1_____
Exemplary   Discredited

APPOINTMENT, ORDINATION, AND CLERGY

"Appoint elders in every city."   Titus 1:5c

Read pages 277-289. Review pages 111-114.

13. List several key reasons why it is wise to avoid using the term "ordination" in reference to elder appointment.

   a. *Ordination in the modern, ecclesiastical sense does not appear in the NT. No such practice existed in the early churches nor was such a practice referred to by the writers of the early second century (p. 286).*

   b. *We foist onto the language of the NT meanings and unscriptural priestly or clerical connotations (ordain) that the words (appoint) do not bear (p. 286).*

   c. *Ordination implies that the position is sacred, an anointed, priestly office or holy, clerical order. Appointment to eldership is not a holy sacrament, and it confers no special grace or empowerment (pp. 284, 285).*

   d. *The term "ordain" creates confusion, misunderstanding, and division (p. 285).*

14. Why is official, public installation of the elder important both to the church and to its officers?

   a. The church:

   Public installation identifies a new pastor elder who will be shepherding the congregation.

   b. The church's officers:

   Formal installation is an official starting point that communicates to the elder the approval, blessing, prayers, recognition, and fellowship of the church. It signals that the pastoral care of the flock rests on his-and his fellow elders'-shoulders. He is assuming the office of leadership and service among God's people.

---

13. Clericalism is an enemy of biblical eldership. Ordination in the modern ecclesiastical sense is the key to the maintenance and perpetuation of clericalism. In *A Theology of the Laity*, Hendrick Kraemer refers to ordination as *"the line of demarcation"* between clergy and laity:

> Particularly has the West, under the leadership of Rome, been very diligent in elaborating this fundamental pattern expressed in the simple but weighty words: *"duo sunt genera Christianorum,"* the clergy including those who choose the monastic life, and the laity, sharply demarcated from each other. The line of demarcation was formed by "ordination." The *"duo genera"* (two bodies or classes) with increasing emphasis meant a superior and inferior class.[10]

The world-renowned Roman Catholic theologian Hans Kung decries the sacralization of the church's ministers and the de facto elevation of ordination over baptism:

> It has likewise become clear that there is neither a sociological nor even theological basis for . . . sacralization of the Church's ministry (which accompanied the formation of a social class) which sets its holder as a sacred person apart from the rest of men and raises him above ordinary Christians to be a mediator with God-thus making ordination appear more important than baptism.[11]

In her classic work on ordination, Marjorie Warkentin echoes the same point:

> Ordination played a key role in consolidating clerical power, so that the priesthood of the church could now lord it over both the "faithful" and the secular authorities. One would have thought that the return to the Scriptures as the sole authority for faith and practice at the time of the Reformation would have restored a semblance of the community relations that had been taught by Christ. Some indeed tried to implement New Testament principles of church government, but they were hounded unmercifully and their leaders killed.[12]

15.   What reasons support the assertion that the clergy-laity division among the people of God is not biblical?

     a.   *No special priestly or clerical class that is distinct from the whole people of God appears in the NT.*

     b.   *The church is a nonclerical family. The NT emphasizes the fact that every believer is a royal priest and united with other believers in the body of Christ. It stresses the oneness of the people of God (Eph. 2:13-19) and the dismantling of the sacred-secular division that existed between priest and people under the old covenant (1 Peter 2:5-10; Rev. 1:6).*

     c.   *Clericalism does not represent biblical, apostolic Christianity. When establishing churches, Paul never ordained a man to perform the church's ministry. Instead, he left behind a council of elders who were chosen from among the believers to share in leadership and to jointly oversee the local church. The church was given a nonclerical structure of government.*

     d.   *When one or more individuals-the ordained ministers-have been raised to an unscriptural status above and apart from their Christian brothers, they have been made Protestant priests. The practice inserts a layer of priests between the one High Priest, Christ, and the one holy priesthood of believers (Heb. 4:14ff.).*

     e.   *A clerical form of government diminishes the direct role of Christ as Lord over His people and demeans the glorious status of a saintly body of people in which every member ministers.*

16.   From your own study and experience, what do you think is the single, most damaging consequence of the clergy-laity division for the local church? Explain your answer.

The most damaging consequence is that it puts in force the strongest disincentive for the members of the congregation to involve themselves in meaningful and responsible ministry. It leads to the corruption of the church, fostering a body of passive attendees who are led by paid professionals. Moreover, this professional staff's pride in their unbiblical position leads to further corruption and God's plan for His church is thwarted.

SCRIPTURE MEMORY ASSIGNMENT:

"For this reason I left you in Crete, that you would set in order what remains and appoint elders in every city as I directed you, namely, if any man is above reproach, the husband of one wife, having children who believe, not accused of dissipation or rebellion. For the overseer must be above reproach as God's steward, not self-willed, not quick-tempered, not addicted to wine, not pugnacious, not fond of sordid gain, but hospitable, loving what is good, sensible, just, devout, self-controlled, holding fast the faithful word which is in accordance with the teaching, so that he will be able both to exhort in sound doctrine and to refute those who contradict."   Titus 1:5-9

[1] Rex A. Koivsto, *One Lord, One Faith* (Wheaton: Victor, 1993), p. 244.

[2] D. E. Hoste, *If I Am to Lead* (London: Overseas Missionary Fellowship, 1968), pp. 16, 17.

[3] Allen P. Ross, "Proverbs," *The Expositor's Bible Commentary*, 12 vols., ed. Frank E. Gaebelein (Grand Rapids: Zondervan, 1991), 5: 990.

[4] Derek Kidner, *Proverbs*, Tyndale Old Testament Commentaries (Downers Grove: InterVarsity, 1964), p. 115.

[5] Ross, "Proverbs," *The Expositor's Bible Commentary*, 5: 1032.

[6] William McKane, *Proverbs: A New Approach* (Philadelphia: Westminster, 1970), p. 530.

[7] Ross, "Proverbs," *The Expositor's Bible Commentary*, 5: 992.

[8] Charles Bridges, *A Modern Study in the Book of Proverbs: Charles' Bridges' Classic Revised for Today's Reader*, by George F. Santa (Milford: Mott Media, 1978), p. 235.

[9] Alexander Strauch, *The Hospitality Commands* (Littleton: Lewis and Roth, 1993), pp. 43, 44.

[10] Hendrick Kraemer, *A Theology of the Laity* (Philadelphia: Westminster, 1958), pp. 53, 54.

[11] Hans Kung, *Why Priest?*, trans. Robert C. Collins (Garden City: Doubleday, 1972), pp. 77, 78.

[12] Marjorie Warkentin, *Ordination: A Biblical-Historical View* (Grand Rapids: Eerdmans, 1982), p. 186.

Lesson 10
Shepherd God's Flock in God's Way

LESSON OVERVIEW

In lesson 10, Peter's farewell exhortations to the elders of northwestern Asia Minor in 1 Peter 5:1-3 are considered. We examine the urgent apostolic imperative for elders to shepherd God's flock, that is, to be all that shepherds should be to the flock. This lesson will help you think practically about your time commitment to the shepherding task and your personal contribution to the shepherding team.

Furthermore, this passage is an urgent call for pastor elders to shepherd the flock in a distinctly Christlike way--willingly, eagerly, and as godly models of Christ--not as authoritarian tyrants or hirelings. Christian elders are to be loving, servant leaders.

SHEPHERD GOD'S FLOCK

"Therefore, I exhort the elders among you, as your fellow elder and witness of the sufferings of Christ, and a partaker also of the glory that is to be revealed, shepherd the flock of God among you." 1 Peter 5:1, 2*a*

Review pages 9-31. Read pages 239-244.

---

1.   What is Peter's purpose in calling himself a "fellow elder" in 1 Peter 5:1?

Peter desired to exhort other elders as their equal, as one of them. He viewed all elders as his colleagues in the work of Christ, thus his appeal is based on their brotherhood and their sharing of the same struggles and the same future reward. Note the fact that Peter considered an appeal based on their mutual responsibility to be more effective than one based on his apostolic authority. This approach encouraged the elders to listen to him, established good communication, and built empathy.

---

1. Point out to your mentoree that the preeminent apostles Peter and Paul both agree on a plurality of elders for shepherding the local church (Acts 20:28; 1 Peter 5:1, 2). Highlight the significant statement on p. 239: "The fact that Peter can address in one letter the elders of churches in five Roman provinces demonstrates that the elder system of government was standard practice." No such scriptural evidence exists for the single-pastor theory. Pastoral leadership of the local church by a plurality of elders is thoroughly biblical.

2. How does the verb "shepherd" (v. 2, p. 149) help you differentiate between the concept of elders that most people and churches have today (see pp. 9-17) and the New Testament concept?

    a. The contemporary view of elders is:

        It is unbiblical. It consists of temporary board members, advisors to a professional staff, men of power and influence, fund raisers, and policymakers of either sex. It conforms to a worldly model of leadership by individualistic, corporate executives.

    b. The New Testament view of elders is:

        They are a leadership team that is primarily responsible to shepherd the church. Elders accomplish this task through corporate and individual teaching, preaching, admonishing, counseling, visitation, and judging. The difference between contemporary and NT elders is the difference between being a detached manager or an involved shepherd who feeds and protects the sheep.

3. Understanding the sense of urgency for the elders' task:

    a. A deep sense of urgency pervades Peter's charge to the Asian elders. According to the entire letter of 1 Peter, what is the cause of this urgency?

        The church is facing external persecution (1:6; 4:14-16; 5:8-9), and Peter desires that the elders lead their flock in standing firm in the faith. Peter believes that "the end of all things is at hand" (4:7).

    b. Do you personally feel a sense of urgency about shepherding God's flock? Why?

        Yes. The church everywhere faces attacks that test the believers' faith. Elders need to equip and protect the church and must give immediate and continuous attention to this imperative.

---

2. Your mentoree needs to understand that one of the major themes of *Biblical Eldership* is that the modern, board concept of eldership contradicts the NT concept of pastoral eldership. Most people have a hard time grasping the NT model of eldership because they have only seen board eldership. For most Christians, the concept of a biblical eldership requires a major paradigm (cognitive model or example) shift, a major change in thinking. To explain how difficult it is to make a paradigm shift, use the following illustration with your mentoree.

> If asked "Who invented the quartz watch?" many people would name the Japanese or Texas Instruments. Amazing as it seems, Swiss watch researchers designed the first quartz watch in 1967. When the designers presented their prototype to Swiss watch manufacturers, however, the executives turned it down because they could not envision a watch without gears, springs, or jeweled bearings. The Japanese, on the other hand, saw the enormous possibilities and began to manufacture the quartz watch. Swiss manufacturers could not conceive of the potential of a watch based on a different design principle, so they failed to have a major role in one of the biggest technological revolutions in time keeping and thus forfeited billions of dollars in sales. At one time the Swiss cornered 90 percent of the world watch trade, but by the early 1980s, they claimed a mere 10 percent of that market.

4.   The shepherding task:

  a.   Describe six responsibilities involved in the shepherding task (pp. 16-31).

      1   *Lead the flock. The elder council must collectively seek the Lord's will and communicate that direction to the congregation. The elders must also lead by personal example.*

      2   *Feed the flock. Teach the congregation the Word and its application to their lives. Admonish the saints in sound doctrine, exhort them to obedience, and encourage their growth into maturity.*

      3   *Be alert to dangers to the flock. Teach the congregation to recognize the dangers and to defend themselves.*

      4   *Judge doctrinal issues. Protect the flock from false teachings and the world's immoral inducements. Pray for the flock.*

      5   *Be courageous in defending the flock. Willingly pursue stragglers and challenge the attackers.*

      6   *Care for the congregation's practical needs. Minister to those who are in ill health and who experience financial need.*

  b.   Which aspects of the shepherding task are you best gifted to perform?

  c.   Which aspects of the shepherding task are you weakest at performing, or least interested in?

  d.   What are you doing, or could you do, to improve your weak areas of shepherding?

  e.   Write the action plan to which you and your mentoring elder have agreed.

5.   The character traits of a good shepherd:

      a.   What were the character traits of a good Palestinian shepherd (pp. 16, 17, 149, and John 10:1-18)?

            Love for the sheep, devotion, perseverance, self-sacrifice, faithfulness, wisdom, watchfulness, courage, and sensitivity to the needs of the sheep

      b.   In which of these character traits are you strongest?

      c.   In which are you weakest?

      d.   In light of your strong character traits, what positive contributions will you be able to make to the shepherding team?

Peter charges the elders to shepherd the flock, which is a time-consuming task. Neil Summerton clearly describes the practical reality of shepherding:

> The demands of personal and group prayer, of meeting in oversight, of preparation for teaching, of pastoral visitation, and of giving necessary leadership and guidance to congregational activities are inevitably very great. A particular individual may have the character and gifts, and even the inclination, to be an elder, *but may not have the time* (italics added).[1]

So, as a prospective elder, you must honestly ask yourself, *Do I have the time to help shepherd God's flock?*

As a busy person, you must acquire effective management skills. We highly recommend reading Charles H. Hummel's short booklet, *The Tyranny of the Urgent*. Hummel reminds us of the principle that the busier we are and the more responsibilities we manage, the more important it is to take time regularly to plan and evaluate our schedule and priorities:

> Ironically, the busier you get the more you need this time of inventory, but the less you seem to be able to take it. You become like the fanatic, who, when unsure of his direction, doubles his speed. And frenetic service for God can become an escape from God. But when you prayerfully take inventory and plan your days, it provides fresh perspective on your work.[2]

> We live in constant tension between the urgent and the important. The problem is that the important task rarely must be done today, or even this week. Extra hours of prayer and Bible study, a visit with that non-Christian friend, careful study of an important book: these projects can wait. But the urgent tasks call for instant action-endless demands pressure every hour and day.[3]

ASSIGNMENT:

Although you are not yet an elder, carefully consider how you would spend the time you have available for serving as a shepherd elder. Be very specific. Write out a monthly schedule that realistically represents the time you would spend in specific pastoral work and personal, spiritual preparation. For example: two nights for two hours a week studying Scripture at home in preparation for teaching a class, one night a week for three hours visiting members in their homes or counseling, one night a week for two hours in small group Bible study, two nights a month at elders' meetings for three hours, one night a week for two hours for corporate prayer, etc. Before you finalize your chart, talk over your time commitments with your wife and children as well as your mentor.

SUNDAY	MONDAY	TUESDAY	WEDNESDAY	THURSDAY	FRIDAY	SATURDAY

ASSIGNMENT This assignment is critically important because most people assess the use of their time unrealistically. Planning how he will use his time for eldering will help your mentoree focus his gifts, limited energies, and time effectively and wisely. Examine his monthly schedule carefully.

6.   What activities and responsibilities in your life need adjustment in order to allow the time needed for your work as a member of the shepherding team? Discuss these adjustments with your wife first, then your mentor.

SHEPHERD GOD'S FLOCK IN GOD'S WAY

"Shepherd the flock of God among you, exercising oversight not under compulsion, but voluntarily, according to the will of God; and not for sordid gain, but with eagerness; nor yet as lording it over those allotted to your charge, but proving to be examples to the flock."   1 Peter 5:2, 3

Read pages 244-248. Review pages 85-98.

7.   Why is Peter deeply concerned about the attitudes and motives of those who lead God's flock?

In the previous chapters, Peter shows his concern for the holy flock that lives in an unholy world. The flock's leaders must be distinctively different; their motives must be holy. Jesus repeatedly taught his disciples about the humble, sacrificial character of the spiritual leader, and Peter urges the elders to be obedient to their Lord's standards and model.

8.   Elders must serve "**not under compulsion**":

      a.   In 1 Peter 5:2, what does Peter mean by the term *compulsion*?

            Responding to external pressure (i.e., the only man available, pressure from the pastor or friends) rather than serving willingly, in response to God's placing the need on his heart.

7.-14. J. Ramsey Michaels succinctly captures Peter's exhortation to the Asian elders, which was given at a time of intense crisis and rising hostile pressure:

The elders have a unique responsibility to prepare the "house of God" for the "judgment" now beginning. Everything demanded of them under "normal" circumstances is demanded with far greater urgency because of the "time" (cf. 1 Peter 4:17). They must guide and shepherd their charges not for financial gain or ego satisfaction but willingly and without complaint. *Instead of taking on themselves more and more "emergency powers," they must become examples of servanthood and humility to the entire "flock of God."* Their congregations in turn must respect the elders' authority, but more than that, follow the elders' example by becoming servants to each other in the face of mounting threats among those hostile to their movement in their respective cities and villages. Once again, as in 3:10-12, Peter articulates his hope of vindication through all this in the words of Scripture: God "opposes the arrogant and gives grace to the humble"-now and forever.[4]

b. Why does Peter prohibit a man from serving as an elder if he serves under compulsion?

He will be serving men rather than God. He will not have staying power when the going is difficult. He will respond to pressure in an ungodly fashion because he was "forced" into the position.

c. What is God's standard for the motives of those who oversee His flock, and why?

God requires that we serve "voluntarily, according to the will of God." This means that we must be convinced that we "aspire to the office of overseer" (1 Tim. 3:1) because we are responding to God's call. Our motivation must be pure-free of the desire for power, control, or monetary gain.

"What is the essential difference between spurious and true Christian leadership? When a man, in virtue of . . . an official position in the church, demands the obedience of another, irrespective of the latter's reason and conscience, this is the spirit of tyranny. When, on the other hand, by the exercise of tact and sympathy, by prayer, spiritual power and sound wisdom, one Christian worker is able to influence and enlighten another, so that the latter, through the medium of his own reason and conscience, is led to alter one course and adopt another, this is true spiritual leadership."

D. E. Hoste[5]

---

9. *Eagerness* is a wonderful quality. How would you describe an elder who *eagerly* shepherds God's flock?

An eager shepherd is one who persistently and cheerfully responds to the needs of the congregation and draws strength for the task from his relationship with the Lord. He is unflagging in his service, has a clear sense of his area of competence and calling, and is a strong influence for good.

"When we consider Paul's example and that of our Lord's, we must agree that biblical elders do not dictate, they direct. True elders do not command the consciences of their brethren, but appeal to their brethren to faithfully follow God's Word. Out of love, true elders suffer and bear the brunt of difficult people and problems so that the lambs are not bruised. They bear the misunderstanding and sins of others so that the assembly may live in peace. They lose sleep so that others may rest. They make great personal sacrifices of time and energy for the welfare of others. They see themselves as men under authority. They depend on God for wisdom and help, not on their own power and cleverness. They face the false teachers' fierce attacks. They guard the community's liberty and freedom in Christ so that the saints are encouraged to develop their gifts, to mature, and to serve one another."

Alexander Strauch[6]

10. An authoritarian style of church leadership is sternly prohibited by Christ and His apostles (Matt. 18:4; 20:20-28; 1 Peter 1:22; 2:16; 3:8-11; 4:8; 5:5, 6; 2 Tim. 2:24, 25). Yet the Lord requires that church leaders diligently lead the church (Rom. 12:8; 1 Tim. 5:17). Thus, pastor elders are to lead diligently and effectively, but not in an authoritarian manner. After reading chapter 5, "Servant Leadership" (pp. 85-98, 114), list the chief distinctives of both the authoritarian style of church leadership, which Christ denounces, and the diligent, servant style of church leadership.

   a. Marks of an authoritarian leadership style:

       Harsh, proud, autocratic, unloving, ambitious, selfish. Exercises unilateral power, lords it over others. Can be legalistic, abusive, evil.

   b. Marks of a diligent, servant leadership style:

       Gentle, humble, submissive, loving, patient, self-sacrificing. Respects his brother elders, defers to them, handles disagreements, works toward consensus, and shares leadership.

11. As you read the following list of the marks of an unhealthy, controlling leader, check your own leadership style for any unhealthy tendencies that need prayer and accountability.

   ___ Self-centered and self-willed
   ___ Shuns genuine, peer accountability
   ___ Must control church finances
   ___ Overly concerned with externals and appearances
   ___ Sees all issues as black and white, operates only in extremes, and views people as for or against himself
   ___ Threatened by legitimate change or differences
   ___ A negative, unaccepting mentality; a closed mind
   ___ Hypercritical of others, but unable to see his own glaring sins, errors, and faults
   ___ Fearful of competent, gifted people
   ___ Cannot delegate genuine authority or significant positions to others
   ___ Lacks balance
   ___ Manipulates people
   ___ Seeks spotlight, recognition

---

10. Before proceeding with this section, carefully reread pp. 95-98 in *Biblical Eldership*. Particularly note the boxed paragraph duplicated here on p. 157. This exhortation best summarizes the attitudes, methods, and leadership styles that are critically important to biblically minded Christians: the very ones we see in Jesus, the very ones Christians need and desire in their servant leaders, and the very ones godly men need to incorporate and espouse. This paragraph should be reviewed routinely as an instructive, and perhaps corrective, reminder.

12. List some of Paul's leadership characteristics (pp. 93-95).

He was gifted and intelligent but, as a loving servant leader, used his gifts to build and promote others. He restrained his use of authority in order to minister to others, avoided self-promotion, and served without pay.

13. Why have Christ's teachings on love, humility, and servanthood been so hard for churches and church leaders to practice?

Love and humility are easy to speak of, but harder to practice. There is a great deal of pressure to be successful in ministry and to do so on a specific schedule, which often means leading by dictatorial control, manipulation, and deception, with fleshly pride, ambition, and argument. It takes greater skill and Christian virtue to lead obediently by love, humility, and servanthood. These leadership characteristics run counter to the spirit of this age, as exemplified in the academic and business arenas.

14. How would you apply the following quotation by Francis A. Schaeffer to Peter's phrase "those allotted to your charge"?

> "As there are no little people in God's sight, so there are no little places. To be wholly committed to God in the place where God wants him-this is the creature glorified . . . . Nowhere more than in America are Christians caught in the twentieth-century syndrome of size. Size will show success. If I am consecrated, there will necessarily be large quantities of people, dollars, etc. This is not so. Not only does God not say that size and spiritual power go together, but he even reverses this (especially in the teaching of Jesus) and tells us to be deliberately careful not to choose a place too big for us. We all tend to emphasize big works and big places, but all such emphasis is of the flesh. To think in such terms is simply to hearken back to the old, unconverted, egoist, self-centered *Me*. This attitude, taken from the world, is more dangerous to the Christian than fleshly amusement or practice. It is the flesh."
>
> Francis A. Schaeffer[7]

a. *We must overcome the sinful tendency to be driven by the world's worship of success and power, which is to practice the politically expedient and cater to the influential and prosperous. No one in our congregation is insignificant; no group is unimportant or too small to deserve our loving attention.*

b. *The congregation does not belong to the elders. The members of the congregation are of infinite worth. They are God's children, whom He has placed into the elders' care.*

SCRIPTURE MEMORY ASSIGNMENT:

"Therefore, I exhort the elders among you, as your fellow elder and witness of the sufferings of Christ, and a partaker also of the glory that is to be revealed, shepherd the flock of God among you, exercising oversight not under compulsion, but voluntarily, according to the will of God; and not for sordid gain, but with eagerness; nor yet as lording it over those allotted to your charge, but proving to be examples to the flock."   1 Peter 5:1-3

---

[1] Neil Summerton, *A Noble Task: Eldership and Ministry in the Local Church*, 2nd ed. (Carlisle: Paternoster, 1994), p. 27.

[2] Charles H. Hummel, *Tyranny of the Urgent* (Downers Grove: InterVarsity, 1967), p. 14.

[3] Ibid., p. 5.

[4] J. Ramsey Michaels, *1 Peter, Word Biblical Commentary* (Waco: Word, 1988), p. 291.

[5] D. E. Hoste, *If I Am to Lead* (London: Overseas Missionary Fellowship, 1968), p. 7.

[6] Alexander Strauch, *Biblical Eldership: An Urgent Call to Restore Biblical Church Leadership* (Littleton: Lewis and Roth, 1995), p. 98.

[7] Francis A. Schaeffer, *No Little People* (Downers Grove: InterVarsity, 1974), p. 18.

Lesson 11
Caring for the Poor
Praying for the Sick

LESSON OVERVIEW

Lesson 11 addresses the elders' attitude toward the poor and needy, and the character qualities necessary in the men who administer the church's charitable funds. The second half of the lesson deals with the elders' responsibility to the sick, as described in James 5:14, 15. To be a Christlike shepherd, the elder must be compassionate toward those who suffer. In ministering to the sick, the pastor elder must be a man of faith, prayer, and wise counsel.

CARING FOR THE POOR

"And in the proportion that any of the disciples [in Antioch] had means, each of them determined to send a contribution for the relief of the brethren living in Judea. And this they did, sending it in charge of Barnabas and Saul to the elders."

Acts 11:29, 30

"In everything I showed you that by working hard in this manner you must help the weak and remember the words of the Lord Jesus, that He Himself said, 'It is more blessed to give than to receive.'"

Acts 20:35

Review pages 156-159.

The first time Luke mentions the Jewish Christian elders (Acts 11:27-30, p. 124), giving to the needy is the subject. The elders in Jerusalem received an offering from the Christians in Antioch for the relief of the destitute saints in Judea. Stressing the significance of our responsibility to the poor, the eighteenth-century American pastor-theologian, Jonathan Edwards (1703-1758), wrote: "I know of scarce any duty which is so much insisted on, so pressed and urged upon us, both in the Old Testament and New, as this duty of charity to the poor."[1] The following Old Testament passages reveal the explicit directions given to Israel concerning the poor and needy:

159

Deut. 15:7-10 If there is a poor man with you, one of your brothers, in any of your towns in your land which the Lord your God is giving you, you shall not harden your heart, nor close your hand from your poor brother; but you shall freely open your hand to him, and shall generously lend him sufficient for his need in whatever he lacks. Beware that there is no base thought in your heart, saying, "The seventh year, the year of remission, is near," and your eye is hostile toward your poor brother, and you give him nothing; then he may cry to the Lord against you, and it will be a sin in you. You shall generously give to him, and your heart shall not be grieved when you give to him, because for this thing the Lord your God will bless you in all your work and in all your undertakings.

Prov. 14:31 He who oppresses the poor reproaches his Maker, but he who is gracious to the needy honors Him.

Prov. 19:17 He who is gracious to a poor man lends to the Lord, and He will repay him for his good deed.

Prov. 21:13 He who shuts his ear to the cry of the poor will also cry himself and not be answered.

Prov. 22:9 He who is generous will be blessed, for he gives some of his food to the poor.

Prov. 29:7 The righteous is concerned for the rights of the poor, the wicked does not understand such concern.

Deut. 15:7-10 This passage is a marvelous summary of the inner attitudes and motives concerning the use of money that God either approves or disapproves. "Note, however," writes P. C. Craige, "that it is not charity, in the sense of almsgiving, that is advocated here; it is a charitable attitude to be expressed by lending the poor man whatever he needs for himself, while [the poor man] pledged to repay the loan in due course."[2]

The year of remission or release, the seventh year or Sabbath year, did not permanently terminate all debts. Rather, during the seventh year, repayment of all loans was suspended for a year or two (Deut. 15:1-6). It is thus a postponement of debts that is in view here.

Moses warned God's people to "not harden your heart, nor close your hand from your poor brother" (v. 7). The Hebrew idiom *close your hand* is similar to the English idioms 'tightfisted' or 'closefisted,' both of which convey the idea of excessive, undue caution in money matters. To "harden your heart" means to be intentionally unresponsive, unsympathetic, uncaring, and unloving to a needy family member. It is a greedy, stingy, selfish, ugly heart that is here described and condemned.

Prov. 21:13 Charles Bridges writes, "When the heart is hard, the ear is deaf."[3] He adds, "Shutting the ears implies cruelty or insensibility, turning away from real and known distress."[4] Here is a person with an unmerciful spirit who refuses to help a drowning fellow human. For a NT example, read the story of the rich man and Lazarus in Luke 16:19-31. In the eyes of God, it is a serious matter to ignore another's cry for help. Note that Prov. 21:13 is similar in thought to 1 John 3:17 (next page).

Prov. 22:9 The key word here and in Deut. 15:10 is *generosity*. Emphasize that we are to give liberally and cheerfully to others. If the church elders are not generous, the church will not be generous. And if the church is not generous, the needy will be ignored and missionaries will suffer want. A tightfisted church is a contradiction of the glorious, free gospel of Jesus Christ.

Prov. 29:7 Job illustrates this passage (Job 29:12-17). Remind your mentoree of what he learned about Job in lesson 1.

This compassion for the poor was also demonstrated by the New Testament church.

> **Acts 4:34, 35** For there was not a needy person among them, for all who were owners of land or houses would sell them and bring the proceeds of the sales and lay them at the apostles' feet, and they would be distributed to each as any had need.

> **Eph. 4:28** He who steals must steal no longer; but rather he must labor, performing with his own hands what is good, so that he will have something to share with one who has need.

> **Gal. 2:10** They [James and John] only asked us [Paul and Barnabas] to remember the poor—the very thing I [Paul] also was eager to do.

> **James 1:27a** Pure and undefiled religion in the sight of our God and Father is this: to visit orphans and widows in their distress.

> **1 John 3:17** But whoever has the world's goods, and sees his brother in need and closes his heart against him, how does the love of God abide in him?

1. In light of these passages, who is your brother?

    My brother is every Christian, especially those whom God has connected to me. The elder bears a special, responsible relationship to those in his charge.

2. Write down the **wrong attitudes or actions** toward the poor brother that you see in these passages.

    a. *Contempt for God; forgetting the fact that God made the poor as well as the rich*

    b. *Hard-hearted, unloving unresponsiveness to the condition of the poor*

    c. *Failure to share with the poor what God has entrusted to us as stewards; withholding what is His from the poor; refusal to lend to the Lord*

    d. *Oppression of the poor (e.g., participation in contracts that are unfair to the poor), or failure to defend their rights when they are oppressed*

    e. *Self-centered calculation of the likelihood of being repaid*

Acts 4:34, 35 A thrilling example of love and generosity is displayed by the first Christian community. Here is costly love, the giving of one's own possessions to help suffering brothers and sisters.

Eph. 4:28 This passage urges the sacrificial sharing of one's earnings and personal possessions with others. Note the emphasis on industry for the sake of supporting the poor. This is not a drop-your-check-in-the-offering-plate Christianity; it is authentic Christianity.

Gal. 2:10 Another key word and attitude is *eagerness*. Paul was eager to help the poor. He went out of his way to raise money from among Gentile churches for the poor in Jerusalem. Such eagerness reminds us again of Job.

3.   What five *positive attitudes or actions* are we to have toward the brother who is in need?

    a.   *Recognition that the poor belong to the Lord*

    b.   *Love, open-heartedness; concern, understanding, attention*

    c.   *Generosity in giving and lending*

    d.   *Free, joyful eagerness in giving*

    e.   *Sacrificial sharing of earnings and possessions*

4.   List the consequences to us of our treatment of our poor brothers.

    a.   Consequences of improper treatment:

        We will be guilty of dishonoring the Lord.
        God will withhold blessings from us.
        Our prayers will be unanswered.
        Our needs will not be met.
        God may inflict other consequences (in response to the petitions of the needy).

    b.   Consequences of proper treatment:

        We will be honoring the Lord.
        God will bless us and our efforts.
        Our prayers will be answered.
        Our needs will be met.
        We will be repaid by God.

5.   Paul instructs the Ephesian elders and, therefore, all shepherd elders, to work hard and share their earnings with poor and needy brothers. Compare Galatians 2:10 and 1 Timothy 3:3*b*.

---

5. By nature we are lazy and greedy, but by the transforming power of the gospel we are to become industrious, financially responsible, and benevolent. The leaders of the church family, the elders, are to set an example of the Christian work ethic and the spirit of mercy and benevolence. The Greeks thought that hard or menial work was demeaning-only for slaves-but Christianity makes all work sacred and honoring to God. We glorify God in our work and employment. Have your mentoree read you Eph. 6:5-8; Col. 3:22-25; 1 Thess. 4: 11, 12; and 2 Thess. 3:6-15. It is important that an elder know these passages.

    Genuine Christian community is displayed by intimate, loving care for one another's needs. The elders are to model our Lord's teaching that it is "more blessed to give than to receive." If the elders display the Christian work ethic and humanitarian spirit, the local church will follow their example.

Acts 20:34, 35 "You [elders] yourselves know that these [Paul's] hands ministered to my own needs and to the men who were with me. In everything I showed you that by working hard in this manner you must help the weak and remember the words of the Lord Jesus, that He Himself said, 'It is more blessed to give than to receive.'"

    a.   Why is it important to the local church that its elders model the practices of hard work and benevolence?

            The congregation must be led to serve the Lord by the strong personal example of its elders. Elders demonstrate their commitment to Christ's work by how they spend their time and use their resources.

    b.   What does leadership in this area imply about the elder's standard of living?

            His standard of living must reflect that he lives modestly, and is not materialistic, or involved in wasteful consumption and the selfish use of leisure. He must not live in luxury while his brothers are forced to forego essentials.

6.   The qualifications of and standards for an elder are listed below.

1 Timothy 3:2-7	Titus 1:6-9	1 Peter 5:1-3
1. Above reproach	1. Above reproach	1. Not shepherding under compulsion, but voluntarily
2. The husband of one wife	2. The husband of one wife	2. Not shepherding for sordid gain, but with eagerness
3. Temperate [self-controlled, balanced]	3. Having children who believe	3. Not lording it over the flock, but proving to be an example
4. Prudent [sensible, good judgment]	4. Not self-willed	
5. Respectable [well-behaved, virtuous]	5. Not quick-tempered	
6. Hospitable	6. Not addicted to wine	
7. Able to teach	7. Not pugnacious	
8. Not addicted to wine	8. Not fond of sordid gain	
9. Not pugnacious [not belligerent]	9. Hospitable	
10. Gentle [forbearing]	10. Lover of what is good [kind, virtuous]	
11. Peaceable [uncontentious]	11. Sensible [see prudent]	
12. Free from the love of money	12. Just [righteous conduct, law-abiding]	
13. Manages his household well	13. Devout [holy, pleasing to God, loyal to His Word]	
14. Not a new convert	14. Self-controlled	
15. A good reputation with those outside the church	15. Holds fast the faithful [trustworthy NIV] Word, both to exhort and to refute	

Those who distribute contributions for the needy and/or receive financial support for the work of ministry are vulnerable to temptation and criticism. List below the requisite qualities for the man who handles the church's benevolence funds. Beside each quality, point out the result: either how the elder should be viewed, or how he should behave.

a. *Above reproach, respectable:*   *Trusted by the congregation*

b. *Prudent, sensible:*   *Wise in the use of funds*

c. *Free from the love of money, not fond of sordid gain, not self-willed:*   *Having right motives, not tempted to steal or misuse funds out of self-interest*

d. *Self-controlled:*   *Not carried away by uncontrolled desires, self-disciplined, balanced*

e. *Just:*   *Righteous in decisions, having financial integrity*

f. *Manages his own household well:*   *Able to decide, set priorities, lead*

g. *A good reputation with those outside the church:*   *Public testimony of financial integrity, trustworthiness*

h. *Not lording it over the flock but proving to be an example:*   *Not proud, exemplifying fiscal responsibility*

7. In Acts 6, the apostles ask the church to choose men (the first deacons or the precursors of deacons) to be responsible for the distribution of food so that the Twelve could devote their attention to the ministry of the Word.

   a. Is it proper for present-day elders to delegate some or all of their responsibility to the poor to a deacon board?

---

7. Make sure your mentoree fully understands the meaning of Acts 6:1-6. From a leadership standpoint, this is one of the most significant NT passages on pastoral priorities. For elders, like the apostles, the ministry of the Word and prayer are top priorities. If your mentoree is unfamiliar with this passage, read it together and explain the leadership principles taught. The lessons of Acts 6:1-6 must be repeatedly rehearsed, as John R. W. Stott so aptly states:

The Church of every generation has to re-learn the lesson of Acts 6. There was nothing wrong with the apostles' zeal for God and his Church. They were busily engaged in a Christlike, compassionate ministry to needy widows. But it was not the ministry to which they, as apostles, had been called. Their vocation was "the ministry of the Word and prayer;" the social care of the widows was the responsibility of others.[5]

Unfortunately, sometimes board elders adopt the opposite posture and wash their hands of their responsibility to minister to the needy by delegating the entire responsibility to a deacon board. In so doing, they fail to lead or set the example.

Yes, it is appropriate to delegate the administration of help for the needy to deacons, as long as the elders continue to provide leadership to the deacons and congregation in this area of concern for the poor. The elders must also be personally involved in some helping of the poor in order to model the right attitudes toward the poor.

b.   What advantage would such delegation have for both the elders and the poor?

Such delegation releases the elders to do their job of teaching, preaching, and caring for the spiritual welfare of the flock. As for the poor, they would receive better attention.

8.   Describe improper delegation (poor leadership by the elders) in the overseeing of care for the needy.

Ignoring the plight of the needy; failing to exercise oversight of the deacons' administration of the caring ministry of the church; failing to personally contribute and assist; failing to see that the deacons give counsel and correction, along with the material aid, so as to keep the recipients properly accountable.

9.   Study Matthew 25:34-40. Explain how this passage should revolutionize your thinking about helping poor, needy believers.

Not one believer is unimportant to Christ: to serve him is to serve Christ. In eternity it will count that the elder has served the ordinary, the "little" people.

---

9. The profound, intimate relationship between Christ and the believer is dramatically illustrated by v. 40. To serve any of Christ's brothers or sisters, even those who are unknown, broken, problem-ridden, or least esteemed, is the same as serving Jesus Christ Himself. Paul discovered this blessed truth on the Damascus road (Acts 9:4, 5). If the glorious Lord Jesus Christ was on earth today, we would be tripping over one another to serve and help Him. Well, He is here-in His people! We are in Christ and Christ is in us. Here are two stories you can use to illustrate this wonderful truth:

There were two men who found this parable [Matt. 25] blessedly true. The one was Francis of Assisi; he was wealthy and high-born and high-spirited. But he was not happy. He felt that life was incomplete. Then one day he was out riding and met a leper, loathsome and repulsive in the ugliness of his disease. Something moved Francis to dismount and fling his arms around this wretched sufferer; and in his arms the face of the leper changed to the face of Christ.

The other was Martin of Tours. He was a Roman soldier and a Christian. One cold winter day, as he was entering a city, a beggar stopped him and asked for alms. Martin had no money; but the beggar was blue and shivering with cold, and Martin gave what he had. He took off his soldier's coat, worn and frayed as it was; he cut it in two and gave half of it to the beggar man. That night he had a dream. In it he saw the heavenly places and all the angels and Jesus in the midst of them; and Jesus was wearing half of a Roman soldier's cloak. One of the angels said to him, "Master, why are you wearing that battered old cloak? Who gave it to you?" And Jesus answered softly, "My servant Martin gave it to me."[6]

PRAYING FOR THE SICK

"Is anyone among you suffering? Then he must pray. Is anyone cheerful? He is to sing praises. Is anyone among you sick? Then he must call for the elders of the church and they are to pray over him, anointing him with oil in the name of the Lord; and the prayer offered in faith will restore the one who is sick, and the Lord will raise him up, and if he has committed sins, they will be forgiven him. Therefore, confess your sins to one another, and pray for one another so that you may be healed. The effective prayer of a righteous man can accomplish much."

James 5:13-16

Review pages 29-31. Read pages 253-263.

Too often we men are not as compassionate as we should be toward those who suffer or are sick. We are like Job's friends, insensitive doctors of the soul. Our supreme model and mentor, however, is the Lord Jesus Christ. He was full of compassion for the sick and weak. The Presbyterian scholar, B. B. Warfield, wrote a significant article entitled, "On the Emotional Life of our Lord." Warfield states that compassion is the chief emotion expressed by our Lord:

> The emotion which we should naturally expect to find most frequently attributed to that Jesus whose whole life was a mission of mercy, and whose ministry was so marked by deeds of beneficience that it was summed up in the memory of his followers as a going through the land "doing good" (Acts 11:48), is no doubt "compassion." In point of fact, this is the emotion which is most frequently attributed to him.[7]

A lack of compassion is actually a lack of love. Warfield says that the fountain-spring of Christ's compassion was His love:

> Jesus' prime characteristic was love, and love is the foundation of compassion . . . . It is characteristic of John's Gospel that it goes with simple directness always to the bottom of things. Love lies at the bottom of compassion. And love is attributed to Jesus only once in the Synoptics, but compassion often; while with John the contrary is true-compassion is attributed to Jesus not even once, but love often. This love is commonly the love of compassion.[8]

Quoting from A. W. Tozer's biography of Robert Jaffrey, J. Oswald Sanders infers that all great spiritual leaders are characterized by compassion and love for people:

> In his biography of Robert A. Jaffrey, who played a major part in opening Vietnam to the gospel, A. W. Tozer pointed out that in one respect all spiritual leaders have been alike. They have all had large hearts. "Nothing can take the place of affection. Those who have it in generous measure have a magic power over men. Intellect will not do. Bible knowledge is not enough. Robert Jaffrey loved people for their own sakes. He was happy in the presence of human beings, whatever their race and colour."[9]

A Christlike shepherd, then, must be a man of love and compassion.

10. Using your concordance, look under the heading "compassion." Spell out for whom Jesus actually felt compassion.

    a. *The sick; the hungry; the confused; the bereaved; the lost*

    b. Choose, from the categories of people you listed above, those for whom you feel the most compassion. Why is this?

        I have the most compassion for the truly unfortunate.

        The amount of compassion I feel depends on the degree to which the person is not responsible for his condition and not able to personally remedy it.

11. Which three elder qualifications most completely represent the concept of compassion or love? Explain why.

    a. *Hospitable:*   *Caring for others, not selfish*

    b. *Gentle:*   *Not judgmental, but forbearing,*
                                                yielding to others, understanding

    c. *Lover of what is good:*   *Virtuous, kind, compassionate, serving*

12. Shepherding the flock of God is a profoundly spiritual work that demands Spirit-filled leaders (Acts 6:3). What does James indicate must be true of elders if they are to participate in an effective ministry to the sick (James 5:13-16)?

    They must be men of prayer (vv. 14, 15), men of faith (v. 15), righteous men (v. 16), and men of discernment and wisdom so as to deal properly with sin (vv. 15, 16).

13. How would you counsel someone who asks why he or she hasn't been healed after fervent, believing prayer? What Scripture texts would you use?

---

10. Remind your mentoree that the goal of every pastor elder is to be like Christ-to be a Christlike pastor. Without compassion, no man can be a Christlike pastor.

13. We must never forget that God's mind and ways are infinitely beyond our sinful, finite thinking and dealings (Isa. 46:5, 9-11; Rom. 11:33, 34). They will remain mysteries to us. As Moses wrote, "The secret things belong to the Lord our God" (Deut. 29:29). But by faith we know that His ways are perfect and just (Deut. 32:4). So with Job we say, "Though He slay me, I will hope in Him" (Job 13:15). We trust in our absolutely trustworthy God, even if we can't understand.

    Moreover, the Bible teaches that God permits suffering in order to develop our character. It is for our good that at times He does not heal our diseases. See Rom. 8:28, 29; Job 23:10; James 1:2-5; 1 Peter 1:6, 7; 2 Cor. 4:16-18.

God can and sometimes does heal. However, at other times, He gives the person the grace to endure the sickness and uses it to sanctify the person. God did not remove the thorn in Paul's side even after he fervently prayed for its removal (2 Cor. 12:7).

14. How would you counsel a sick person who asks if his or her sickness is the result of personal sin? What Scripture texts would you use?

    Sickness is not necessarily related to personal sin. Job protested this interpretation of his condition and was vindicated by God. Paul advised Timothy to take some wine for his stomach, and did not accuse him of sin (1 Tim. 5:23). However, God occasionally allows sickness to discipline us as a result of our personal sin. We are warned, in 1 Cor. 11:27–30, that some people who had unconfessed sin and participated in the Lord's Supper became sick or died as a result. Therefore, the sick person should examine himself, and confess and repent of any unconfessed sin.

15. What are the two main, contending views put forth today concerning application of oil to the sick by the elders? Indicate the view you support.

    a. *As was common at the time of James' instruction, oil was used for medicinal purposes.*

    b. *In the Jewish culture, oil had a symbolic, spiritual significance and was used to set apart the sick person in the same way that leaders and priests were dedicated for service.*

    c. Explain why you hold the position you do.

    Position b. Because James instructs that the anointing was to be done "in the name of the Lord," this means that the anointing with oil is symbolic rather than medicinal. The anointing with oil symbolizes the setting apart of the sick person through prayer to God's care and healing.

16. What are some practical benefits for both the sick person and the elders of praying in the sick person's presence (at his bedside) rather than praying at a distance, in a church building?

    The expenditure of effort and time in gathering with the sick person communicates the elders' concern and love to him. Since the elders represent the church, it also conveys the concern of the congregation. Furthermore, this procedure demonstrates the elders' care to the congregation.

---

15. We will never persuade everyone to agree on James' meaning of anointing the sick with oil. But what we must all agree to, and faithfully act upon, is compassionate prayer and care for the sick. On this point there should be no disagreement. This is certainly not a matter to divide the eldership or the church.

The personal, face-to-face contact fosters more fervent and effective prayer.

The elders can counsel the sick person, comfort him and his family.

ASSIGNMENTS:

Write a short list of specific, practical guidelines that will help you be effective when you visit the sick, whether they are at home or in the hospital. Ask your elders for their ideas, practices, and procedures. List some key Scripture references to read to the sick. Ask your elders to include you the next time they are called to pray for the sick so that you can learn how to minister to the sick. When our congregation's elders are called to a home or hospital to pray for a sick person, these are specific aspects of our practice:

- We take songbooks along and sing appropriate songs. This establishes a good atmosphere for prayer and seeking the Lord's intervention.

- Each elder shares from the Word (see questions **13** and **14**) and gives encouragement and counsel to the one who is sick and his or her family, if present. At this time, one of the elders lovingly asks about the person's relationship to the Lord and if there is unconfessed sin. We have not experienced any adverse reaction to this question. Most sick people who call for the elders are willing to face honestly their relationship to the Lord.

- One of the elders explains the significance of the oil (see question **15**) and applies oil to the sick person.

- We all kneel and pray. Each elder prays at least once.

- While they pray, one or two of the elders will lay hands on or hold the hand of the person who is sick, communicating our love and affection.

SCRIPTURE MEMORY ASSIGNMENT:

"Is anyone among you sick? Then he must call for the elders of the church and they are to pray over him, anointing him with oil in the name of the Lord; and the prayer offered in faith will restore the one who is sick, and the Lord will raise him up, and if he has committed sins, they will be forgiven him. Therefore, confess your sins to one another, and pray for one another so that you may be healed. The effective prayer of a righteous man can accomplish much." James 5:14-16

---

[1] Jonathan Edwards, *The Works of Jonathan Edwards*, 2 Vols. (1834; repr. Edinburgh: The Banner of Truth Trust, 1974), 2:164.

[2] P. C. Craige, *Deuteronomy*, NICOT (Grand Rapids: Eerdmans, 1976), p. 237.

[3] Charles Bridges, *A Modern Study in the Book of Proverbs: Charles Bridges' Classic Revised for Today's Reader*, by George F. Santa (Milford: Mott Media, 1978), p. 445.

[4] Ibid., p. 444.

[5] John R. W. Stott, *Between Two Worlds: The Art of Preaching in the Twentieth Century* (Grand Rapids: Eerdmans, 1965), p. 206.

[6] William Barclay, *The Gospel of Matthew*, vol. 2, rev. ed. (Philadelphia: Westminster, 1975), 2: 326.

[7] B. B. Warfield, "On the Emotional Life of Our Lord," in *The Person and Work of Christ* (Philadelphia: Presbyterian and Reformed, 1950), p. 104.

[8] Ibid., p. 101.

[9] J. Oswald Sanders, *Spiritual Leadership* (Chicago: Moody, 1980), p. 90.

Lesson 12
Spiritual Watchmen
Submission to Authority
Male Leadership

LESSON OVERVIEW

The final lesson explores Hebrews 13:17. We discuss the institutional church model versus the community church model, and the joys and heartaches of leading God's people. In addition, the subject of submission to church elders, a matter of great disdain to modern man, is studied.

The lesson also reviews chapter 3 of *Biblical Eldership*, "Male Leadership." This is not only an issue related to God's plan for male-female relationships in the home and church, but is an issue of biblical integrity and authority that is of utmost importance to the Lord's people.

SPIRITUAL WATCHMEN

"Obey your leaders and submit to them, for they keep watch over your souls as those who will give an account. Let them do this with joy and not with grief, for this would be unprofitable for you."

Hebrews 13:17

> Read pages 265-273.

In his description of the differences between the institutional church model and the community church model, Stephen B. Clark writes:

Heb. 13:17 As we near the end of our study, the content of this passage provides a good review of many of the basic principles of biblical eldership. Heb. 13:17 demonstrates beyond question that the NT elder is a pastor of souls, not an executive board member. It refers to a plurality of leaders for the local church and shows the close community nature of the local congregation and its responsibility to obey and submit to its leadership body.

In most churches in the Western world, the institutional elements predominate over communal elements. The reverse was true among the early Christians. . . . In a communal grouping like that of the early Christians, the overall leadership of the community governed the people. The heads of the Christian communities functioned in a way similar to fathers in a family; they did not treat the community members like children, but they did lead and direct them personally. They governed (cared for) the people. They taught them and watched over their lives. When members of the community were in need, the elders saw that the need was met. When the lives of the community members did not conform to the Lord's way of life, the heads would personally discuss the issue with those members. If a major transgression occurred, the elders would discipline the person. They governed and led the people, not the institution.

By contrast, the leaders of most modern churches concern themselves more directly with the institution than with the people, and their leadership consists primarily of administration, decision-making, and opinion-forming. The people's lives are a private matter. The leader will counsel someone upon request. The leader will run a program for those who want something enough to sign up and participate. The leader thus provides services for some individuals when they express a personal interest. The authority of church leaders extends over the institution-the common activities-but not the lives of the church members. The leaders can influence the direction of their members' lives through educational activities, but their primary authoritative functions are either administrative or policy-making for the institution (decision-making about budgets, hiring personnel, types of programs to use, etc.)[1].

1.   Show that the community concept of church life is the only valid understanding of Hebrews 13:17.

      There was a close, intimate, accountability relationship between the spiritual leaders and their people. The church elders guarded the spiritual lives of the people. The elders were more like fathers than managers.

2.   This passage contains two important Greek words that are essential to a proper understanding of biblical eldership.

      a.   What is the meaning of the Greek term *agryneō* in this context?

---

1. The biblical concept of the local church is that it is a redeemed family of brothers and sisters who are closely related to their spiritual leaders. This family is to be marked by *agapē* love: mutual care and accountability, intimate relationships, and humble service (review pp. 109-115). It is less demanding to be an elder in an institutional church than it is to be an elder in a church that is a community because the latter requires its pastor elders to deal personally and directly with their brothers' and sisters' sins, doctrinal errors, and family problems. An authentic, NT community, however, should demand no less of its elders.
2. Reinforce the fact that the shepherd elder's work is of a deeply serious nature, because so much is at stake. He watches over the spiritual condition and development of God's dear people. He is engaged in spiritual warfare and the battleground is people's souls.

Literally, "keep one's self awake;" metaphorically, "watch," "guard, " or "care" for people, in the manner of ancient city watchmen

b.   What is the meaning of *psychē* in this context?

Literally, "soul," or equivalent to "person" or "oneself." It relates to the inward, spiritual dimension of life.

c.   What do you learn about the significance of the elders' work from these two terms?

Keeping watch means that the elders deal with the spiritual dimension of the lives of God's children, which is a profound responsibility. Keeping watch also implies that the flock is in danger. The elders must consistently watch over the spiritual development of God's people in order to secure their safety. The flock is valuable to God and He will hold His shepherds accountable for its well-being and protection.

3.   How will the fact that elders must give an account of their stewardship to the Lord affect your efforts as a spiritual caregiver and leader?

My priorities for the use of my time and resources must be shaped by God's values rather than by my personality or natural inclinations.

I must work hard at shepherding the flock because if I fail, God's people will be hurt.

I bear a greater responsibility that will result in stricter scrutiny from God (Luke 12:48b).

I will not fear men's criticisms or evaluations because God's evaluation is the one that counts.

4.   What aspects of shepherding bring the greatest joy to the elder's heart?

Seeing Christians mature in the Lord, especially as they in turn begin to shepherd others.

---

3. Refer to 1 Cor. 4:1-5 for Paul's own answer to this question.

4. Although this lesson deals with the negative aspects of the shepherding responsibility (because it is carried out in a sinful environment), there are profound, lasting joys in shepherding God's people. Shepherding God's flock is a significant, worthwhile, and meaningful expenditure of one's life. Great joy comes from seeing God's people, as a close community, grow in the knowledge and love of Christ. Despite heartaches, pressures, and weariness of spirit, those who have served God's people are the most fulfilled and rewarded in life. Paul, for example, spoke of his beloved brethren as "my joy and crown" (Phil. 4:1).

"Something has already been said regarding the character of the pastor. In Paul's eyes he must be a patient and gentle teacher who is firmly committed to the truth. But [Paul's] troubles with the church at Corinth caused him to reveal a much deeper side to pastoral life than this. *Pastoral life can be painful and costly and [no one] can be more vulnerable to the wounds inflicted by others than the true pastor.*

"[Paul] reveals in 2 Corinthians how some of his own children had criticized him for being fickle (1:15-17), speaking with a double tongue (1:13; 10:1, 10), of lacking credentials (3:1), of being untrustworthy with money (8:20, 21), of acting in a worldly fashion (10:2), of being proud and deceitful (10:8; 12:16), of not being an original apostle (11:5) and of lacking dignity (11:7). The misunderstandings had led to a rupture in relationships, with the Corinthians not communicating with Paul in any meaningful way (7:2). It was all the harder because it was a family relationship which was disrupted and because Paul took such delight in them (12:14, 15; 7:3, 4). It was also hard because it came on top of all his other pressures (11:22-28). What is more, he was innocent. The strife had been stirred up by impostors (11:13), who in contrast to Paul had no legitimate place in the church at Corinth (10:13)" (italics added).   Derek J. Tidball[2]

The emotional stresses and heavy burdens of caring for the spiritual welfare of people can break a man's health and his resolve to do the work. It is not the hard work or long hours that defeat a man; it is the emotional and spiritual stress that crushes a man's spirit. To be specific, constant fighting among believers, complaints, unbelief, and disobedience ultimately wear down a Christian elder.

If you are inexperienced in the shepherding ministry, the Scripture references that follow will inform you of the harsh realities of working with people. Even the mighty Moses was broken by the people's incessant complaining and unbelief (Num. 11:15). Unrealistic or romantic ideas of Christian ministry eventually lead to disillusionment and discouragement.

5.   Based on the passages below, list the major problems with the people and their attitudes that elders can expect to face when leading God's people.

   Ex. 14:10-12 As Pharaoh drew near, the sons of Israel looked, and behold, the Egyptians were marching after them, and they became very frightened; so the sons of Israel cried out to the Lord. Then they said to Moses, "Is it because there were no graves in Egypt that you have taken us away to die in the wilderness? Why have you dealt with us in this way, bringing us out of Egypt? Is this not the word that we spoke to you in Egypt, saying, 'Leave us alone that we may serve the Egyptians?' For it would have been better for us to serve the Egyptians than to die in the wilderness."

---

5. According to these texts, the core issue is unbelief. The people did not trust God (Deut. 1: 32; Heb. 3:19; 4:2). This sin led to senseless complaining, murmuring, irrational fears, stubborn rebellion, outright disobedience, and accusing their spiritual leaders of wrongdoing. "Without faith it is impossible to please Him" (Heb. 11:6*a*).

People will resist and resent the elders because the congregation does not share the elders' faith in God's providence. When people are frightened, they say and do irrational things. They cannot make rational decisions based on facts and evidence.

Num. 11:4-6, 10-15 The rabble who were among them had greedy desires; and also the sons of Israel wept again and said, "Who will give us meat to eat? We remember the fish which we used to eat free in Egypt, the cucumbers and the melons and the leeks and the onions and the garlic, but now our appetite is gone. There is nothing at all to look at except this manna."

Now Moses heard the people weeping throughout their families, each man at the doorway of his tent; and the anger of the Lord was kindled greatly, and Moses was displeased. So Moses said to the Lord, "Why have You been so hard on Your servant? And why have I not found favor in Your sight, that you have laid the burden of all this people on me? Was it I who conceived all this people? Was it I who brought them forth, that You should say to me, 'Carry them in your bosom as a nurse carries a nursing infant, to the land which You swore to their fathers?' Where am I to get meat to give to all this people? For they weep before me, saying, 'Give us meat that we may eat!' I alone am not able to carry all this people, because it is too burdensome for me. So if You are going to deal thus with me, please kill me at once, if I have found favor in Your sight, and do not let me see my wretchedness."

The congregation will have a self-centered, consumer orientation. They will be concerned with their own needs and will fear hardship and will complain. Faced with such a negative environment, their leaders will be discouraged and want to escape from their responsibility.

Num. 12:1-3, 5, 8b Then Miriam and Aaron [Moses' sister and brother] spoke against Moses because of the Cushite woman whom he had married . . . and they said, "Has the Lord indeed spoken only through Moses? Has He not spoken through us as well?" And the Lord heard it. (Now the man Moses was very humble, more than any man who was on the face of the earth.) . . . Then the Lord came down in a pillar of cloud and stood at the doorway of the tent, and He called Aaron and Miriam. When they had both come forward, . . . [He said] "Why then were you not afraid to speak against My servant, against Moses?"

The people will be jealous, proud, and insubordinate. They will disregard God's shepherds and question their calling. The greatest pain will be inflicted by those who are closest to us, by the very ones who should be the most supportive.

Num. 14:1-4 Then all the congregation lifted up their voices and cried, and the people wept that night. All the sons of Israel grumbled against Moses and Aaron; and the whole congregation said to them, "Would that we had died in the land of Egypt! Or would that we had died in this wilderness! Why is the Lord bringing us into this land, to fall by the sword? Our wives and our little ones will become plunder; would it not be better for us to return to Egypt?" So they said to one another, "Let us appoint a leader and return to Egypt."

The people will be more concerned with their comforts than with God's plan. They will refuse to submit to the leaders and their decisions, and will try to appoint other leaders who will advocate their cause.

Num. 16:1-4, 7b, 9, 12-14 Now Korah . . . with Dathan and Abiram . . . rose up before Moses, together with . . . two hundred and fifty leaders of the congregation, chosen in the assembly, men of renown. They assembled together against Moses and Aaron, and said to them, "You have gone far enough, for all the congregation are holy, every one of them, and the Lord is in their midst; so why do you exalt yourselves above the assembly of the Lord?" When Moses heard this, he fell on his face. . . . [He said] "You have gone far enough, you sons of Levi! . . . Is it not enough for you that the God of Israel has separated you from the rest of the congregation of Israel, to bring you near to Himself, to do the service of the tabernacle of the Lord, and to stand before the congregation to minister to them?"

Then Moses sent a summons to Dathan and Abiram, the sons of Eliab; but they said, "We will not come up. Is it not enough that you have brought us up out of a land flowing with milk and honey to have us die in the wilderness, but you would also lord it over us? Indeed, you have not brought us into a land flowing with milk and honey, nor have you given us an inheritance of fields and vineyards. Would you put out the eyes of these men? We will not come up!"

The people will accuse the elders of exercising authority improperly. They will organize an insurrection and make ultimatums. When these are not met, the people will refuse to communicate.

Num. 21:4, 5 Then they set out from Mount Hor by the way of the Red Sea, to go around the land of Edom; and the people became impatient because of the journey. The people spoke against God and Moses, "Why have you brought us up out of Egypt to die in the wilderness? For there is no food and no water, and we loathe this miserable food."

The congregation will voice their dissatisfaction with the rigors of the Christian walk and the type of provision God makes.

Deut. 1:42, 43 "And the Lord said to me [Moses], 'Say to them, "Do not go up nor fight, for I am not among you; otherwise you will be defeated before your enemies."' So I spoke to you, but you would not listen. Instead you rebelled against the command of the Lord, and acted presumptuously and went up into the hill country."

The people's rebellion will lead them to presumption and disobedience.

Judg. 8:34, 35 Thus the sons of Israel did not remember the Lord their God, who had delivered them from the hands of all their enemies on every side; nor did they show kindness to the household of Jerubbaal (that is, Gideon), in accord with all the good that he had done to Israel.

The people will not learn to trust God even after experiencing deliverance under the leadership of able shepherds. They will be ungrateful to both God and His servants.

1 Sam. 8:19, 20 Nevertheless, the people refused to listen to the voice of Samuel, and they said, "No, but there shall be a king over us, that we also may be like all the nations, that our king may judge us and go out before us and fight our battles."

The people will be stubborn, arrogant, and ambitious for worldly status. They will capitulate to cultural standards. They will want professionals to do the work.

1 Sam. 30:6 Moreover David was greatly distressed because the people spoke of stoning him, for all the people were embittered, each one because of his sons and his daughters. But David strengthened himself in the Lord his God.

When the people experience hardship, they will become impatient and blame their misfortunes on their elders. They may become vindictive and plan treachery against the elders.

2 Sam. 17:1-4 Furthermore, Ahithophel [one of David's chief counselors] said to Absalom [David's son], "Please let me choose 12,000 men that I may arise and pursue David tonight. I will come upon him while he is weary and exhausted and will terrify him so that all the people who are with him will flee. Then I will strike down the king alone, and I will bring back all the people to you. The return of everyone depends on the man you seek; then all the people shall be at peace." So the plan pleased Absalom and all the elders of Israel.

Those who are closest to the leaders may betray them and influence other leaders to capitulate.

2 Chron. 36:15, 16 The Lord, the God of their fathers, sent word to them again and again by His messengers, because He had compassion on His people and on His dwelling place; but they continually mocked the messengers of God, despised His words and scoffed at His prophets, until the wrath of the Lord arose against His people, until there was no remedy.

The unfaithful people will despise and reject God's messengers, thereby incurring God's wrath.

Matt. 26:56b Then all the disciples left Him and fled.

In a crisis, the people will give into fear and abandon their leaders.

1 Cor. 4:18 Now some have become arrogant, as though I were not coming to you.

People will arrogantly challenge their leaders, and moral disorder will occur in the church when busy elders cannot immediately attend to every problem.

2 Cor. 11:20, 21 For you tolerate it if anyone enslaves you, anyone devours you, anyone takes advantage of you, anyone exalts himself, anyone hits you in the face. To my shame I must say that we have been weak by comparison. But in whatever respect anyone else is bold--I speak in foolishness--I am just as bold myself.

The people will follow cult leaders who have charisma while rejecting truthful leaders who may appear to be weak and ineffective.

Gal. 4:16 Have I become your enemy by telling you the truth?

Because the people will not hear or tolerate the truth, the elders will be rejected as the enemy.

Phil. 1:15, 17 Some, to be sure, are preaching Christ even from envy and strife, but some also from good will; . . . the former proclaim Christ out of selfish ambition rather than from pure motives, thinking to cause me distress in my imprisonment.

Motivated by personal ambition, others in leadership will attempt to harm the elders.

2 Tim. 1:15 You are aware of the fact that all who are in Asia turned away from me, among whom are Phygelus and Hermogenes.

The elders may face situations in which the pressures and problems will turn the entire congregation against or away from them. Out of cowardice, people may turn against their leaders because of the dangers involved in being associated with them or in coming to their defense.

6. From the above list of difficulties, which problems will you find it most difficult to manage and why?

7. From the list of elder qualifications, select those that will help you cope with the hurts and aggravations of working with people. Explain why each qualification will help.

1 Timothy 3:2-7

1. Above reproach
2. The husband of one wife
3. Temperate [self-controlled, balanced]
4. Prudent [sensible, good judgment]
5. Respectable [well-behaved, virtuous]
6. Hospitable
7. Able to teach
8. Not addicted to wine
9. Not pugnacious [not belligerent]
10. Gentle [forbearing]
11. Peaceable [uncontentious]
12. Free from the love of money
13. Manages his household well
14. Not a new convert
15. A good reputation with those outside the church

Titus 1:6-9

1. Above reproach
2. The husband of one wife
3. Having children who believe
4. Not self-willed
5. Not quick-tempered
6. Not addicted to wine
7. Not pugnacious
8. Not fond of sordid gain
9. Hospitable
10. Lover of what is good [kind, virtuous]
11. Sensible [see prudent]
12. Just [righteous conduct, law-abiding]
13. Devout [holy, pleasing to God, loyal to His Word]
14. Self-controlled
15. Holds fast the faithful [trustworthy NIV] Word, both to exhort and to refute

1 Peter 5:1-3

1. Not shepherding under compulsion, but voluntarily
2. Not shepherding for sordid gain, but with eagerness
3. Not lording it over the flock, but proving to be an example

---

7. Review the emphasis that we have placed previously on the quality of self-control. Christlike shepherd elders must be Spirit-controlled leaders. If an elder is not under the Spirit's disciplining power, he will not only damage the people, but he simply will not hold up under the horrendous pressures of his responsibility.

a. *An elder must be peaceable [uncontentious], not quick-tempered, temperate, and self-controlled in responding to people's demands and insults.*

b. *An elder must be sensible, prudent, and gentle, answering with balanced judgment when he is attacked or accused. He must realize that it is his responsibility to minister to people's true needs.*

c. *The elder must be just and devout so that he will act righteously in situations (not lie, wound, or manipulate) and take his bearings from the Lord.*

SUBMISSION TO AUTHORITY

"Obey your leaders and submit to them, for they keep watch over your souls as those who will give an account. Let them do this with joy and not with grief, for this would be unprofitable for you."

Hebrews 13:17

Review pages 270-273.

Contemporary personal values and attitudes about authority differ radically from those taught in the Bible. For the most part, modern man rejects the authority of Scripture, denies objective standards of right and wrong, and refuses to accept the moral absolutes of good and evil. As J. I. Packer points out, there is growing contempt for all forms of authority: "Undisguised contempt for restrictions and directions, and truculent defiance which bucks all systems when it is not busy exploiting them, have become almost conventional, and anyone who respects authority stands out as odd."[3]

Describing modern man's contempt for submission, his self-centeredness, and his relativistic thinking, Stephen B. Clark writes:

> Contemporary society, however, does not value personal submission. Rather, it teaches that the ideal, the highest position a human being can attain, is that of personal autonomy. The human being who decides for himself, who is creative, that is, who devises novel opinions or viewpoints, the human being who is "adult," taking the responsibility to make his own decisions-this is the human being who is valued.... For the modern mentality, freedom is the ability to set one's own standards, to submit to no person, to chart one's own course.[4]

8. How have such ideas affected what Christians think about the elders' involvement in their personal lives?

Church people want their needs serviced but resist being directed or admonished regarding their sins, erroneous philosophy or teaching, family behavior, lifestyle, or priorities. They resent any challenge to their self-determination.

9.   Why is it vitally important to the spiritual development of a believer that he or she obey and submit to the elders of the church?

   a.   *Obedience and submission are fundamental to Christian living. They are the mark of the Spirit-led life.*

   b.   *The church is a family, and its family relationships depend on voluntary submission to the leadership of the elders.*

   c.   *Christ set His personal example of submission to the Father for all Christians to follow.*

   d.   *We receive guidance and biblical correction through our church leaders. God uses the elders in our sanctification process.*

   e.   *If we circumvent the church's spiritual leadership, we will not grow in holiness as we should. God's plan for our growth and sanctification is for us to listen to those who have spiritual authority over us. The elders' authority is delegated to them by God. Therefore, submission to the elders is submission to God.*

   f.   *Those who make the elders' work a grief bring spiritual disaster upon themselves.*

MALE LEADERSHIP

"Likewise, I want women to adorn themselves with proper clothing, modestly and discreetly, not with braided hair and gold or pearls or costly garments, but rather by means of good works, as is proper for women making a claim to godliness. A woman must quietly receive instruction with entire submissiveness. But I do not allow a woman to teach or exercise authority over a man, but to remain quiet. For it was Adam who was first created, and then Eve. And it was not Adam who was deceived, but the woman being deceived, fell into transgression. But women shall be preserved through the bearing of children if they continue in faith and love and sanctity with self-restraint. It is a trustworthy statement: if any man aspires to the office of overseer, it is a fine work he desires to do. An overseer, then, must be above reproach, the husband of one wife."   1 Timothy 2:9-3:2a

Review pages 51-66.

---

9. The eldership must instruct the flock not only to obey the church elders but to ask for counsel and prayer. James exhorts Christians to call on their elders for prayer and spiritual counsel concerning sickness and sin (James 5:14, 15). Although they need to draw upon their elders for prayer, counsel, or direction, people avoid this. They are more concerned with protecting their privacy, anonymity, and autonomy. They do not understand the nature of true, Christian community.

ASSIGNMENT:

Because the concept of male leadership continues to be a source of intense, heated debate among God's people, and the world continues to escalate its godless, feminist philosophy, you will need to be well informed about this controversy. As a protector of God's people, keep up with the current debate on feminism (both secular and religious), biblical gender roles, homosexuality, and related issues. One way to be advised of current thought regarding these issues is to subscribe to CBMW News[5] (Council on Biblical Manhood and Womanhood). Elders cannot watch over the souls of the Lord's people today and remain uninformed about these matters. Our families and churches are at stake. Our young people need teaching and guidance regarding God's design for gender and sexuality. Those who are uncertain about the Scripture's answers to these questions are nearsighted, crippled shepherds who will be unable to protect God's flock.

10.   Why do we insist that Jesus Christ had to be born male?

   a.   *It was a theological necessity, absolutely essential to His person and work. Jesus had to be a first-born male, "holy to the Lord" (Luke 2:23). Jesus was born as the Son of God so that He would be "the last Adam" (1 Cor. 15:45, 47), the first-born son of the lineage of Abraham and David, the true son of promise. Jesus Christ alone is Head of the Church and King of kings.*

   b.   *According to the creation order, Jesus could not be a woman. In the male-female relationship, the male partner alone is invested with the headship-authority role (Gen. 2:20, 22, 23; 1 Cor. 11:3; 1 Tim. 2:12). All leadership structures in Scripture are based on male leadership.*

11.   What does this statement from *Biblical Eldership* mean: "If Jesus is the supreme egalitarian that some would like Him to be, He surely failed women at a crucial moment"?

   The crucial moment was when Jesus appointed only men to be His twelve disciples (apostles). At that moment, Jesus should have appointed at least one woman apostle—if not six—to show His egalitarian viewpoint. By appointing not one woman to the apostolate, He sent the strongest possible message to His church for the ages to come that only males are to serve in positions of authority in His church. In so doing, Jesus ratified the OT creation order of male leadership and established the prototype for church leadership.

---

11. Jesus Christ is the founder and leader of the church, the cornerstone of all doctrine. Christ personally established the foundational office of the apostolate for the church, choosing twelve males (Eph. 2:20, 3:5; Rev. 21:14). Therefore, feminist teaching is a direct attack on the character of Jesus Christ and His choice of a male apostolate. In one form or another, so-called biblical feminists ultimately accuse Jesus Christ of accommodation to His corrupt culture or of failing women at the crucial starting point of building His church.

12.   Which sentences or clauses in Paul's epistles demonstrate that his teaching on male leadership in the church is universally binding on local churches today and is not a culturally conditioned instruction?

    a.   *"I want you to understand that **Christ is the head of every man**, and **the man is the head of a woman**, and **God is the head of Christ**" (1 Cor. 11:3).*

    b.   *"The women are to keep silent in the churches; for they are not permitted to speak, but are to subject themselves, just as the Law also says. . . . **The things which I write to you are the Lord's commandment**" (1 Cor. 14:34, 37b).*

    c.   *"For the husband is head of the wife, **as Christ also is the head of the church**" (Eph. 5:23).*

    d.   *"I do not allow a woman to teach or exercise authority over a man, . . . **For it was Adam who was first created, and then Eve. And it was not Adam who was deceived, but the woman being deceived, fell into transgression**" (1 Tim. 2:12-14).*

13.   Western, twentieth-century people despise the words *submission* and *subordination*. Explain the biblical, positive concept of submission in the home and church (pp. 300, 301).

Submission is the humble response to God's order for the family and the church. It does not in any sense imply inferiority. Our willingness to submit to parents and to the elders in the church expresses our personal obedience to Christ and our readiness to fulfill the roles He has ordained.

14.   In *Biblical Eldership*, the following statement pertaining to the erroneous interpretation of the phrase, "there is neither male nor female" (Gal. 3:28), is made: "Following the same methodology of interpretation as the [so-called] biblical feminists, so-called Christian homosexuals claim the right to same-sex relationships." What is that methodology?

If there is no difference between male and female (as is falsely alleged from this passage), then there can be no prohibition against same-sex marriages. The false methodology consists of taking the verse out of context to address issues that are not being discussed. This passage deals with equality only as it relates to our access to salvation.

---

12.   Encourage your mentoree to thoroughly study 1 Tim. 2: 12-14, the key passage in the debate regarding women elders. Understanding the arguments in the controversy about this passage will arm elders for protecting the church from false, feminist doctrine.

15.   According to *Biblical Eldership*, what is the advantage to the local church of an all-male eldership?

      a.   *When it has an all-male eldership, the church is obedient to the teachings of Scripture. Moreover, all-male eldership models the leadership God established for the family.*

      b.   *Godly men are better equipped to protect the church from false teaching (1 Peter 3:7).*

We close this examination of God's standards for biblical eldership with a call for you and your mentor to join us in praying great King Solomon's prayer for a wise and discerning heart:

"Now O Lord my God, You have made Your servant king in place of my father David, yet I am but a little child; I do not know how to go out or come in. Your servant is in the midst of Your people which You have chosen, a great people who cannot be numbered or counted for multitude. So give Your servant an understanding heart to judge Your people to discern between good and evil. For who is able to judge this great people of Yours?"

                                                    1 Kings 3:7-9

SCRIPTURE MEMORY ASSIGNMENT:

"Obey your leaders and submit to them, for they keep watch over your souls as those who will give an account. Let them do this with joy and not with grief, for this would be unprofitable for you."

                                                Hebrews 13:17

---

15. Examine the ultimate problem in the male-female debate with your mentoree. The problem is not with women's liberation but with male irresponsibility and abdication of leadership. John Piper addresses the heart of the problem:

If I were to put my finger on one devastating sin today, it would not be the so-called women's movement, but the lack of spiritual leadership by men at home and in the church. Satan has achieved an amazing tactical victory by disseminating the notion that the summons for male leadership is born of pride and fallenness, when in fact pride is precisely what prevents spiritual leadership. The spiritual aimlessness and weakness and lethargy and loss of nerve among men is the major issue, not the upsurge of interest in women's ministries.

Pride and self-pity and fear and laziness and confusion are luring many men into self-protecting, self-exalting cocoons of silence. And to the degree that this makes room for women to take more leadership it is sometimes even endorsed as a virtue. But I believe that deep down the men—and the women—know better. Where are the men with a moral vision for their families, a zeal for the house of the Lord, a magnificent commitment to the advancement of the kingdom, an articulate dream for the mission of the church, and a tenderhearted tenacity to make it real?[6]

[1] Stephen B. Clark, *Man and Woman in Christ: An Examination of the Roles of Men and Women in Light of Scripture and the Social Sciences* (Ann Arbor: Servant, 1980), p. 124.

[2] Derek J. Tidball, *Skillful Shepherds: An Introduction to Pastoral Theology* (Grand Rapids: Zondervan, 1986), p. 188.

[3] J. I. Packer, *Freedom and Authority* (Oakland: International Council on Biblical Inerrancy, 1981), p. 7.

[4] Clark, *Man and Woman in Christ*, pp. 334, 335.

[5] Council on Biblical Manhood and Womanhood, P. O. Box 317, Wheaton, IL 60189

[6] John Piper, "A Vision of Biblical Complementarity," in *Recovering Biblical Manhood and Womanhood: A Response to Evangelical Feminism* (Wheaton: Crossway, 1991), pp. 53, 54.

Appendix 1
Scripture Abbreviations

Old Testament

Gen. ....Genesis
Ex. ....Exodus
Lev. ....Leviticus
Num. ....Numbers
Deut. ....Deuteronomy
Josh. ....Joshua
Judg. ....Judges
Ruth ....Ruth
1 Sam. ....1 Samuel
2 Sam. ....2 Samuel
1 Kings............................1 Kings
2 Kings............................2 Kings
1 Chron............................2 Chronicles
2 Chron............................2 Chronicles
Ezra ....Ezra
Neh..............................Nehemiah
Est. ....Esther
Job..Job
Ps.......................................Psalms
Prov..................................Proverbs
Eccl..............................Ecclesiastes
Song ....Song of Solomon
Isa. ....Isaiah
Jer. ....Jeremiah
Lam.............................Lamentations
Ezek. ....Ezekiel
Dan...................................Daniel
Hos...................................Hosea
Joel ....Joel
Amos ....Amos
Obad. ....Obadiah
Jonah ....Jonah
Mic. ....Micah
Nah. ....Nahum

Hab. ....Habakkuk
Zeph................................Zephaniah
Hag. ....Haggai
Zech.................................Zechariah
Mal.....................................Malachi

New Testament

Matt.................................Matthew
Mark....................................Mark
Luke.....................................Luke
John ....John
Acts ....Acts of the Apostles
Rom. ....Romans
1 Cor. ....1 Corinthians
2 Cor. ....2 Corinthians
Gal. ....Galatians
Eph. ....Ephesians
Phil....................................Philippians
Col.....................................Colossians
1 Thess.....................1 Thessalonians
2 Thess.....................2 Thessalonians
1 Tim. ....1 Timothy
2 Tim. ....2 Timothy
Titus ....Titus
Philem. ....Philemon
Heb. ....Hebrews
James...................................James
1 Peter ....1 Peter
2 Peter ....2 Peter
1 John ....1 John
2 John ....2 John
3 John ....3 John
Jude ....Jude
Rev. ....The Revelation to John (Apocalypse)

Appendix 2
Scripture Index

Appendix 3
General Index

It is not enough merely to have an eldership; the eldership must be actively functioning, competent, and spiritually alive.

Understand the value of eldership.

With over 130,000 copies sold, this comprehensive look at the role and function of elders brings all the advantages of shared leadership into focus. Beginning with the four broad categories of eldering (leading, feeding, caring, and protecting), *Biblical Eldership* explores the essential work of elders, their qualifications (including why qualifications are necessary), their relationships with each other, and each of the biblical passages related to eldership. Written for those seeking a clear understanding of the mandate for biblical eldership, this book defines it accurately, practically, and according to Scripture.

Biblical Eldership
  Alexander Strauch; ISBN 093608-3115;
  340 pages
Biblical Eldership Booklet (an overview)
  Alexander Strauch; ISBN 093608-3158;
  48 pages

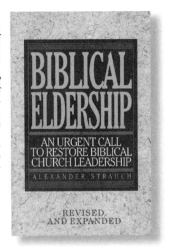

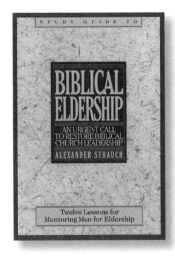

An eldership training package.

It's not enough merely to have an eldership. Elders must be actively functioning, competent, and spiritually alive. Unfortunately, most churches do not possess the tools to adequately train their elders, so they remain under-equipped for their work. This training guide provides twelve comprehensive lessons covering a full range of biblical eldership principles, and can be used by prospective, new, or existing elders. (The *Mentor's Guide* is designed for the leader and provides extensive answers to all the *Study Guide* questions and practical tips for mentoring. For group or one-on-one use.)

Biblical Eldership Study Guide
  Alexander Strauch; ISBN 093608-3131;
  176 pages.
Biblical Eldership Mentoring Guide
  Strauch & Swartley; ISBN 093608-3123;
  194 pages

Your house, Christ's home.

Christian hospitality is a *very* effective tool for evangelism and building a loving Christian community. It can help your church grow and become a friendlier, more caring place. Ideal for all church leaders, this short book will also make a profound difference among the members of your congregation. Unique among books on hospitality, *The Hospitality Commands* expounds every Scripture on the subject, explores all the Biblical examples, and lists the various biblical fruits of Christian hospitality. Also included are study questions and assignments for group discussion, making it an excellent resource for adult Sunday school classes or small group fellowships.

The Hospitality Commands
  Alexander Strauch; ISBN 093608-3093;
  68 pages

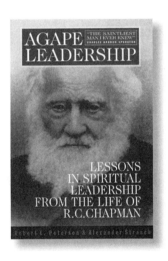

LOVE: the key to great leadership.

As we train new generations of church leaders, we desperately need examples of what Christian leadership is supposed to look like. Robert Chapman (1803-1902) provides an extraordinary example of loving, Christlike leadership. Though largely unknown today, Chapman became legendary in his own time for his patience, kindness, gracious ways, balanced judgment, ability to reconcile conflict, absolute fidelity to Scripture, and his loving pastoral care. Featuring twelve "leadership lessons" drawn from Chapman's life, this inspiring little book can make a profound difference in the fruit of every elder's leadership.

Agape Leadership
  Strauch & Peterson; ISBN 093608-3050;
  76 pages

Who has time to care for others?

There's not a single person in any of our churches who doesn't want to be loved and cared for. That's why the role of "deacon" is so vitally important. It's through the deacons' ministry of caring for the needy, poor, sick, and suffering that we make Christ's love a reality for many people. This is a matter dear to the heart of God. *The New Testament Deacon* is the most thorough book available today on the role of deacons from a New Testament perspective. A fresh and ground-breaking study of all the biblical texts on the subject, this guide will help you build a strong ministry in your church. (Study guide also available.)

The New Testament Deacon
  Alexander Strauch; ISBN 093608-3077;
  192 pages
The NT Deacon Study Guide
  Alexander Strauch; ISBN 093608-3107;
  96 pages

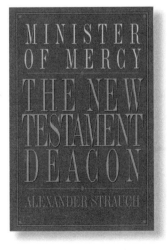

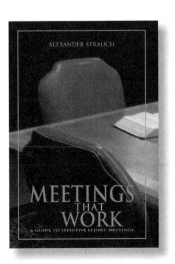

Do you look forward to meetings?

If you are less than satisfied with the quality of your elders' meetings, you are not alone. The fact is, good meetings don't just happen. People have to learn how to lead and how to participate in meetings effectively. This book is designed to help you do just that. It describes, step-by-step, how to implement changes that can significantly improve your elders' meetings. It provides insightful information that every participant needs to know. Although *Meetings That Work* is written primarily for church elders, the practical ideas can be readily adapted by any church committee to improve the quality of their meetings.

Meetings That Work
  Alexander Strauch; ISBN 093608-3174;
  96 pages

More essential tools for effective shepherds.

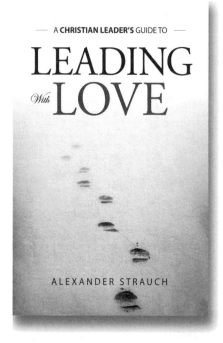

"Pursue Love..."

Though a wealth of good material is available on the leadership qualities of courage, charisma, discipline, vision and decisiveness, few books for church leaders include anything about love. This is a major oversight since the New Testament is clear that love is indispensable to service. In the absence of love, Christian leadership counts for nothing (1 Cor. 1:1-3).

If you lead or teach people--whether as a Sunday School teacher, youth worker, small group leader, administrator, worship leader, elder, deacon, pastor, evangelist or missionary--this book will help provide you with a clear understanding of what the Bible teaches about love, improve your relational skills, enhance your effectiveness, diminish senseless conflict and divisions, build a healthier church family and promote evangelism.

"This book was incredibly practical and very clear. As a pastor I was inspired to love my flock better and lead with love.... This was honestly one of the best books I have ever read and it has just become required reading for all leaders at our church."
— David Anderson, Pastor, Calvary Baptist Church, Englewood, CO

"*Leading with Love* demonstrates that love is indispensable for effective spiritual leadership. I hope this insightful study will received the enthusiastic response it deserves and that it will be widely read."
— Dr. Vernon Grounds, Chancellor, Denver Seminary

"This message is urgently needed by all of us. You may have many talents and spiritual gifts, but without the love that this book speaks about, you don't really have much at all."
— George Verwer, Founder, Operation Mobilization

Leading With Love
  Alexander Strauch; ISBN 093608-3212; 208 pages

Leading With Love Study Guide
  Alexander Strauch; ISBN 093608-3220; 108 pages

Leading With Love Teacher's Guide
  Alexander Strauch; ISBN 093608-3239

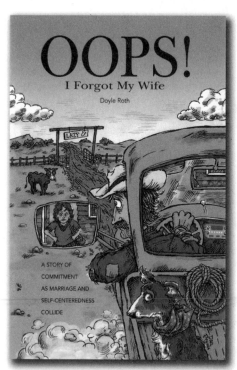

A different kind of marriage book

Combining humor, decades of real-life counseling experience and solid Biblical instruction, Doyle Roth weaves together a fun and easy-to-read story that helps couples to see themselves and their marriages from a fresh perspective.

Written as an exchange of emails between a church elder and a young man whose marriage is crash landing, *Oops!* features short chapters that fit the busy pace of men's lives and a "straight-talk" style that hits the issues head on. In addition, it:
--Equips men for spiritual leadership in the home.
--Challenges marriages to face their #1 enemy: self-centeredness
--Encourages friends and mentors to intentionally "bear one another's burdens"
--Provides a helpful resource for counseling, discipleship and group study with a quick, no-homework discussion guide
--Creates a "user-friendly" approach for evangelism

Oops! I Forgot My Wife
  Doyle Roth; ISBN 093608-3182; 304 pages

Oops! I Forgot My Wife Discussion Guide
  Doyle Roth; ISBN 093608-3190; 48 pages

Oops! I Forgot My Wife Audio Book
  Doyle Roth; ISBN 093608-3247;
  2 Audio CDs; 158 minutes

Additional resources on previous page . . .